BEHIND THE CURTAIN OF
SCHOLARLY PUBLISHING

BEHIND THE CURTAIN OF SCHOLARLY PUBLISHING

Editors in Writing Studies

EDITED BY
GREG GIBERSON
MEGAN SCHOEN
CHRISTIAN WEISSER

UTAH STATE UNIVERSITY PRESS
Logan

© 2022 by University Press of Colorado

Published by Utah State University Press
An imprint of University Press of Colorado
245 Century Circle, Suite 202
Louisville, Colorado 80027

All rights reserved

 The University Press of Colorado is a proud member of the Association of University Presses.

The University Press of Colorado is a cooperative publishing enterprise supported, in part, by Adams State University, Colorado State University, Fort Lewis College, Metropolitan State University of Denver, University of Alaska Fairbanks, University of Colorado, University of Denver, University of Northern Colorado, University of Wyoming, Utah State University, and Western Colorado University.

ISBN: 978-1-64642-216-6 (paperback)
ISBN: 978-1-64642-217-3 (ebook)
https://doi.org/10.7330/9781646422173

Library of Congress Cataloging-in-Publication Data

Names: Giberson, Greg, editor. | Schoen, Megan, editor. | Weisser, Christian R., 1970– editor.
Title: Behind the curtain of scholarly publishing : editors in writing / edited by Greg Giberson, Megan Schoen, Christian Weisser.
Description: Logan : Utah State University Press, [2022] | Includes bibliographical references and index.
Identifiers: LCCN 2022000311 (print) | LCCN 2022000312 (ebook) | ISBN 9781646422166 (paperback) | ISBN 9781646422173 (ebook)
Subjects: LCSH: Editors. | Editing. | Scholarly publishing. | English language—Rhetoric—Study and teaching (Higher)—Authorship.
Classification: LCC PN162 .B435 2022 (print) | LCC PN162 (ebook) | DDC 808.02/7—dc23/eng/20220314
LC record available at https://lccn.loc.gov/2022000311
LC ebook record available at https://lccn.loc.gov/2022000312

Cover photograph © Mario Lisovski/Shutterstock.

CONTENTS

Foreword: The Shape of Editorial Work
   Michael Spooner   vii

Acknowledgments   xv

Introduction: Why Consider the Role of Editor?
   Megan Schoen and Greg Giberson   3

PART ONE: EDITING JOURNALS IN WRITING STUDIES

1. The Journal You Have
   Kelly Ritter   15

2. Minutiae Matters: On Editing an Independent Journal
   Laura R. Micciche   29

3. Growing a Community of Colleagues: Editing *WLN: A Journal of Writing Center Scholarship*
   Muriel Harris   39

4. PRE/TEXT
   Victor J. Vitanza   57

5. Getting Up from a Fall: Five Years as Editor of *WPA: Writing Program Administration*
   Alice S. Horning   69

6. Opening Spaces in Writing Studies: An Impetus for Change at *Composition Forum*
   Christian Weisser   78

7. Greater Than the Sum of Its Parts: Enacting an Editorial Philosophy at *College Composition and Communication*
   Kathleen Blake Yancey   92

PART TWO: EDITING BOOKS AND BOOK SERIES IN WRITING STUDIES

8. The University of Pittsburgh Press Series: Composition, Literacy, Culture
   David Bartholomae and Jean Ferguson Carr   105

9. Opening a New Chapter: Open-Access Publishing in Writing Studies
   Mike Palmquist   118

10. Gatekeeper, Guardian, or Guide? Negotiating the Dynamics of Power as an Editor
    Michael A. Pemberton   139

PART THREE: PULLING BACK THE CURTAIN: REFLECTIONS ON EDITING IN WRITING STUDIES

11. Reflections: Edit to Learn
    Victor Villanueva   155

12. Everything Is Rhetoric: Design, Editing, and Multimodal Scholarship
    Douglas Eyman and Cheryl E. Ball   164

13. *enculturation* and Scholarly Editing as Network Coordination
    Byron Hawk   181

14. Building a Field through Editorial Work: The Case of Second Language Writing
    Paul Kei Matsuda   192

15. Making Space for Diverse Knowledges: Building Cultural Rhetorics Editorial Practices
    Malea Powell   202

16. Won't You Be My Neighbor? How to Build Scholarly Community
    Charles Bazerman   213

Afterword: On "Becoming" an Editor
   Greg Giberson   229

Index   237

FOREWORD

The Shape of Editorial Work

Michael Spooner
   University Press of Colorado / Utah State University Press (retired)

The Editor (Rowley 2019), a novel, opens with a scene of a young writer trying to land a publisher for his own novel. After scores of rejections, he hears from a very well-established, very famous, very influential editor. "I like your manuscript," she says, "but it needs work."

The rapport that Rowley develops between his writer and editor reprises a stereotype, a theme in vernacular culture that I find strange, or at least strangely persistent. Rowley's hero sees his editor as judicious, tasteful, supportive, disciplined and disciplining, maternal. Authoritative. He feels unworthy, but she will see something in him. It is as if she knows something she isn't telling him. She will push him to create his best work, and yes—spoiler alert—he will find his best self in the process.

I mean.

I wonder if, in the folklore of writers, we have imagined this editor to express our yearning for the perfect reader. Response, of course, is vital to writers, and the work of writing becomes a little easier when we invent a superaddressee who knows exactly what we mean and who will nourish and teach and bless us from a place of higher wisdom. From a pedestal, if you will. But for an editor, the danger of a pedestal is that it can become too comfortable; it can turn you into the classic old-timer who presumes a right to advise any youth who clambers onto the next barstool. As I approach full geezerhood myself, I can see the appeal, but good manners suggest that one abstain, and most editors do abstain, I believe.

At the same time, this projection does perceive something real about editorial work. An editor makes judgments, and those judgments can make or break a career. And I don't mean the easy stuff like "needs

https://doi.org/10.7330/9781646422173.c000a

work" or Browning's fabulous "here you miss/Or there exceed the mark" (first quoted to me by an editor). Larger judgments are more telling, like where a manuscript might deepen or extend, where to find its center, whether to protect its innovations or rein them in. All the developmental possibilities that live in the relation among author, editor, audience, and text. Ultimately, these inform the judgment of whether to publish or not.

I almost wrote "of whether a work warrants publishing or not," but what goes into editorial judgment is more textured than the simple idea of *deserving* publication. In scholarly and commercial work alike, a great many proposed articles and books are indeed *worthy* to be published—that is, they offer serious subjects maturely reasoned and well expressed—but are declined by an editor for reasons beyond publishability. For example, size of the audience must be considered, and size of the manuscript. The complexity of production is a factor (medium, tables, images, graphs, color, translations, fact-checking, permissions). Staffing and other limitations at the publisher impinge. Profit is the primary question for many publishers. For others, overlap with already published work is part of the calculus. Room in the queue. Fit with the list or the journal.

I want to focus on "fit" here because in it we have a metaphor that very clearly reveals the role and risk of editorial judgment. It is not the final criterion, but, in the dimension of fit, every submission is regarded in light of how well it addresses the editor's or the publisher's larger purposes. Does it fit? Rejection letters almost ritually ward off submissions with this idea. "Ultimately, we didn't feel it was a good fit for us. All best."

Often, less deliberation goes into the question of fit than one might wish. I have heard editors complain about needing to publish almost whatever comes over the transom. Times can be that lean or quotas that demanding. "Who has time to read a manuscript?" one editor said to me at a conference, lighting up a smoke. "Let the referees do that. I gotta sign thirty contracts this year." At other moments, editors might find themselves wealthy in submissions and might publish only the trendiest ones, regardless of how "fitting" they might be. At any time, an editor might go into the field actively commissioning work that might fit. And sometimes, say at a vanity press, editorial purposes might deliberately not filter anything.

What is fundamental in fit for scholarly publishers is that an editor operates from some working sense of the discipline they are serving, alongside a sense of their own positionality in relation to that discipline. Greg Giberson, Megan Schoen, and Christian Weisser, with the contributors to *Behind the Curtain of Scholarly Publishing* know this experientially: an editor reviews more than manuscripts. They judge the discipline, too—where it needs work, where it might be missing or overshooting some mark—and they judge what impact they are personally positioned to have. In 2007, the MLA Task Force on Evaluating Scholarship for Tenure and Promotion made a similar point, lamenting that institutions in their survey seriously undervalued editing in tenure and promotion decisions. To undervalue editorial work in scholarly journals and essay collections, the committee writes, is especially problematic

> when we consider that editors disseminate new scholarship and further the arts, stimulate and direct inquiry in their fields of study, help produce new knowledge, and create communities for discussion and debate within and among disciplines. *Undoubtedly, editors play a critical role in shaping their disciplines.* (40; emphasis added)

***

When Laura Di Ferrante, Katie Bernstein, and Elisa Gironzetti founded *E-JournALL: Euro-American Journal of Applied Linguistics and Languages* in 2014, their vision of fit and of their role in shaping their discipline was explicit. They intended to decenter English as the language of international publication in applied linguistics. As they report in their self-study of the first four years of the journal (2019), they felt a critical need for a venue that represented the international character of the field and that leveraged the non-English research conducted in it. They reasoned that valuable work was produced every year by Spanish and Italian linguists, and therefore the field needed a journal as hospitable to work in *those* languages as it was to work in English. They committed to publish at least one article in each of these three languages in every issue of *E-JournALL*. Not translations. They wanted a trilingual journal.

The scope of the challenge they faced was daunting; one might call their mission quixotic if it weren't so deeply substantial. Not only do almost all academic journals in their discipline (as well as in writing studies and many other disciplines) publish monolingually in English, but this dominance of English also creates a double bind for scholarship. First, research published in English is less accessible to readers in non-English and so-called periphery contexts (Canagarajah 1996). And further, authors from "periphery" communities now routinely neglect those journals that do exist in other languages, electing instead to write for English-only journals.

Describing the situation, Di Ferrante, Bernstein, and Gironzetti (2019) argue that A. Suresh Canagarajah's center/periphery conception is just as apt in 2019 as it was in 1996 when he first wrote of it. Despite the many advantages of evolving communication that have come with globalization, they point out, most of the economic, technological, colonialist, and other forces that set conditions in place for English-language dominance remain today. And distortions in the demographics of published work are accumulating as a consequence. They write,

> While the internet, exchanges via email, and online publishing opportunities have reduced the exclusion and isolation of peripheral communities, the hegemony of English-language publications over any other language remains a strong influence in scholars' choice of publication venues, topics, and styles of scholarly debate. (106).

I mention these coeditors' self-study here because it shows editors not just acknowledging but also truly forwarding their responsibility to make judgments and embracing the clear ideological shape of the judgments they make. If English is becoming hegemonic as it institutionalizes across the global academy, these coeditors say, then individual editors and publishers must examine their *solamente inglés* choices.[1] In this context, then, the choice to hold open a multilingual niche in their own discipline is a necessary, important gesture of critique and reparation. It argues that the erasure—that is, the accumulating ignorance—of what is discoverable via non-English languages is deforming their field because, remember, they perceive the hegemony of English beyond the simple choice of venue, arguing it also influences the "topics and styles of scholarly debate." In this context, their experiment with *E-JournALL* exposes the illiteracy at the root of monolingualism.[2] This is what informs their idea of editorial fit, and it becomes the shape of their influence on the discipline.

Closer to home for this volume, Sandra Tarabochia, Aja Martinez, and Michele Eodice describe the vision that led them to establish the online journal *Writers: Craft & Context*. Their first issue was released in 2020, and in their editors' introduction, they use precisely the terms I am interested in here: *fit* and *shape*. "The three of us are aware of meaningful work, including our own, that would never 'fit' in the current landscape of scholarly publishing. . . . [T]he field is missing out by failing to be shaped by those [unrepresented] voices and projects" (1). These coeditors' purpose, like that of Di Ferrante, Bernstein, and Gironzetti, is quite consciously to re/shape their field in some way, to have an impact with new editorial choices. The time has come, they say, for writing studies to make itself hospitable to "new knowers who resist privileging only argument and evidence bound in traditional forms and genres. We wanted to show, not tell, how we value lived experience, epistemic diversity, and the ways art can help us understand writers and writing" (2).

Di Ferrante and colleagues' choice, and Tarabochia and colleagues' choice, remind us that editors work within the same context that writers do. We are all constrained by context, yes, and of course we want to be relevant to it. But we are not only bound; we also address our context, and our editorial choices incrementally challenge it, transform it, reshape it. Di Ferrante, Bernstein, and Gironzetti have already made a difference. At this writing, Tarabochia, Martinez, and Eodice are just setting out to do so. Quixotic or not, and whether or not they ultimately displace the windmills they aim for, they are changing the shape of what is possible to think in their disciplines. Not just for the present moment, either; their impact will be visible for some time to come.

***

I have complained elsewhere that those of us who make a career in editorial acquisitions too rarely get a chance to consider our profession in systematic, theoretical ways (Spooner 2002). We may be—indeed I believe we *are*—serious and reflective thinkers, but professional editors seldom produce published scholarly reflection *on editing*. We work at the threshold of academe, yet we seem not to think of our profession as a domain of knowledge-making in the way (true) academics think of their disciplines. In addition, of course, our institutions reward only the *practice* of acquisitions, not building a knowledge base under it; possibly, they see a risk of intellectual distraction should editors turn to writing.

By contrast, when writing scholars turn to editing, they write about their editorial work with great interest, as we can see in the current volume. Among other purposes, the chapters that follow mean to take us behind what may seem a few mysteries of scholarly publishing—choosing a venue, preparing for submission, interpreting a response, and others. Between the lines here as well, we can see the contributors examining the contours of the individual niches they set out to make.

It strikes me that writing scholars are especially suited for this kind of reflection and even for editorial work itself, because writing studies is steeped in response theory, and an editor is, if nothing else, a professional responder. Never the perfect one, never the "real" reader. But through our judgments, we function as a proxy for an audience, and we live with the knowledge that our judgments are always contingent and always depend on how well we anticipate that audience. Therefore, the editor's first task is not to advise, correct, or persuade, but to understand—to understand both the writer and the audience they imagine—from a place much like what Lisa Blankenship calls "rhetorical empathy" (2019). This place may be on a barstool, but I don't think it will be on a pedestal, because alongside the writer—not above—is the angle from which one can best review a manuscript, assess the needs of a discipline, and judge the possibilities in one's own relation to both. And it is this turn of mind that predisposes scholars of writing to keep an ongoing eye on their own editorial practice. Ideally, they discipline themselves as much as they do a writer. It is their occupation to understand writers, but even more it is their *pre*occupation because they identify as writers themselves. So, where writing scholars do editorial work, we hope to find editors who do not accept the pedestal, whose conceptual stances cannot be captured in a convenient archetype. In the hands of writing scholars, then, editorial practice should become rhetorical practice, and we can see in this volume how that can happen.

The contributors here understand the many shades of response to writing like Cyrano understands the expressive potential of his nose, to borrow Louise W. Phelps's amusing metaphor (Phelps 2000). That is, in framing a response to an individual text, their approach is multiple and nuanced. These editors appreciate that a response is a text, too—a text that will be, in Phelps's terms, hermeneutic, rhetorical, transactional, critical, aesthetic, and so on. And in the larger sense, each of the editors writing here understands that the long bibliography of works they have acquired amounts to their own ambitious text of response to their entire discipline. Each contributor to *Behind the Curtain of Scholarly Publishing* is one of those judicious editors whose judgments, which may have seemed quixotic even to themselves at times, in the end framed a significant and unique niche—one that in turn added shape to the discipline of writing studies.

Quixote, of course, is more than a caricature, and a discipline is more than a windmill. My hopeful view is that a discipline is much less static, much more dynamic and responsive than we often feel it is. And I read the collective role of the editors here from this perspective. Each one in their own way has shaped what is possible to think in writing studies, and the impact of their presence will be visible for years to come.

NOTES

1. Hat tip to Victor Villanueva, the first one I heard use this ironic wordplay.
2. One wonders what the field of writing studies might learn if it were possible for our journals to publish an article in Spanish, Arabic, or Japanese in each issue, or if books like this one could always include a non-English chapter.

REFERENCES

Blankenship, Lisa. 2019. *Changing the Subject: A Theory of Rhetorical Empathy.* Logan: Utah State University Press.

Browning, Robert. 1989. "My Last Duchess." In *Robert Browning: Selected Poems*, 25–26. London: Penguin.

Canagarajah, A. Suresh. 1996. "'Nondiscursive' Requirements in Academic Publishing, Material Resources of Periphery Scholars, and the Politics of Knowledge Production." *Written Communication* 13 (4): 435–472.

Di Ferrante, Laura, Katie A. Bernstein, and Elisa Gironzetti. 2019. "Towards Decentering English: Practices and Challenges of a Multilingual Academic Journal." *Critical Multilingualism Studies* 7 (1): 105–123.

MLA Task Force on Evaluating Scholarship for Tenure and Promotion. 2007. "Report of the MLA Task Force on Evaluating Scholarship for Tenure and Promotion." Modern Language Association. file:///C:/Users/Owner/AppData/Local/Temp/taskforcereport0608.pdf.

Phelps, Louise W. 2000. "Cyrano's Nose." *Assessing Writing* 7 (1): 91–110.

Rowley, Steven. 2019. *The Editor.* New York: Putnam.

Spooner, Michael. 2002. "An Essay We're Learning to Read: Responding to Alt.style." In *ALT DIS: Alternative Discourses and the Academy*, 155–177. Portsmouth, NH: Boynton/Cook-Heinemann.

Tarabochia, Sandra L., Martinez, Aja Y., Eodice, Michele. 2020. "Editors' Introduction." *Writers: Craft & Context* 1 (1): 1–5.

ACKNOWLEDGMENTS

We would like to acknowledge and thank all of the people who responded to Greg's original listserv request for the names of important and influential editors in the field. He received over one hundred separate responses, which often included heartfelt stories about how an editor or editors had a significant impact on their lives and careers that have always stuck with them.

We would also like to acknowledge and thank the countless other people behind that editorial and publishing curtain that make it possible for us scholars and editors to share our work with the world. While this volume focused primarily on the work of the editor "in charge," we recognize that the vetting and publishing of scholarship, like the production of it, is a complex and collaborative effort. Without all of those people, some of whom are paid, while most are not, none of us could do our work.

We would also like to thank Mandy Olejnik, a newly minted PhD as of the printing of this volume, for her work on developing and editing the index for this collection. Congratulations, Mandy!

Finally, we would like to thank the contributors. It was a pleasure to work with you all.

BEHIND THE CURTAIN OF SCHOLARLY PUBLISHING

Introduction
WHY CONSIDER THE ROLE OF EDITOR?

Megan Schoen
Oakland University

Greg Giberson
Oakland University

The purpose of this book is to elucidate the often behind-the-scenes work of editors in the field of writing studies to help both new and seasoned scholars, as well as the field's future editors, to understand this important role in shaping the discipline and how to successfully enter into publishing in the discipline. We believe the book will be useful to anyone currently working to publish in writing studies, or who hopes to someday work as an editor in writing studies, or who simply wants to better understand what editors in writing studies do on a day-to-day and year-to-year basis and how that work has contributed to the growth and development of the field itself historically. For readers to better understand the genesis of this collection and to provide some context for it, we first would like to add very brief versions of our own editorial histories and how we came to believe there is value in the personal histories, philosophies, experiences, and advice we have gathered in the following chapters.

***

MEGAN

When Greg first invited me to collaborate with him on this book, I immediately thought of my own initiation into the world of editing. I can still remember the bright summer afternoon when I received the excited call from my friend and fellow Purdue graduate student Joshua Prenosil, a call that launched my work with what would become *Present Tense*. I was sitting in my parents' backyard in Ohio while home visiting when I picked up my phone. Josh had been inspired by John Schilb's 2008 James Berlin Memorial Lecture in which Schilb notes a dearth of timely publications in writing studies about sovereign political power, partially due to the length of the publishing process. Josh was afire with inspiration to fill this gap with a new journal that would quickly publish rhetoric studies on contemporary political and social issues. The editorial team Josh began assembling that day consisted entirely of graduate students, including me. What this opportunity meant for us was that we had to learn how to become editors at the same time we were learning how to write and publish in the field. So, for me, the roles of editor and scholar have always been inextricably linked since my early days as a burgeoning academic—even as I made lots of mistakes developing into both. At the time, a collection like this one would have been extremely useful to help me understand the experiences of the field's most prominent and long-standing editors as I tried to learn how to become both a researcher and an editor myself.

GREG

Much as it did for Megan, journal editing is something that sort of came to me, as opposed to something I sought out. When Alice Horning took over as editor of *WPA* in 2009, I was in my third year as an assistant professor at Oakland University. I remember one day bumping into her in the hall, and she pretty much informed me (and two other junior faculty peers in the Department of Writing and Rhetoric) that we were to be the new assistant editors of the journal. I'm sure there was more of a discussion/invitation, but that is how I remember it. When Alice brought me on, I was (patiently) waiting for my first edited volume to be officially published (*The Knowledge Economy Academic*) and was finalizing the manuscript for my second (*What We Are Becoming*) (Giberson and Moriarty 2012). When my coeditor of *The Knowledge Economy Academic* (Giberson and Giberson 2009), who happens to be my brother, and I began work on that first collection, neither of us had any experience with editorial work. After developing the idea, we stumbled around in the dark for several months trying to figure out how to disseminate our CFP, what processes to put in place to vet submissions (assuming we ever got any), how to write a prospectus, how to select potential publishers, and so on. That collection is somewhat unique, as it is international in scope and inherently interdisciplinary, so there were unique challenges relating to all the questions and gaps we had to fill in pursuit of publication, but after much trial and error, we were able to do so.

Upon reflection, one of the things we were really lacking throughout that project was an understanding of what it means to work as editors. We had to figure it out on our own, step by step, sometimes forward, many times back. Needless to say, the second and third collections went much more smoothly for me, as I had gained some important experience and perspective on editorial work that, in no small part, led me to conceive this collection. I'll write in much more detail in the "Afterword" about the development of this collection, but suffice it to say that, like Megan, I would have benefited immensely as an emerging scholar and editor from such a volume. As a new editor, I could have avoided many of the mistakes I made and pitfalls I encountered. As a new scholar, I would have had a better understanding of what editors really do, why they make decisions they make, and how to better prepare my own work before submitting it for consideration. When we first dip our toes into the world of academic publishing, everything is new and confusing. The work editors do is central to making that world work, and until now, it has been rather opaque and hidden. We hope this volume opens that world up a bit.

***

To the best of our knowledge, there are no other published books that duplicate the content and scope of this project. Numerous advice books abound on general academic publishing (Belcher 2009; Henson 2005; Rocco and Hatcher 2011), but there are no current books about publishing in writing studies solely and explicitly from the perspectives of journal and book editors in the field. In the 1990s, there were a handful of books by writing studies scholars on academic publishing. For example, Joseph M. Moxley authored *Publish, Don't Perish: The Scholar's Guide to Writing and Publishing* (1992) and *Becoming an Academic Writer: A Modern Rhetoric* (1994). Moxley went on to coedit with Todd Taylor *Writing and Publishing for Academic Audiences* (1997). While these scholarly publishing texts were composed by writing studies scholars, the books were designed primarily for a general academic audience, and the perspectives were largely those of successful authors rather than those of editors. Gary Olson and Taylor's (1997) edited collection *Publishing in Rhetoric and Composition* offers advice about academic publishing specific to the field and from editors' perspectives but with a focus on later-stage composing and final manuscript submission. Moreover, in the more than twenty years since its publication, the landscape of academic publishing in writing studies has vastly changed. Maureen Goggin's (2000) *Authoring a Discipline: Scholarly Journals and the Post-World War II Emergence of Rhetoric and Composition* recounts a history of the field's development through its scholarly journals and their editors, but the book's scope does not include practical advice for writing studies scholars trying to publish in these journals. Some articles and book chapters provide editing perspectives about specific subfields within writing studies, such as George Hayhoe's (2010) "Editing a Technical Journal" in Avon Murphy's edited collection *New Perspectives on Technical Editing*, but what has been missing in the field is a compilation centered entirely on the perspective of editors across the spectrum of writing studies.

More recently, the March 2019 special issue of *College English* with the theme "Scholarly Editing: History, Performance, Future" (Ianetta 2019) brings together articles by multiple editors in the field to discuss their role in shaping the past, current, and future directions of writing studies. Like this important special issue, *Behind the Curtain of Scholarly Publishing* extends insights about the role of editors and publications in writing studies but with a larger cross-section of editors and publications represented and with a specific goal of bringing to light the often unknown aspects of journal and book editing for those hoping to better understand how to make their own meaningful contributions to scholarly conversations in the discipline.

Two other recent publications from Utah State University Press / University Press of Colorado are useful companions to *Behind the Curtain of Scholarly Publishing*. The first, *Explanation Points: Publishing in Rhetoric and Composition* (Gallagher and DeVoss 2019) gives advice from successful scholars about best practices for publishing in the field. The second, *Talking Back: Senior Scholars and Their Colleagues Deliberate the Past, Present, and Future of Writing Studies* (Elliot and Horning 2020), provides insights from many of the field's best-known scholars about the discipline's history and ongoing development. Both suggest practical wisdom about the field, including publishing in it, from many of the field's most notable members, many of whom are or have also been editors.

While similarly sharing the collective knowledge of seasoned scholars in the field, *Behind the Curtain of Scholarly Publishing: Editors in Writing Studies* is distinct in focusing exclusively on the perspectives of journal and book editors in writing studies for an audience of both new and seasoned scholars in the field hoping to better understand the editor's role and the publishing process in our discipline. Additionally, we believe the book offers deep historical context, sound practical advice, and inspiration for the field's next generations of journal and book editors.

***

Writing studies scholarship has a rich history, and one way to trace that history is through the progression of its publication venues, including journals and book presses. Such a tracing was famously performed by Robert J. Connors in "Journals in Composition Studies" (1984). Douglas Hesse revisited and updated Connors's project in 2019 with his article "Journals in Composition Studies, Thirty-Five Years After." Because publications are so central to the shaping of any discipline, the editors who helm those journals and book presses are both reflections and vanguards of the discipline at a particular moment of its history. The authors featured in this book have served as editors for many of the extant journals both Connors and Hesse chronicled, including *College English, College Composition and Communication*, and *Composition Studies*. They also represent newer publishing platforms Hesse acknowledges came into being long after Connors surveyed the field's publications, such as *Kairos, enculturation*, and *constellations*. These editors have helped shape the field's scholarship and, by extension, the discipline itself. Their stories illustrate the history of writing studies while also providing insights about the current status and future direction of the field, which is eminently useful for other scholars wishing to publish, as well as for burgeoning editors who will someday assume these mantles of editorial leadership. Moreover, many impressions of the field Hesse gleaned from studying its publications are themes explored by the editors in this collection, including the continued growth of subdisciplines like writing across the curriculum, the rising impetus to interrogate power and politics in our scholarship, the increased focus on second language learners and writing in languages beyond English, the expanding prominence of independent journals, the ascending influence of digitality and online publication, and the surge of open-source scholarship. Finally, both Connors and Hesse identify the proliferation of journals and other publishing platforms as a sign of writing studies becoming fully instantiated as a discipline—a boon perhaps for academic respectability but also a challenge in maintaining a cohesive scholarly identity. The variety of journals and books represented by the editors in this collection seems to underscore Connors's prediction and Hesse's confirmation that writing studies has asserted a rightful place in academic discourse through its growing body of diverse scholarship, though perhaps at the expense of a unified scholarly community with shared knowledge and purpose (Hesse 2019, 392–393). The fact that so many journals and book series now exist means writing studies scholars have many options for submitting their work, a welcome circumstance to be sure. But such an abundance of choice also requires thorough research about how and where to submit. The chapters in *Behind the Curtain of Scholarly Publishing* offer the wisdom of editors across the spectrum of our field's work to assist scholars in preparing and sending out their manuscripts.

All the editors featured in this book develop a conceptual framework based on their personal experiences and the particular publications for which they have worked; within that specific framework, they present concrete advice for scholars. In doing so, they provide insights into editing and publishing in writing studies grounded in the ethos of individual publishing venues in the field while also providing wisdom that transcends particular publications to create a vision for successful scholarship in our discipline. Each chapter explores, in different ways based on the unique experiences and styles of the individual authors, the following:

- individual authors' editorial histories and philosophies and the different influences and experiences that contributed to those histories and philosophies;
- reflections on their editorial accomplishments, contributions, and influences as editors and how they understand their role in relation to the text, content, the scholar, and the many other considerations inherent in the complex work of scholarly production;
- advice for new, emerging, and seasoned scholars designed to offer insight into the relationship editors have with the authors they work with, the scholarship they help produce, the decisions and interventions they must make, and the challenges they face(d).

The book is divided into three sections, starting with concrete historical accounts and moving toward broader, more theoretical explorations of the role of editors in writing studies. Part 1, "Editing Journals in Writing Studies," includes historical retrospectives of editors reflecting on their work at prominent scholarly journals in the field and advice for authors and editors based on that work. In chapter 1, "The Journal You Have," Kelly Ritter discusses her position as editor of *College English* from 2012 to 2017 and her belief in the importance of editors serving the journal's mission rather than their own scholarly agendas. Chapter 2, "Minutia Matters: On Editing an Independent Journal," features Laura Micciche providing insights gained from her role as editor of the discipline's longest-running independent print journal, *Composition Studies*. Next, Muriel Harris recalls the concomitant emergence of writing center studies and *WLN* in chapter 3, "Growing a Community of Colleagues: Editing *WLN: A Journal of Writing Center Scholarship*." Victor Vitanza follows with chapter 4, "*PRE/TEXT*," an innovative and experimental history of the equally innovative and experimental journal it chronicles. In chapter 5, "Getting Up from a Fall: Five Years as Editor of *WPA: Writing Program Administration*," Alice Horning reflects on her editorial position at *WPA* and the role of editors as sponsors in the discipline. Christian Weisser, longstanding and still current editor at *Composition Forum*, expounds on the growth of open-access journals in chapter 6, "Opening Spaces in Writing Studies: An Impetus for Change at *Composition Forum*." In chapter 7, "Greater Than the Sum of Its Parts: Enacting an Editorial Philosophy at *College Composition and Communication*," Kathleen Blake Yancey recollects her editorship at *CCC*, including the differences between her initial plans and the actual unfolding of her work on one of the field's most prominent journals.

Part 2, "Editing Books and Book Series in Writing Studies," moves beyond individual journals to include the perspectives of book-series editors and presses to provide rich histories and sound advice about editing and publishing in these venues. In chapter 8, David Bartholomae and Jean Ferguson Carr explain their roles as editors of the Composition, Literacy, Culture series at the University of Pittsburgh Press, recounting their efforts to find and publish books they "believe in." Next, in chapter 9, "Opening a New Chapter: Open-Access Publishing in Writing Studies," Mike Palmquist gives a fascinating account of the emergence of writing across the curriculum as a field of study and the WAC Clearinghouse as a burgeoning home for much of that nascent field's work; central to that story was the decision to make available the clearinghouse's books and journals in open-access format. In chapter 10, "Gatekeeper, Guardian, or Guide?: Negotiating the Dynamics of Power as an Editor," Michael A. Pemberton explores the issue of editorial authority and control through his experience as editor of both the journal *Across the Disciplines* and the book series *Across the Disciplines Books*.

In part 3, "Pulling Back the Curtain: Reflections on Editing in Writing Studies," prominent journal editors portray a theme of editing through the lens of personal editing experience, moving from the more historical accounts of parts 1 and 2 to more explicit theorizing of editorial work. Many of the authors in part 3 draw on experience in editing multiple publications in the field. Each chapter develops a conceptual framework of editing through which to understand the editorial role. In chapter 11, "Reflections: Edit to Learn," Victor Villanueva describes how his desire to work as an editor for multiple special issues, book collections, and book series was fueled by excitement to broaden his own disciplinary knowledge and also to foster more research from scholars of color. Douglas Eyman and Cheryl E. Ball contribute chapter 12, "Everything Is Rhetoric: Design, Editing, and Multimodal Scholarship," which offers their collaborative philosophy of rhetoric's centrality to all good scholarship, including the multimodal scholarship they have edited and published for years at *Kairos: A Journal of Rhetoric, Technology and Pedagogy*. Next, Byron Hawk's chapter 13, "*enculturation* and Scholarly Editing as Network Coordination," describes the origin of *enculturation: a journal of rhetoric, writing, and culture* as a distributed network of labor. In chapter 14, "Building a Field through Editorial Work: The Case of Second Language Writing," Paul Kei Matsuda recalls his editorial history as an effort to grow scholarship on second language writing. Next, Malea Powell, founding editor of *constellations: a cultural rhetorics publishing space* and current editor of *CCC*, seeks to "highlight some ways to engage in Indigenous and cultural rhetorics practices as an editor" in chapter 15, "Making Space for Diverse Knowledges: Building Cultural Rhetorics Editorial Practice." Finally, Charles Bazerman concludes the collection with chapter 16, "Won't You be My Neighbor? How to Build Scholarly Community," which pulls from his experiences editing special issues and book series to demonstrate the myriad ways editing contributes to the establishment and maintenance of scholarship as communal practice.

We hope readers enjoy drawing back the curtain to see the often-occluded but deeply significant work of writing studies editors through the years as they forged the publications and scholarly trajectories that continue to define our discipline.

REFERENCES

Belcher, Wendy Laura. 2009. *Writing Your Journal Article in 12 Weeks: A Guide to Academic Publishing Success*. Thousand Oaks, CA: SAGE.
Connors, Robert J. 1984. "Journals in Composition Studies." *College English* 46 (4): 348–365.
Elliot, Norbert, and Alice Horning, eds. 2020. *Talking Back: Senior Scholars and Their Colleagues Deliberate the Past, Present, and Future of Writing Studies*. Logan: Utah State University Press.
Gallagher, John, and Dànielle Nicole DeVoss, eds. 2019. *Explanation Points: Publishing in Rhetoric and Composition*. Logan: Utah State University Press.
Giberson, Tom, and Greg Giberson, eds. 2009. *The Knowledge Economy Academic and the Commodification of Higher Education*. New York: Hampton.
Giberson, Greg, and Tom Moriarty, eds. 2012. *What We Are Becoming: Developments in Undergraduate Writing Majors*. Logan: Utah State University Press.
Goggin, Maureen Daly. 2000. *Authoring a Discipline: Scholarly Journals and the Post-World War II Emergence of Rhetoric and Composition*. New York: Routledge.
Hayhoe, George F. 2010. "Editing a Technical Journal." In *New Perspectives on Technical Editing*, edited by Avon J. Murphy, 155–180. New York: Routledge.
Henson, Kenneth T. 2005. *Writing for Publication: Road to Academic Advancement*. Boston: Pearson/Allyn and Bacon.
Hesse, Douglas. 2019. "Journals in Composition Studies, Thirty-Five Years After." *College English* 81 (4): 367–396.

Ianetta, Melissa, ed. 2019. "Scholarly Editing: History, Performance, Future." Special issue, *College English* 81 (4).
Moxley, Joseph M. 1992. *Publish, Don't Perish: The Scholars Guide to Academic Writing and Publishing.* Westport, CT: Greenwood.
Moxley, Joseph. 1994. *Becoming an Academic Writer: A Modern Rhetoric.* Lexington, MA: DC Heath.
Olson, Gary A., and Todd W. Taylor. 1997. *Publishing in Rhetoric and Composition.* Albany: SUNY Press.
Rocco, Tonette S., and Timothy Gary Hatcher. 2011. *The Handbook of Scholarly Writing and Publishing.* San Francisco, CA: Jossey-Bass.
Taylor, Todd W., and Joseph Moxley. 1996. *Writing and Publishing for Academic Authors.* 2nd ed. Lanham, MD: Rowman & Littlefield.

PART ONE

Editing Journals in Writing Studies

1
THE JOURNAL YOU HAVE

Kelly Ritter
   University of Illinois at Urbana–Champaign

My origin story, as both an editor and a scholar, is framed by a life lived outside the typical pathways to academia. I come from a working-class family. I was a first-generation student who began my PhD largely ignorant of what the professorial life would entail, though I knew I was interested in teaching and, somewhat secondarily, research and scholarship. I was also trained as more of a poet than a scholar. My undergraduate degree in English was characterized by that cafeteria-style curriculum of the 1980s, which gave me an unreasonable amount of freedom to take writing courses over period-based literature or theory courses. And both my graduate degrees are in creative writing. Entering my first full-time (non-tenure-track) faculty job at the age of twenty-seven, I had little idea of what my career would look like, or whether I would have one at all.

In these years since—including the initial leap onto the tenure track, and intentional (self-) retraining from creative writing to rhetoric and composition, *and* the sheer will to often tip the delicate balance between "work" and "life" (as if those categories were ever mutually exclusive)—I have found myself a tenured professor with a respectable publication record, standing in my field, and a career now chiefly in administration. But the trajectory that truly set this course I'm currently on began one late December evening in 2011 after I returned from a pleasant but by no means uniformly awesome interview at the NCTE convention in Orlando, Florida, for the position of next editor of *College English*. I opened an email that began *Congratulations!*, and I was astounded at my sudden good fortune, if a little terrified at the prospect. At that point—as fellow editors know—the proverbial needle skidded off the record and the direction of my professional life, as well as my perspective on the profession, changed, essentially for good.

I was privileged to be the editor of *College English* from 2012 to 2017, across two faculty appointments and institutional structures (the

University of North Carolina at Greensboro and the University of Illinois Urbana–Champaign). I was the third woman to hold this position and, from what I can ascertain, also one of the youngest to do so. It's not that being an editor of this, or any, academic journal would be considered a disruption to, or a departure from, what most would label a *successful* career. In fact, many senior scholars find themselves in leadership positions of this sort around the time they achieve the rank of full professor. Such is the duty of being "senior": an elder, safe on the other side of the career mountain, who has made it over the peak and now is responsible for pulling others up behind them. To become an editor is not unusual, or, for some, even wholly unexpected. Rather, becoming and *being* an editor require a surprisingly dramatic shift of expectations—of one's self, of others—that fairly irreparably changes the way your career moves forward and how you view the arena of scholarly publication in relation to it.

As I've written elsewhere,[1] being an editor means *you may no longer be (just) yourself.* But being an editor also means you will forever look at your work, and the work of others, with a set of newly opened eyes. You will understand the front and the back of the house equally, in theatre terms. You will reposition yourself in your field—whatever it is—now realizing your research agenda may be far different from everyone else's, or right in line with the crowd, and/or a trend, fad, or wave amongst other waves equally powerful and quick, bright yet fleeting arrhythmic tsunamis. You will ultimately realize that regardless of what or how much it has meant to the field, *your* research doesn't matter to how you must be an editor now. *Your* scholarly identity cannot and should not guide the way you edit the journal you have been assigned for safekeeping. Instead, your role is surprisingly prescribed: you can only accept the work you are sent, reject the work that won't fit (and come to understand that not everything rejected is *not* good), and edit the journal you have.

My editorial philosophy, born of these limitations and realizations, is fairly simple. Unlike how you have chosen to make your career through your own scholarship—the questions you want to answer or the problems you want to solve—the journal you edit is beholden to its readers and other field stakeholders. It is not *yours.* It is not a publication you mold into the one you personally or professionally want as rooted in your own particular positionality in the field. And it will live and thrive long after you are gone—unless you are the founding and only editor of a publication whose ongoing livelihood therefore depends upon you. That particular editorial experience is beyond my ken; all I will say here is that a publication, position, program—really *anything* controlled by and dependent upon *one* person—must be especially vigilant about its relevance, internal health, and viability. Such a philosophy that privileges the greater good is part and parcel, I argue, for leadership work in general in academia.

Maybe it's just old age talking (I turned fifty-two last December), but rarely does good come from a vision that is the conjuring of one person and what they want. Editors do not move the field so much as move with it. In this, I follow M. H. Abrams's (1958) terms of the mirror over the lamp. It's important for editors to realize the journal they have is the one they must edit, especially when working as part of an organization, such as NCTE, that has some visionary and fiduciary control over what the journal means and what it *is*. And it's important for authors, and manuscript readers, to remember as they navigate the review and publication process that no editor is a Supreme Being.

When I began as editor, I knew a lot about my field, but I didn't know much about this kind of leadership role. I was still figuring out how I wanted to balance procedural items, for example. What would be my stated response time for reading and responding to manuscripts? Who would serve as my assistant editors, my right-hand people? How would I handle revise-and-resubmit decisions, recalcitrant readers or authors (luckily, those were extremely rare in my years with *CE*), and other logistics? These felt like enormous responsibilities for which I needed consultation and advice from colleagues. Fortunately, this help I readily received. But as far as the "vision" thing, I had one holistic wish, likely born of my background as a creative writer and my current scholarly bent as a historian of writing programs and pedagogy (which revealed the many intertwined reasons the past really does shape the present): I *really, really* wanted to change the title of the journal, straight away.

College English. "What does that even *mean* anymore?," I asked out loud, smug in my progressive stance on disciplinary histories. So many departments, it's true, are no longer called "English," evident at the very least by the history of work in rhetoric and composition (or writing studies, if you prefer—though of course that is not precise and equivalent nomenclature, either; such is the fate of naming progress) within English departments. There is little in colleges and universities today exactly equivalent to the study of English, as this category of study itself no longer means what it did in, say, the nineteenth century, when such departments came into institutional prominence and when English became as legitimate a field of study as others on the elite college map. And furthermore, "English" as a term is often not readily inclusive of the other cultures and perspectives that now constitute the people and the work of our twenty-first-century English departments. But *College English*, as I have written about elsewhere,[2] has had a long and storied history as the college publication—a sort of spin-off, in modern terms—of an even older NCTE publication, *English Journal*. So readers have come to it for these past seventy-odd years with certain expectations—each with their own internal truths *as* readers. And having that "big-tent" title allowed a kind of open, welcoming stance wherein many authors could see themselves in the publication in ways that, say, *The Wallace Stevens Journal* did not (no offense to any Stevens scholars out there). Changing the name now would mean changing a lot of things far beyond the scope of my lone editorial appointment—because what we call something matters.

So, I quickly determined that pursuing a name change was out. Vision #1: Fail. But I was not going to be that editor who upended the publication structures and histories of NCTE with one fell swoop, and I wasn't going to close doors to authors and scholarship I had not yet met. I won't rule out that such a global visioning change might eventually come for *CE*. But I realized I would need to instead grapple with the journal I had, which was an extremely capacious publication possessing an airplane-hangar capacity of a title. *CE* was and is a journal that has emphasized (and deemphasized) certain aspects of English studies over its seven-decade run but was at the time of my editorship seen as chiefly a venue for scholars in rhetoric and composition and associated subfields to publish groundbreaking research related to writing, language, culture, and pedagogy. Or at least that had been my relationship to the journal as a two-time contributor, one-time guest editor of a special issue, and an avid subscriber for the twenty-plus years I had been in the profession, including during my doctoral work at the University of Illinois at Chicago. *CE* was where I had published my early scholarship on creative writing pedagogy, my first "major" article publication, shortly before also landing my first tenure-track job. I came into the editorship thinking I had been so, so lucky. The journal had, in many ways, helped launch my career. I was lucky that with its low acceptance rate and tough and brilliant editor (Jeanne Gunner), I was let into the club where, surely, the lines were long outside of those the bouncers had summarily turned away. And surely, I imagined, Jeanne herself was actively shaping the journal's content from an overwhelming sea of competing manuscripts, choosing only those that struck her fancy, or met with her own scholarly preferences, in order to shape the journal's issues as she solely wished.

To be fair—and to clarify how my imagination works, too frequently in relation to my own variable self-esteem—this is how I thought *all* publications worked, across the board, when I began my career. Publishing was good fortune and kind fates, and maybe a little bit of magic, far less than the value of my or anyone's contribution to a body of scholarship, or line of research. I thought little of supply and demand in the mundane sense, of the work and churn of scholarship moving its way through and among editors of journals and reviewers. And I never imagined truly good scholarly work (by other people, of course) was ever, finally, rejected. I had been (minimally) trained, as a junior scholar, to carefully study the backgrounds and publications of the editors to whom I was submitting my work before targeting a venue. Looking at literary magazines even earlier than this—when I was in graduate school and still thinking I would make a living writing poetry and creative nonfiction and teaching creative writing to undergraduates in a lovely little liberal arts college—I had found this assumption in most cases to hold true.

As an MFA student and, to a lesser extent, later as a PhD candidate (since by then I had a couple of literature and rhetoric faculty helping me develop publications outside poetry, in preparation for a broader career), I was trained to always have my work in circulation. I was to always start at the top of the magazine food chain and ruthlessly work my way downward through it (send to Big Journal One and Big Journal Two, and when they reject your poems in a week, don't delay—send them some more!). Always, always be In The Churn, because on any given day, you might look "right" to an editor, sort of like the underlying eat-or-be-eaten theme of representations of the Life of an Artist (see, for example, *A Chorus Line*). So I learned *Magazine X*, with its history of privileging language poetry, would not look kindly on my New York School-influenced work, for example. Nor would *Journal Z*, with its family-tree-like, traceable list of published authors who were born into fame and bred for it, be interested in a twenty-three-year-old woman with only a handful of poems published in her career, even if she was getting her MFA from Iowa (and there's a whole other essay about the anxiety of influence and graduate school and academic careers that focuses on *this*, but luckily, that's not the purpose of this collection).

Further, working as an assistant manuscript reader on the *Iowa Review*—my first foray into the world of publishing as an MFA student—I witnessed the graduate student editors in charge push and pull poems and short stories to and from the final reject pile we lower-level assistants created. This was done in a manner that seemed to rely heavily on aesthetic preferences and not much on qualitative, holistic discussion about overall issue composition, various schools, movements, or styles represented in the work. Such a position was a funny job for someone like me, whose working-class family made its decisions based on logic and practicality. I thought there was a system and that it could be learned; I still took notes on responses to other students' poems in graduate workshops and tried to apply them regularly to my own work. In the journal office, though, I wasn't seeing much of what I heard in workshops and seminars applied to the manuscripts under review. I will say that much of what they chose to publish was very good, and I did see the lead editors reject at least one "famous" author. But quite honestly, the work in that case was inarguably terrible. For the most part, how we made decisions very rarely went beyond what we "liked," and most manuscripts moved very quickly from intake to trash, not unlike the affective review process often experienced in the broader assessment of art. You either get it or you don't.

These experiences—and my own lack of belief in myself and my work, and a faith in good old serendipity—heavily influenced my early publication pursuits as a scholar of rhetoric and composition in looking almost solely to the editor-as-decider for preemptive judgments regarding my authorial chances. I saw all these gatekeepers as mysterious, but undeniably bright, lamps. Flood lights, if you will, the kind attached to cranes atop big trucks that light up traveling carnivals and other such outdoor nighttime events (readers may observe that the link I make here between circuses and academic publishing is neither accidental nor new).

Of course, as an *N* of one, I can't make any kind of broad claim here that I was always wrong, or right. My own publication success has been, I think, very much the result of carefully targeting *venues* that made sense to my work *while* I was writing it and slowly getting wize to the presence of conscientious and rather selfless editors who graciously expressed interest in my work, in many cases helping me make it better. I've always believed, however, that one doesn't write on spec, and this is advice I give freely to authors, including graduate students under my direction. Like the bust of the housing market c. 2008, wherein builders could no longer afford to construct entire tracts of homes that would be filled immediately by eager buyers, so too can junior scholars no longer assume their work will be universally appealing to all journals and published eventually. Good work is good work, but fields are highly specialized. Space is limited. And journal editors, it turns out, are similarly bound by these two limitations when filling their own issues. The journal you have is a mirror that can only reflect what the field is producing; it cannot make trends where there are none, and it cannot control the past or, really, the future of your field. Or at least that was my particular view, but I do not think mine was a necessarily unique experience. Let me say a bit more about that particular editorial experience now.

College English is considered a Tier 1 journal due to its very low acceptance rate. When I was editing, our acceptance rate was around 10 percent, or approximately 27–30 manuscripts published per year out of about 300–350 submitted. Following on this ranking accordant to selectivity, there are Tier 2 (~20–40 percent acceptance rate) and Tier 3 (~40–60 percent) journals. I suppose there are more tiers below this, but I don't hear those discussed *per se*. Thus, those are probably venues lacking peer review and/or accepting all or nearly all submissions. Here is a good place to point out that, however, in definitional terms, *open access* (i.e., journals that have content online available without a paywall or subscription) does not mean *no peer review*, or below Tier 3. People get those terms confused quite a bit. Tiers are ways of sorting selectivity of publications, not access. Unfortunately, publishing (still) costs money, so journals like *CE*, who have no budgets beyond subscriptions and membership dues (from NCTE), therefore have very small margins and are *not* as a consequence open access.[3] This may seem like a side point to raise now, but it is important to keep in mind later when I talk more about capacity and constructing individual issues of the journal. I just want to clarify now how *CE* operates. Selectivity is not equated with open access (or lack thereof), nor should it be. But in my case, because *CE* was and is limited to a certain number of printed pages each year within its assigned organizational budget (by NCTE), its accessibility to readers—and how those readers keep it afloat—is important to any discussion of editorial control and constraints.

Being Tier 1 means also a high volume of submissions because, quite frankly, many scholars operate accordant to my own early training and ambitions and thus want to start at the "top" of journals in terms of perceived and relative prestige of venue before moving down to lesser-ranked or higher-accepting venues. As I say more about these realities and constraints, I should make clear: I didn't make these rules, but I do believe in them. The job market for anyone in or near English studies today is highly competitive (even, I argue, for rhetoric and composition studies—though that, too, is another essay for another day). Graduate directors rightly counsel their students to seek out highly visible venues for their work, to go to nationally peer-reviewed conferences, to be able to distinguish among and between different journals with different rates of acceptance and, in some fields, varying impact factors. It's great to pretend all journals are the same, but those of us who have sat on promotion and tenure or hiring committees know that just isn't true.

Volume and venue are what matter—how much you have published and where you have published it. If you are working on a campus or in a department where visibility and prestige matter at all (and even if you are not—witness the promotion and tenure requirements at so-called teaching schools these days and you'll be surprised to find they often include multiple articles and/or a book from a peer-reviewed press), you would be fooling yourself to say that at least *trying* to publish in the Tier 1 journal(s) in your field isn't important. It is. I'm sorry.

As you might imagine, then, being an editor at one of these journals can be a bit high pressure in terms of being mindful of turnaround time for reviews, providing guidance for junior authors (including graduate students), and possessing sensitivity in rejection. This is not to say editorial work isn't hard at *every* journal; it certainly is. But when you know—or in some cases are *told*—that publication in *CE* ("or similar," as they say in those Hertz rental car agreements) is a requirement for that person's tenure, and you know the submission isn't going to make it through, regardless—well, that's a difficult decision to communicate. Said message is made even more difficult when the author thinks it's solely about what *you* want rather than what's good for the journal. That you are picking and choosing manuscripts because of that whole lamp-spotlight thing rather than making the best judgments according to what you have in front of you and what's right for the journal *as* a journal. That you are seeing the journal as a mirror.

Let me outline some related principles from my time as editor that I hope might illustrate the tension between thinking of editors as "owners" of journals versus keepers, shepherds, or other less-charged roles. I don't question that editors have power; obviously this is true, and we would be irresponsible to deny this entirely. But the reality of influence is often overstated, in my experience, and for that reason, it's similarly irresponsible to reveal all the players and their roles in particular power dynamics/specific occasions. I hope my stated principles are therefore appropriately broad enough to protect the innocent (and not-so) or even appropriately fictionalized to gloss over the rough edges. I'm a big believer in editors being the keepers of vaults, being the *consiglieres* to their journals (mafia overtones noted, but for a variety of reasons having to do with the "peacekeeping" part of that job, the shoe here fits). Someone authors can trust, to the end. This is because scholarship is often critically important to a variety of publics—especially when it exposes quiet lies or loud truths, or shapes discoveries that make life better in any number of ways not always material. But it is also messy, and personal, and the result of sometimes much pain and sacrifice. So whoever is charged with the true honor of reading, reviewing, and refereeing scholarship as it enters those public spaces should be someone you can actually trust. This burden makes it hard to tell *actual* stories. But I'll relay some of my own principles that live around the margins, as it were.

PRINCIPAL 1: TELL THE TRUTH (AND PROTECT OTHERS FROM THE LIE)

Many a day I opened my online editorial portal and downloaded a manuscript that was, to put it no other way, a train wreck, whether due to a wild mismatch for our focus (indeed, your close reading of a minor Beckett play is not really what *CE* readers long for these days), or to a strange misunderstanding of our procedures ("Here is the first chapter of my memoir. I think you will find it delightful! Please let me know in which issue it will appear"), or to a sadly insufficient screening process prior to submission ("This chapter of my dissertation will examine . . ."), sometimes an editor has no choice other than to Reject. I saw myself as a sometimes-developmental editor, meaning that if a manuscript showed promise but was moderately rough around the edges, I'd get reviews and try to work with the author to polish it toward a shinier center, especially junior authors who might have not yet published an article. But I did not see it as my responsibility to comb through layers and layers of *no* to get to *yes*, as it were. I cannot publish a genre we don't feature or even consider (hello, poetry!). I cannot reshape a sixty-page essay that has no research foundations into a twenty-five-page scholarly article. And unfortunately, I usually cannot help an unrevised dissertation chapter highly dependent upon its fellow chapters not in evidence to become a journal article. I'm not that good.

So I practiced the principle of Telling the Truth. I'm sorry, dear author, but I can't use this work and revising it won't help. I'll explain why, and I'll try not to hurt you in the process. But I also won't (usually) suggest you send it somewhere else because I want to Protect Others from The Lie. The Lie is this: if I let a manuscript kick around without appropriate critical feedback, some editor out there will accept it anyway. The Truth: many other editors will also *reject* it, and then a lot of people's time will have been wasted—including the author's—yet the work will never have improved. So, when an editor tries to tell you what's wrong, first, please listen, and second, please understand that the practice I outlined above, taught in creative writing programs—to just put those poems right into another envelope and send them back out!—is not a good one for scholarly work. If your manuscript has been rejected, it's the case at least 9.8 times out of 10 that *something is wrong and you can make improvements*. If you don't believe that, you aren't being honest with yourself. If I don't tell you that, I'm pushing the Truth onto some other editor down the road. And that's unethical. And for the work that *does* eventually get published somewhere, without revisions and with existing major flaws—maybe somewhere below Tier 3 where there is no legitimate peer review? That work does you *no good* as an author. No one benefits from poor scholarship seeing the light of day (by poor, I mean work multiple people besides me have deemed not ready for publication without serious and deep revision). Not the author, not the journal, not the field. To engage in this system is to tell the biggest lie of all.

PRINCIPLE 2: I MAY NOT LOVE WHAT YOU SAY, BUT I'LL GIVE YOU THE RIGHT (AND SPACE) TO SAY IT

Returning directly to the point I made at the outset of this essay about editors and control: as an editor of a journal that represents a very broad and diverse field of scholarship, sometimes I'm going to publish work I'm not invested in personally and may not even like. In fact, *that's my job*. I won't give specific examples because my point here is certainly not to rank work in various subfields, or even show any preference to X or Y approach. It's the opposite. Because I am, at this point in my career, largely an historian of writing does not mean I will only publish historical or archival work about writing. To do so would be boring and irresponsible to readers. Why should only the work I do be what the journal promotes solely or primarily? But this also does not mean I will publish *all* historical work submitted—and in fact, I did not as *CE* editor. Like all scholarship, some historical work isn't good, or more accurately, isn't *ready*. So I didn't publish it.

My editorial philosophy also means I'll publish work I strongly disagree with but feel others will find valuable and/or influential. This goes back to the principle we *all* agreed to, first, as citizens in a democracy and, second, as teachers of writing: I may find what you are arguing unacceptable to my own personal beliefs (or interests, or just predilections), but I will practice an openness to your saying it, if you say it well. I should be clear that to *disagree with* here means I disagree with your scholarly argument or don't share your viewpoint for whatever reason. I am *not* talking about publishing work with which good and reasonable people disagree on a fundamental, moral/ethical basis—such as work that promotes racist, sexist, ableist, and/or homophobic ideas or arguments or states harm done or implied. So I'm not talking about publishing eloquent fringe or hate speech here but about acknowledging reasonable scholarly disagreements.

For editors who struggle with this principle, for whatever reason, I suggest a greater use of special issues. The special issues I commissioned for *CE* (or rather that were presented to me as proposals—because that was my process; I didn't do CFPs for these) sometimes reflected a subfield that I either just didn't know enough about to be critical or that I wasn't fully invested in as a scholar myself. So it was better to have other experts make careful judgments about the content of those issues. I can't recall any of those issues saying anything outright that alarmed or troubled me, or gave me pause, either as a scholar or a person. But I would have been open to being troubled or alarmed if the work was good.

So again, while I can only speak for myself and not the mass of other editors out there, I would say to new and emerging authors: pay attention to how the journals you are targeting represent a range of voices and perspectives and how they organize issues that focus on themes or subfields. Contrary to some criticism I've read of special issues, I never thought of these as quarantined or marginalized spaces for authors who were otherwise unwelcome in the journal. Instead, for these authors—and others I published as part of so-called regular issues, guided by strong and wise reviewers who helped me understand what quality looked like in X or Y subfield—I always hoped the space in our pages of *CE* was welcoming and without significant constraints, regardless of the path one took to get there.

PRINCIPLE 3: TRUST YOUR REVIEWERS, EXCEPT WHEN YOU CAN'T, A.K.A. THE RIGHT THING IS OFTEN THE HARDEST THING

If you've edited a journal, you already know this secret: the equation of Fame=Useful Critical Perspective is faulty. Prestige in a field does not always bring with it appropriate critical distance, generosity of time or spirit, or selflessness in disciplinary perspective. Similarly, relative lack of prestige or reputation does not mean one has no ability to judge. But I think this is a principle many readers and prospective authors might not know, so I want to discuss it here.

Not all reviewers are created equal. Beyond the many memes about fabled reviewer 2, which highlight the frequent discrepancy between two readers' critical experiences with a manuscript, it should be known that occasionally a reviewer doesn't do their work, and, at least in my experience, that correlation is higher when dealing with those we might call the Academic Rich and Famous. People can be fantastic, insightful, generous authors and even mentors but can fall down when it comes to deciding among reject, revise and resubmit, and accept. These three categories are super clearly distinguishable in my mind, but as I've learned, are less so in the minds of others. At the same time, as we get older (and more secure in ourselves and our scholarship), many of us feel less inclined to put in the effort to Take a Stand. So as much as anything the job requires, the job of an editor is to interpret, synthesize, and sometimes ditch commentary in order to serve a greater good, for authors' sakes.

Of course, experience does matter in a broader sense. I still maintain that assigning graduate students as reviewers is not a sound practice—for reasons related to power balance/imbalance, especially for those students who have never published. It's okay to sit back and take notes and observe for a while before jumping into the reviewer fray (whether for journal reviewing or conference, book, or other scholarly proposal reviewing). But I also believe the most senior scholars are sometimes not the best reviewers. This truth manifests itself in one-paragraph (or one-sentence!) reviews; reviews that complain that the reviewer's own scholarship isn't central enough to the author's argument, so this manuscript is a reject; reviews that line edit or proofread work but say nothing about content; or reviews that make broad, glowing, unhelpful remarks and vote to Accept Without Changes. To readers out there: it's appropriately rare to see an Accept Without Changes decision. Barely any work I've seen in my reasonably long life thus far has been of that quality. Every manuscript can be better. So the Accept decisions I received for initial submissions—not entirely unfrequently—I usually did not trust. Such reviews triggered the need for reviewer 3, who—unsurprisingly—rarely if ever agreed with the other reviewer's sunshine-filled assessment. Even if the sunshine came from someone Very Famous, which it usually did.

The unfortunate corollary to the not-critical famous reviewer is the not-*self*-critical famous author, the kind who literally demands publication in your journal Or Else. Maybe I'm just lucky, but the two times this happened to me, no harm or great misfortune resulted as a consequence of saying no to the manuscript, though much was threatened. I do suspect women editors like myself, and also editors from underrepresented groups, face this threat more than do white male (cisgender) editors. Frankly, it's shocking to see such demands in your inbox, especially if you've been otherwise insulated from these behaviors in your professional life outside your own institution, as I had. I can say one such a demand was characterized as "doing [me] a favor" because I was still relatively new to the position. Upon discussion with my fellow assistant graduate student editors, we decided the cost-benefit analysis didn't actually compute in that direction. We instead wished that person well and thanked him for considering our journal.

Since this principle, in illustration, veers dangerously close to revealing sources, I want to clarify why I am discussing it at all: to let readers know that even though editors are largely beholden to the trends and needs of their publication's home field(s), as I've stated previously, editors still must be strong enough to say no when it's really important to do so. And wouldn't you know it? Those authors who demand publication of their work are almost always (a) not presenting what I know to be their best work, which in itself is sort of insulting to me and to the journal I'm editing, and (b) not presenting something the journal's readers are currently invested in, based on what I'm reading elsewhere in the field, what the submissions are showing in terms of focus and area, and what I'm hearing at conferences and in graduate seminars. Mirrors all the way down, people. As I've told my own daughter many times, in my attempt to be moral in my parenting, as well as in my career, the right thing is often the hardest thing.

***

It's difficult to determine, in the advice genre, what is truly useful to readers, especially readers who may have come to my essay, or this book as a whole, looking for specific help and insight into their own publishing pursuits or struggles. As much as I can wax on about my own experiences, there's no substitution for engaging in the work yourself. If there were pieces of advice I could shape from my narrative and accompanying principles above, I suppose it would be to (a) always trust your own scholarship and its merits, but do not close yourself off to editorial guidance that will inevitably make the work better; (b) look for opportunities to join with like-minded scholars in developing and sustaining field trends that can then be visible in field journals. In other words, build yourself a hall of mirrors (but hopefully avoid the attendant problems of the French monarchy) that can help editors see what scholars are valuing and arguing about because good arguments can be very good; and (c) understand that not all reviews are created equal and that if you don't understand one you've received, *ask the editor for help*. In this chapter, I didn't even discuss signed versus unsigned reviews, for example, which is a fruitful topic to be sure. But in the case that a review *is* signed by a scholar you respect (or fear), do not be discouraged from inquiring should you find the review isn't clear. Journals are neither built nor sustained in the absence of productive and respectful conversation among editors, reviewers, and authors. If you can't find that respect at a particular journal, pack your things and politely move on.

And most of all, if I am promoting the notion that an editor should lead the journal they have, and not one that is simply a spotlight on their own subfield or the special interests, or those of a select group of others, know this: in order to engage widely with the field as it stands, then I say to authors, write the work you *have* inside you. Send out for publication the work you have developed by listening to field arguments, identifying where you can intervene, and risking a little where you might disrupt enough to cause a movement (or countermovement). Do not write the essay or article you think other people (including your advisors) want. Do not write the dissertation you think will get you a job. Do not undertake the overall scholarly trajectory you hope will make you famous. Write the thing you love, not the thing you hate or do not even recognize. Only then will editors have the best work to choose from, developed by a true community of scholars—and that will make these editors' work so much easier. Listen to your instincts, and train the mirror on yourself.

NOTES

1. See my "From the Editor" column for the July 2017 issue of *College English*, my final issue as editor of that journal, for more reflection relevant to editors' identities and the self-definition that accompanies the job.
2. See my contribution to the collection *Microhistories in Composition*, edited by Bruce McComiskey (2016).
3. Each issue of *CE* under my editorship (and ongoing) included one to two pieces free to all (including nonsubscribers) via the journal's web page. This typically included my editor's introduction to the issue plus one of the three or four other articles in the issue I and my assistant editor(s) thought had the broadest appeal to subscribers and nonsubscribers alike. But the journal overall was behind a subscribers' paywall, with issues older than two years being indexed for open viewing on the NCTE website; more recent issues were also available, per other journals' processes and procedures, in online databases such as JSTOR, to be accessed by members of university communities who may or may not be individual subscribers to the journal itself.

REFERENCES

Abrams, M. H. 1958. *The Mirror and the Lamp: Romantic Theory and the Critical Tradition.* New York: W. W. Norton.

Ritter, Kelly. 2016. "Journal Editors in the Archives: Microhistory as Reportage." In *Microhistories of Composition*, edited by Bruce McComiskey, 90–115. Logan: Utah State University Press.

Ritter, Kelly. 2017. "From the Editor." *College English* 79 (6): 535–549.

2
MINUTIAE MATTERS
On Editing an Independent Journal

Laura R. Micciche
> University of Cincinnati

My editorship of *Composition Studies* (*CS*), the longest-running independent print journal in the field, began in 2013 with a paper archive shipped to my office in approximately thirty cardboard boxes from previous editor Jennifer Clary-Lemon. The archive included binders of subscription forms dating back decades, personal correspondence with previous editors, and receipts from subscription companies. Also included were microfilm reels of early issues and print copies of the journal beginning with 1.1, a zine-like collection of photocopied, stapled pages published in 1972. Outlines of editorial processes emerged from these materials and informed my work as an editor, as did Clary-Lemon's advice and my previous editing experiences.

When I began, I had been practicing to be an editor for over three decades. As an undergraduate student, I coedited a literary magazine, during graduate school I served as poetry coeditor of *The Cream City Review*, and in my first year of a tenure-track job, I coedited *A Way to Move: Rhetorics of Emotion and Composition Studies* (Jacobs and Micciche 2003) with my colleague Dale Jacobs. The importance of collaboration, communication, emotional intelligence, organization, DIY ethics, and creative problem solving travelled with me across these different experiences and was amplified when editing *CS*. In addition, editing *CS* taught me that big-picture contributions of editors are made possible by sometimes excruciating attention to detail—mundane tasks that form the backbone of extraordinary contributions to a scholarly community.

While editors are regularly characterized as gatekeepers, hosts, facilitators, and conversation starters (Connors 1984; Enos 1997; Gale 1998; Olson 1997; Sparks 2014), these descriptors risk obscuring some of the ordinary yet essential roles editors of independent journals perform. We are emailers in chief, conflict resolvers, copyeditors,[1] emotion managers, policy makers, bookkeepers, marketers, nags, archivists, coders, liaisons between authors and reviewers, mentors, reviewers, task managers, technicians, indexers, and organizers. We do this work because we care about the field and its scholarship and want to support new and veteran researchers; we don't do it for the compensation, of which there is little to none. Some of us get course releases, some hire student workers; others have neither luxury.

Editorial work fits in the seams between teaching, administration, family, and the busyness of everyday life. Drawing on my experiences from 2013 to 2019 as editor of *CS*, and those of four open-access independent journal editors representing *Present Tense: A Journal of Rhetoric in Society* (*PT*), *Reflections: A Journal of Community-Engaged Writing and Rhetoric*, *Literacy in Composition Studies* (*LiCS*), and *Across the Disciplines* (*ATD*), I provide a glimpse into the everydayness of being an indie journal editor in writing studies. Representatives from each journal participated with me in a private google group chat focused on the nuts and bolts of editing. Our conversation was organized around three questions a new editor might ask: What skill sets will I use or develop? What is editing in the context of an independent journal? How will I spend my time as an editor? I draw from that conversation to describe the small, largely unseen actions of editors and their teams that make possible the scholarship we read in independent journals. This view of editors' actions can inform how prospective authors approach submission and production processes.

COPYEDITING OR BUST

"Copyediting is for the damned"—so goes a saying amongst the *LiCS* editorial staff, as shared by managing editor Brenda Glascott. Having spent countless hours copyediting articles, reviews, course designs, and other contributions to *CS*, I understand too well this half-joking, half on-the-nose description of copyediting. For indie journals, which largely function as one-stop shops, copyediting often gets blurred with developmental and content editing, a collaborative process with authors that can focus on issues like reorganizing, rewriting, revising, and reconceptualizing key terms, concepts, or sections of an article. Copyediting is typically the next step in preparing a manuscript for publication after those content issues have been resolved. Copyediting can mean any of—and more than—the following: correcting grammar, spelling, citation, formatting, and usage errors; ensuring a text adheres to house style and design constraints; checking format and layout consistency across a manuscript; reviewing copyright guidelines; fact-checking; and resolving issues with html code (for online publishing).

Prior to becoming editor of *CS*, I knew how to read closely and provide feedback on scholarship, knowledge I had gleaned from my experience as a teacher and peer reviewer. I had edited a book and worked on literary-journal editorial teams, but my experience was on the front end—reading and developing content—not on the back end, polishing content in preparation for publication, though I knew what copyediting looked like from an author's perspective. Upon receiving a copyedited version of my article "More Than a Feeling: Disappointment and WPA Work" (Micciche 2002), I was stunned by the difference isolated changes at the sentence-level made to the overall argument. Yet, when I became a journal editor, I realized these experiences had not prepared me to copyedit. I learned on the job, particularly from my editorial assistant Christina LaVecchia, who had worked as a professional copyeditor and modeled the practice for me, and from *The Copyeditor's Handbook* (Einsohn and Schwartz 2019). I learned that reading and writing scholarship does not automatically qualify one to be a good copyeditor. A tedious, slow, hyperattentive process aimed at consistency and readability, copyediting is not reducible to writing or close reading. It requires a much more disciplined identification with audience that ends up making strange every phrase, every syntactical habit, every grammatical move and design element.

While journals hosted by a professional organization—that is, *Rhetoric Society Quarterly*, *College English*, and *College Composition and Communication* (see Yancey, this volume)—typically have established processes and professional copyeditors, indie journal editors create their own organizational systems and workflows to match the ebb and flow of submissions, review processes, publication schedules, and available personnel. For instance, Glascott provides the following detailed account of the copyediting process at *LiCS*:

1. Our grad student intern takes a first pass and looks up every quotation to verify it and carefully checks the works cited.
2. The editor who is lead copyeditor does a round of copyediting on all the issue's pieces (we want one person looking at all the content to ensure consistency).
3. A second editor does a copyedit on each piece.
4. The manuscript is sent to the author.
5. The second editor resolves the manuscript once it is back from the author.
6. The manuscripts are formatted.

7. The second editor proofreads the formatted manuscript.
8. The lead copyeditor proofreads the issue.
9. Authors and editors do a "clickthrough" on the website before the issue is officially published.

This multistep process involving a team of people gives you an idea of the protracted, labor-intensive nature of copyediting. When copyediting a full-length article of twenty-five to thirty typewritten pages for *CS*, I typically allotted four to six hours for a first pass, three to five for a second. The article was then sent back to the author for corrections, after which an editorial team member reviewed it again. Using track changes in Microsoft Word, we returned to authors their manuscripts framed by layers of comments and editing suggestions. Multiply this process by, say, four articles, ten book reviews, and two course designs, each of lengths varying from six to thirty pages, and repeat the whole copyediting process two or three times a year, depending on a journal's publication cycle. In effect, copyediting ends up being a task that has no end. If editors are not preparing manuscripts for a current issue, they are likely preparing for a forthcoming one—another way of saying yes, copyediting *is* for the damned.

Don't get me wrong: what might seem like divine punishment and torment to some is the epicenter of reward and satisfaction to others. Copyediting shows you transformation in slow motion; it reveals microchanges that produce macrodifferences, taking writing from pretty good to compelling and memorable. That transformation can be exciting and powerful to witness, especially when working with junior scholars and first-time authors.

EMAIL, ASSIGN REVIEWERS, REPEAT

In competition with copyediting for editors' time and attention is email, that seemingly antiquated mode of communication still alive and well in academia, especially for indie journal editors, many of whom use noninstitutional email accounts like Gmail to allow shared access across institutions (and/or to avoid the cost of an institutional email account—my university charged my department $20 a month for a journal-affiliated email account). *Reflections* editor Deborah Mutnick says she and coeditor Laurie Grobman "have thousands of emails on [their gmail] account—3,166 to be exact." Michael Pemberton, editor of *ATD*, describes the centrality of email to his work as an editor:

> Since *ATD* doesn't use an automated submission system—it's all done by emails sent to me directly—I have to go through a series of emails and

recordkeeping steps for everything that comes in. I acknowledge receipt of the submission with a personalized email and, if my quick skim of the piece indicates that it just doesn't fit the journal's editorial focus (which happens more often than people might expect), I also give regrets and say I won't be sending it out for review. Then I have to record the submission information and identify reviewers who are well suited to read the manuscript. . . . Then there are email invitations to the potential reviewers, emails when they agree to review, emails if they don't get reviews in on time, emails to authors about the reviews they've received, and on and on and on.

Ehren Pflugfelder, managing editor of *PT*, also details the time it takes to prepare a manuscript for review and the role of email in that process. After determining a submission appropriate for the journal, the editors

clean it of any identifying information, send it to two possible reviewers, (in all likelihood) send it to another possible reviewer once one reviewer is unable to review the article, remind the reviewers once their reviews are due, corral the suggestions made by reviewers into one document, (sometimes) find another reviewer that I trust to resolve any major conflicts, write an email to the original author, and then repeat that process once a revision or changes are made. . . . I'm always surprised when I think that I send a lot of email and then see my co-Managing Editor Megan Schoen's email output. Between us, we probably send 50–100 journal-related emails on a monthly basis.

Working with a submission manager like Open Journal Systems (OJS) can reduce the amount of emailing an editor does, but this system must be hosted on a server, which may not be feasible for all journals, in part, I've found, because many universities (the most likely hosts) are unfamiliar with OJS and its function and/or they might charge a monthly fee for hosting.

In addition to email, making spreadsheets is another skill editors named as part of their daily work lives. Spreadsheets, most often Excel or Google Sheets, are used to keep track of submissions, the production cycle, and active reviewers. As is probably becoming clear at this point, finding and assigning reviewers, as well as collating and parsing reviewer comments in order to provide authors with directed feedback, is a significant part of the job. The organizational element is only one part of the reviewing process; editors also need a broad understanding of the field and its subfields, an appreciation for a diverse range of scholarly practices, and a recognition that sometimes we need to do research in order to assign appropriate reviewers. And editors also function as reviewers, meaning some person or a group of persons on an editorial staff reads *every manuscript* at least once, and multiple times if it goes through review.

On the subject of reviews, editors had a lot to say about the intellectual and emotional work attached to this responsibility. They noted diversity is at the forefront of reviewer selection (and, as Pemberton put it, at the "forefront of everything [a] journal does"), as are soft skills like empathy, patience, emotional intelligence, and conflict management. Pflugfelder writes, for instance, "As independent editors, we're not in the business of shutting people out of conversations, but [we] work with authors to find the features in their articles that are the most powerful, meaningful, or significant. We do a lot of developmental editing, especially for graduate students writing their first article, and try to help authors create an article that, through revision, they can publish." Megan Schoen, cofounder and comanager of *PT*, notes that when responding to authors who are frustrated with the reviewing timeline or with a reviewer's decision, she tries to be patient and understanding: "This is probably someone's tenure clock talking, and I remind myself what that pressure feels like . . . before I respond."

FINANCES AND SUSTAINABILITY

On the edges of this talk about journal editing is money. Economics is inseparable from scholarly editing. It drives decision-making, publication venues and schedules, and final products. For those journals that do not outsource copyediting, expense is the most likely reason to handle it in-house. Not everyone may realize indie journals typically have a very small or nonexistent budget. While graduate student assistants are mentioned above in the context of *CS* and *LiCS*, funding to support their work is not guaranteed for every indie journal (though volunteerism is usually welcome, and the professional experience can be really valuable). Pemberton notes that "there is almost no money available, and sometimes very little institutional support." As an open-access journal, *ATD* generates no subscription income. While WAC Clearinghouse supports an undergraduate intern for the journal and, crucially, website hosting, Pemberton reports, "Cost-consciousness is always at the forefront of my mind." Likewise, Pflugfelder says *PT*'s annual budget is "less than $100." Reliant on "the good will of our reviewers and editors," the journal depends on an editor's university to pay for site hosting. He continues, "[*PT*] sometimes feels like it's held together with rubber bands and chewing gum," a remark that resonates with other participants as well. This by-the-seat-of-our-pants reality is likely experienced by a lot of new journal editors. Schoen notes that when the cofounders of *PT* established the journal, they were a group of graduate students from Purdue desperately trying to create a journal that would be well respected in the field and through which we could pursue our own vision for a new publishing venue. When we were trying to spread awareness about this new journal, we would pool our own money for promotional materials like bookmarks and pens that we could distribute at conferences to get the word out.

In a similar vein, Glascott describes the uneven resources distributed across the *LiCS* editorial team:

> Between the five members of the collective (not all the same as in 2012), we have patched together some support for the journal. One person has a grad assistant, another sometimes is able to get undergrad research assistant support, a third person has a budget from her university that we use to modestly pay the editor who does our layout and web publication and to do some marketing. Otherwise, none of the editors has release time for this work.

For an indie print journal like *CS*, financial sustainability is dependent on subscriptions, user browsing habits on scholarly databases, and, to a much lesser extent, advertisers. The subscription base is very small; for *CS*, it's currently under fifty individual subscribers and around eighty institutional (mostly libraries). Since 2013, individual subscribers have dropped 20 percent, and institutional ones 38 percent. However, because *CS* is indexed in Gale and JSTOR, it earns revenue when users view or download a manuscript. It probably comes as no surprise that the revenue stream from electronic databases has increased considerably during the same time period subscriptions have decreased, reflecting the reality that users increasingly interact with print periodicals digitally. It's not my purpose here to debate the merits and limitations of print journals. Suffice it to say that issues of access and affordability are important ones when considering the future of print journals (see Weisser, this volume). Online journals, too, must address sustainability. As Glascott remarks, open-access journals must develop a strategy for long-term preservation of online content and a succession plan for the next editorial team so a journal and its content don't disappear over time.

Sustainability also requires that indie editors establish and periodically update submission policies, reviewer guidelines to solicit feedback the editors value, a review process and timeline, house style guidelines, an editorial board and description of the board's duties, and copyright processes. New journals need an ISSN so they are distinguishable from other periodicals and findable by automated systems and by readers. In addition, to be included in CompPile, the field's primary online inventory, editors must index each issue using the inventory's specific key words and phrases—initially a labor-intensive process. Specific to print journals, my team and I sent pdfs of *CS* issues to databases that index the journal: EBSCO, ProQuest, ERIC, Gale/Cengage, and JSTOR. Before doing this, I never gave any thought to how scholarship appears in these databases. It shouldn't have been a revelation that behind the screen is a human being who sends the content through email or uploads it to a file-transfer protocol system. Sometimes materiality seems like magic until you're the one who makes it happen.

WHY MUNDANITIES SHOULD MATTER TO AUTHORS

Understanding what it takes to create and circulate the indie journals many of us depend on for research, teaching, and engagement with emerging conversations brings fresh significance to publishing advice. Awareness of the material practices of publishing—from copyediting and emailing to scrounging resources and soliciting reviewers—grounds writers in the real processes underway when a submission appears in editors' inboxes. Before I published my first article, I crossed my fingers and figured I'd hear back within a journal's stated six-week turnaround time. I gave no thought to the many steps my article had to go through before I received word on its status; if I had, I might have been more careful to support my claims, scrutinize my language choices, and ask readers for feedback. In hindsight, I deserved that desk rejection.

What I've since learned is that editors *want* to send work out for review; we want a successful outcome from the review process. In order to create the conditions for both to happen, the process works best when authors know what a journal publishes and doesn't, submit manuscripts that advance ongoing conversations, and adhere to formatting guidelines specific to a particular venue. Beyond this overly familiar advice, authors might address the following when submitting work to indie journals.

Solicit feedback on your work before submitting.

In her discussion of how doctoral students can work toward publishing, Laura Gonzales (2019) underscores the importance of developing a "sustainable community of feedback" writers can "turn to for ideas, encouragement, and motivation," as well as for direct feedback on writing in progress (110). Simultaneously, valuable feedback can sometimes come from unlikely sources, as Asao Inoue (2019) offers in "Embrace the Opposition." Inoue recommends that, before submitting work for review, writers "seek feedback from readers who seem most opposed to your views or position in the draft, then practice compassionately listening to what they say, not merely to use the feedback, but to understand it as a gift" (140).

Gathering feedback from trusted readers, whether coaches or critics, and whether for immediate improvement or for ongoing writerly development, is important to publishing success. That's because exchanges with a reader connect writers to an embodied audience, not abstract "readers in the field" or anonymous reviewers. Writers must imagine a world in which their logic might not win the day, might not even be recognized as logic. While getting feedback prior to submitting is important for publishing in any venue, it's especially important for indie journals because the editorial team is so time strapped they may not be able to give you the feedback you need and want to develop your argument.

Adopt a view of copyeditors as your writing partners.

Copyeditors know your manuscript better than anyone else—oftentimes, better than you as writer. They are simultaneously insiders, deeply familiar with your claims and writerly habits, and outsiders who, through the act of copyediting, can't help but make strange what you likely consider straightforward and given. You need both perspectives to help your writing reach a wide audience in the field.

While you can question suggested editorial changes or clarify your purpose when a copyeditor seems to misunderstand it, try not to be defensive about your writing. Remember multiple editors have spent *hours* reading and reviewing your manuscript. Chances are that if two or more readers trip over a sentence, it should be edited. House style rules will dictate other edits; if accessible, review a venue's style guide to make sure you understand expectations (if not accessible, request a copy).

Respond to email messages, whether as an author or reviewer.

When you receive email correspondence from editors, respond promptly. Acknowledge receipt and follow instructions, if there are any. Indie editors without staff support don't have time to contact you three or four times reminding you to complete the publication agreement or send your bio.

Understand that a late response to your work may be due to a reviewer's lateness; if you write to ask for an update on the status of your manuscript (and you should if the stated timeline has expired), don't start with anger or frustration. My experience is that editors try to keep authors informed about delays when they happen, but given all we're juggling, we sometimes fall short. Tread lightly when seeking information about your submission.

If contacted to be a reviewer, confirm or decline within a week of the request. If you agree to be a reviewer, respond to the email correspondence in a timely fashion and let editors know if you can't make the deadline. While they may be able to stretch a deadline, they can also reassign a submission to another reviewer if you end up unable to fulfill your obligation this time around. Better to give editors a heads-up in advance than to avoid making that decision until time is short.

Support indie journals with more than submissions.
To support the growth and sustainability of indie journals, read them and teach and cite works published in them. If you want these publications as options for your own work and for the wider field, then support them as a writer and a reader. Field diversity needs publication diversity, a reality that is unattainable if our collective attention and support goes primarily to flagship and/or organization-sponsored journals. The field needs the energy and fresh vision enabled by editorial teams like those of *PT* and *LiCS* if it is to be representative of the field's changing demographics.

Acknowledgments. I am indebted to Brenda Glascott, Deborah Mutnick, Michael Pemberton, Ehren Pflugfelder, and Megan Schoen for their participation in a private google chat discussion about their editing experiences. Their views helped me enlarge my own. Greg Giberson and Schoen provided helpful comments for revision.

NOTE

1. I follow *The Copyeditor's Handbook* (Einsohn and Schwartz 2019) in using the compounds *copyeditor* and *copyediting* for both noun and verb (rather than formatting as two separate words). Oddly enough, there is no spelling consistency within the publishing industry.

REFERENCES

Connors, Robert J. 1984. "Journals in Composition Studies." *College English* 46 (4): 348–365.
Einsohn, Amy, and Marilyn Schwartz. 2019. *The Copyeditor's Handbook: A Guide for Book Publishing and Corporate Communications*. 4th ed. Oakland: University of California Press.
Enos, Theresa. 1997. "Gender and Publishing Scholarship in Rhetoric and Composition." In *Publishing in Rhetoric and Composition*, edited by Gary A. Olson and Todd W. Taylor, 57–72. Albany: SUNY Press.
Gale, Frederic G. 1998. "Composition Journals and the Politics of Knowledge-Making: A Conversation with Journal Editors." *JAC* 18 (2): 197–211.
Gonzales, Laura. 2019. "Publishing as a PhD Student by Building Knowledge Across Communities." In *Explanation Points: Publishing in Rhetoric and Composition*, edited by John R. Gallagher and Dànielle Nicole Devoss, 107–110. Logan: Utah State University Press.
Inoue, Asao B. "Embrace the Opposition." 2019. In *Explanation Points: Publishing in Rhetoric and Composition*, edited by John R. Gallagher and Dànielle Nicole Devoss, 140–144. Logan: Utah State University Press.
Jacobs, Dale, and Laura R. Micciche, eds. 2003. *A Way to Move: Rhetorics of Emotion and Composition Studies*. Portsmouth, NH: Boynton/Cook.
Micciche, Laura R. 2002. "More Than a Feeling: Disappointment and WPA Work." *College English* 64 (4): 432–458.
Olson, Gary A., and Todd W. Taylor, eds. 1997. *Publishing in Rhetoric and Composition*. Albany: SUNY Press.
Sparks, Summer C. 2014. "From Gatekeepers to Facilitators: Understanding the Role of the Journal Editor." *College English* 77 (2): 153–157.

3
GROWING A COMMUNITY OF COLLEAGUES
Editing WLN: A Journal of Writing Center Scholarship

Muriel Harris
  Purdue University (retired)

> *There is always a mixture of reasons for founding a new journal. Most obviously, journals are founded because some particular group of academics wishes to proclaim and formalize its existence as a discipline. We might call these "manifesto foundings."*
>
>   —Robert J. Connors

In 1984, when Robert Connors reviewed composition journals and pondered the question of why they are started, he decided the most obvious reason was to announce that a new field or special-interest subfield was "here to stay" (350). He notes that *College English* was established to cover both literature and composition, but then a special-interest group—intent on identifying the field of teaching communications and written expression as separate from literature—launched *College Composition and Communication*. As Connors (1984) explains, "Establishing a journal was a primary interest of the founders [of *CCC*]" (349). From that point, the rapid appearance of more specialized journals Connors identifies illustrated the need for announcing specific interests within the special interest of college composition. However, although Connors includes *the Writing Lab Newsletter* (*WLN*) among a spate of special-interest journals within college composition that appeared in the 1970s, *WLN* didn't start as a journal and wasn't a "manifesto" proclaiming the existence of a new field. Its origin story is worth rehashing because it explains much of *WLN*'s ethos and growth. Certainly, Connors's analysis of why some (or many) journals start is valid, but I wasn't thinking of inaugurating a journal when the first issues of *WLN* appeared because there simply wasn't a field of writing center studies as an identifiable subset of composition studies. I was, instead, intent on finding a way for a small group

https://doi.org/10.7330/9781646422173.c003

of people—most of whom were newcomers to writing center work—to keep in contact with each other and to share what we were learning. Because I was a new writing center director whose doctoral studies in English sixteenth-century literature didn't adequately prepare me for the exciting new world I was discovering, I was intent on keeping together a group of like-minded colleagues who also weren't well versed and were also encountering a new learning environment that seemed to hold great promise. *Collaboration* wasn't yet a frequently touted term, so we probably talked about being eager to interact, share, and help each other. How we started that collaboration is a story that begins at a CCCC conference.

THE UNPLANNED BEGINNING

Before there was a subset of composition scholarship identified as writing center studies, I was invited to join several women who were working as writing center directors[1] and who had proposed a session on writing centers at the 1977 Conference on College Composition and Communication. Given that writing centers studies was not a "field," the CCCC planning committee assigned our session to a small room at the end of a long corridor. That seemed a bit dismissive, but we hoped some conference-goers would find us. Initially gratified that a few people hesitantly came in and took seats, we began to sense something important was happening as the room rapidly filled to capacity, the walls disappeared behind people leaning against them, and the doorway was blocked with yet more people sitting on the floor and then even more people congregating out in the hallway, straining to hear what was going on. It was an invigorating session in which much was shared, especially a gratifying sense that we each had so many colleagues also interested in writing centers. Without a scholarly body of publications about writing centers to refer to, without any organizational structure, and without any academic preparation because our advanced degrees were in literature, we were in a situation we referred to as "playing a violin while constructing it." And so, having found each other, we knew we needed to keep in contact instead of waiting for next year's CCCC meeting. During the planning for the session, I had offered to bring along a sheet of paper to take down the names of anyone who might show up. So, after the session ended, in an effort for all of us—presenters and attendees—to stay connected in those pre-internet days, I sent around that sheet for those who wanted to sign up with their names and addresses. I wasn't exactly sure what I was going to do with that list of names, but I knew it would involve sending out lists of those names along with an invitation for others to join us. And I knew, as others did, that we had to share what we were doing and learning and thinking as we were formulating theory and practice for work we were finding so incredibly rewarding and, well, fascinating.

Initially, what I sent out, under the heading of the *Writing Lab Newsletter*, was merely a few mimeographed sheets of names and addresses to help people learn about each other's existence, plus announcements, short pieces about resources readers wanted to share or practices and ideas they wanted to contribute to the discussion.[2] I assumed there should be a title to those stapled sheets, so I labeled it the *Writing Lab Newsletter* because, in choosing the term *newsletter*, my initial goal was mainly to keep us all connected to each other, to help form a community, and to share our burgeoning knowledge and experience—to learn from each other. *Newsletter* seemed like an apt term. I chose the word *lab* to draw on the connotation of a lab as I knew it on my science- and engineering-oriented campus: a place to do hands-on work, try out possibilities, and break a few Erlenmeyer flasks or an oscilloscope. A few graduate students (all lit majors) and I who had recently started the Writing Lab at our institution had that connotation of a *lab* in mind when we chose the name for our new place. The terms *writing center* and *writing lab* coexisted, but I chose *lab* for the newsletter for the same reasons we called our new place on campus the Writing Lab.

As more people entered the world of writing center work and contacted me to get on the list, I published their names in forthcoming monthly issues so others could connect to them. *WLN* was helping to bring an expanding cadre of people together as we explored and worked at defining this intriguing approach to assisting student writers and creating a physical space where we would meet and interact with those writers. As I've noted, none of us had prepared ourselves for such work through graduate studies because there was no such field to study when we were students. In the 70s, the graduate major of rhetoric/composition didn't exist, much less writing center studies. But slowly, as we worked through ideas, tried resources, and offered important insights into what one-to-one tutorial interaction with writers was—and could be—about, *WLN* started to publish contributions that were morphing into articles. At first, I didn't intercede in any editorial way to offer revision advice, both because I didn't feel qualified to offer any advice and because I didn't want to discourage authors from contributing. We were thinking through the large and small questions, and *WLN* was a publication in which to share them. *WLN* was, most probably, the only publication that would print those initial contributions. But without those early pieces, *WLN* wouldn't have continued to exist. I viewed *WLN* as a group project engaged in building a community of people working in writing centers who could share and contribute to each other's knowledge. Group projects don't do well when one person's contribution is to judge the contributions of others. Clearly, the concept of *WLN* as a journal hadn't really jelled in my mind. I had many questions that needed answers and many new colleagues whose contributions to *WLN* I wanted to read. The early years of *WLN* issues were not exactly "scholarly." But slowly the contributions to *WLN* were beginning to grow a body of writing center scholarship as characteristics of tutoring, resources needed for the center, and responsibilities of the director were getting articulated. Plus, more and more names of others who wanted to connect to the group were coming in. There was a general sense of commitment by the contributors, editor, and readers to supporting each other, to focusing on helping but not evaluating (an alien response because we knew evaluating a piece of writing is not the job of a tutor), to staying flexible and open to meeting various needs and accommodating new directions. We were definitely forming a community, as well as working to build an academic area of study that held as foundational principles the value of collaborating and the value of supporting and helping writers improve rather than evaluating their drafts. I managed to appease administrators in my department, who didn't view *WLN* as a journal or as professional scholarship or service, by asking readers for donations that paid for printing and mailing. Robert Connors, in his 1984 review of composition journals, also didn't view *WLN* in those early years as a journal.

> *WLN* publishes few long essays and few essays concentrating on theory, specializing instead in practical articles describing ways in which writing labs can be run and improved. Practical help and hand-holding are the important contents. The newsletter's readership writes in almost like a mutual-aid club, describing their programs with modest pride, suggesting ways to go about organizing, improving, and evaluating lab programs, providing answers to the always pressing questions of funding. *WLN* acts like a bulletin-board for writing lab administrators, keeping them in touch, announcing who's had a baby or lost a relative, offering help at home and handy-dandy tips. Though *WLN* remains a very specialized publication, . . . it serves its special purpose well. . . . It is the only writing journal that makes its readers feel like friends. (359)

That description by Connors is well worth close study because it both encapsulates an accurate sense of what many of us newly anointed writing center directors needed and what I hoped those stapled sheets would accomplish. While Connors's assumption was that most journals start when a group wants to be publicly recognized with a journal of its own, higher education was changing rapidly with new challenges and no ready-made solutions or specialists to meet those challenges. As a result, those challenges were (and continue to be) taken up by people who may not have the appropriate academic background but are eager to try out solutions—and become enthused and invigorated by the solutions they are engaged in. We couldn't begin to write theoretical or research articles until we had some solid ground under our feet. We couldn't theorize what we hadn't yet done and weren't adequately prepared to do. Even becoming versed in composition scholarship wasn't sufficient entry into writing center work because that work involves far more than having a content area to share with students. We also had physical spaces to create and administrative responsibilities to handle. Writing center directors needed to know how to recruit and train tutors, publicize a new service around a large campus, help instructors know what we offered as writing assistance, figure out a budget, write reports to justify that budget, set up a room for tutoring, get needed reception staff, acquire helpful materials, keep records, decide how tutors should communicate with instructors, evaluate our effectiveness, and so on and so on. Collaboration, sharing what we were learning, seemed to me to be key to growing a successful field, and that's what I hoped *WLN* would help each of us do—collaborate in learning how to be administrators, learning how effective tutoring is done, learning how to set up a physical facility, and finding out what else we needed to know.

Several years after I had been sending out those stapled sheets with the *WLN* title, a small group of writing center colleagues sensed the need for an organization and named it the Writing Center Association—later renamed the East Central Writing Center Association when more regional groups began to meet. Eventually, a national group was organized, the National Writing Centers Association (NWCA, later changed to the International Writing Centers Association, IWCA) in the early 80s. As the only publication focusing on writing centers, *WLN* was informally considered the journal affiliated with the organization. I didn't think about any formal connection with the organization, as it seemed unnecessary. The field and *WLN* were on the way to being a definable subset of composition studies. Those authors whose essays were published in *WLN* appreciated the fact that *WLN* was now an "affiliate" of NWCA, which, in turn, had become an affiliate of the National Council of Teachers of English. That gave cachet to the *WLN* articles authors listed on their CVs. At some point, I realized being an affiliate of NCTE introduced a more formal need for some sort of review process to determine whether an essay was publishable. But, as I have noted, evaluating writing wasn't and isn't the work of writing centers. Clearly, a new and somewhat disruptive element had appeared, and it was changing the process of submissions being revised for publication. Colleagues who were kind enough to read essays that came in often had comments and suggestions for revision and occasionally worked with the authors during the revision process. But, for a variety of reasons, some authors were never heard from again, and the process of reviewing essays was in constant flux. It would be difficult—and perhaps impossible—to trace all the permutations of how submissions were dealt with, as each new essay presented new opportunities and procedures, a situation that mirrors the many permutations of tutoring and echoes the constant tutors' comment that no two tutorials are ever alike. In the one-to-one context of a tutorial, individual differences are always present. Just as response to writing varies with every student, the review process for *WLN* has remained in constant flux. Every submission seemed to raise new questions as to how to proceed, a state of flux that continues to the present. Whether one considers that flux to be a sign of flexibility, a hopeless lack of organization, or an adherence to writing center principles depends on one's perspective.

While reviewing as a form of responding to writers' writing is an ongoing area of scholarship, I knew early on, from my experience as a tutor talking with students frustrated by long waits for instructor feedback, that authors should have reasonably quick reviewer responses. Sometimes that meant reminding a reviewer to send a response, and sometimes I offered authors feedback before review. At other times, an overly generous reader, opposed to offering any comment that would be perceived as negative (in keeping with a tutoring principle of being supportive and offering suggestions rather than negative responses), would accept an essay that was far from being a publishable draft. Different situations kept arising that needed individual solutions. Again, that was entirely appropriate because responding to individual writers presents different needs that call for unique interactions. So, I was comfortable with the fact that each submission seemed to give rise to a path to possible revision, and perhaps publication. At best, all I can offer at a later point in this essay is a summary of our current review process—which still echoes that same lack of rigorous protocol because most manuscripts seem to still need different solutions as to how they should be handled. The editorial staff of *WLN*, composed of people steeped in writing center theory and practice, continue to think and act under the same guiding principles they espouse when training tutors.

GROWING PAINS, BOTH APPROPRIATE AND DIRE

The *WLN* staff for the first few decades was myself and the Writing Lab's secretary, who split her time between Writing Lab work and *WLN*. Somehow, she managed both sets of responsibilities. She sent subscribers' funds to the English Department's business office to pay for *WLN*'s copying and mailing, kept the mailing list up to date, sent out manuscripts to readers and reader comments to authors, and functioned as a superbly competent manager for *WLN* while I tried to keep up with the editorial work. As the editor, I was able to keep my distance from the managerial end of the journal. Eventually, printing and mailing of *WLN* was moved to the university's printing office, where they also developed a template as they computerized publication. Only in retrospect did I realize starting a journal includes managerial skills and responsibilities, such as handling subscription money, lists, records of submissions, a website, printing and mailing, and so on, a realization that became apparent when our competent Writing Lab secretary retired. The inept person who moved in proceeded to badly bungle the mailing list, funding reports, and communications with authors and readers. But suddenly and unexpectedly, that all paled when compared to a dire problem that made the continued existence of *WLN* highly unlikely. For no reason ever communicated to me, an administrator at my university abruptly decided *WLN* would no longer be supported by the institution beyond the next issue that was about to go to the university's printing office. That led to my panicked call on WCenter, the listserv for writing center folk, asking where *WLN* could be moved to. Those who wanted their institution to support *WLN* quickly expressed interest but were hindered by requests from higher up for proposals that included items such as a budget, staffing and space needs, and other types of documentation that, given *WLN*'s informal nature, were not readily available. Clearly none of the institutional offers of support was likely to come through quickly—if at all—and I wondered if *WLN* was going to go on hiatus or disappear altogether.

Within a few days, while I was still reeling from that unexpected administrative dismissal, Richard Hay (formerly a graduate writing center tutor at Marquette University who had gone on to start his own company providing academic technology services) offered to have his company, The RiCH Company, handle the managerial end pro bono, with subscription costs paying for printing and mailing. He rapidly corrected the mailing list, cleaned up the financial mess, produced a vastly improved website, and seamlessly printed and mailed the next issue. It was a clear-cut case of a door being slammed shut only to have a far better door open with a vastly increased potential for *WLN*'s growth. It also meant I had to weather some angry backlash from people who felt I had "sold out" to commercial interests, even though The RiCH Company was adamant it would work only at the managerial end and not charge for its work. At present, with one of their companies now named Twenty Six Design, Richard and Carla Hay continue their practice of offering their company's support at no cost (including a website they continue to improve) and using subscription funds to cover printing and mailing. So, having served as an editor for decades, I still am not knowledgeable about the managerial end of keeping a journal going. But having Richard and Carla's skills and receptivity to helping *WLN* grow in new directions was crucial to *WLN*'s ability to find new ways to continue its mission of helping writing center specialists communicate and learn from each other.

As *WLN* continued to develop and manuscript submissions became more complex to handle, it became ever clearer I could not pedal fast enough to keep up with all the editorial work myself. When I finally accepted this reality, I asked colleagues to join me, and thus, an editorial staff for *WLN* began—and continues—to expand. When a journal's editorial staff is more than just a single person, new questions about operating principles surface. Most important, what will be the hierarchy or lack of it among the staff? As in writing center tutorials, where the constant effort is to maintain some peer relationship and avoid hierarchy, I viewed the people who joined me as equals. I had more historical knowledge of how things worked, as well as seniority and all that entails, but they each brought new knowledge and skills. And that continues to be true. There were and are instances in which I have to control the situation, but a writing center journal staffed by writing center people should operate as much as possible as a party of equals. But even a group of colleagues or peers needs someone to stand at the side to view the whole operation, make final calls (preferably in accord with the majority vote by the staff), coordinate all branches of the journal, and handle endless matters that don't fit neatly into anyone else's bailiwick (e.g., coordinate with the company that manages *WLN* about numerous matters, acknowledge receipt of new submissions, collect files and send them to the printer, watch that the work flow and deadlines are kept, respond to an author who wants to know when their article will be published or someone who sends in a query about a possible article, write letters to review committees, write nomination packets for academic awards, etc.). The current staff, who are editors, formalized my position as editor in chief. At some point the burgeoning editorial staff realized we had to acknowledge *WLN* had long since become a scholarly journal and needed a new name, but for reasons of nostalgia, we kept *WLN* in that new name: *WLN: A Journal of Writing Center Scholarship*. Accompanying the renaming, at the start of the fourth decade of publication, there was a major format change, designed by Richard Hay's company.

A CONSISTENT PHILOSOPHY

Much has changed over the decades *WLN* has been publishing, but the original goals have remained the same. In that set of stapled sheets that constituted the first issue of *WLN*, I offered what I thought would define the goals and contents of this new newsletter: "Our intention is to keep the newsletter brief, useful, and informative" (*WLN*, vol. 1, no. 1, p. 1). The original readership I had in mind, newcomers like myself, expanded as the field grew to include articles from people whose insights, theorizing, and research deepened the pool of writing center scholarship. Articles submitted now tend to mirror this spectrum, from relative newcomers to authors whose work is well known in the field. It's necessary to remember that some readers of *WLN* continue to be people stepping into writing center positions without extensive backgrounds. In the current move toward hiring ever more part timers and people in staff positions, rather than tenure-track faculty, such newcomers become directors with minimal experience and not enough time to read the extensive body of writing center scholarship that now exists. (I suspect some readers will catch whiffs of a process repeating itself here—that is, the reason I started *WLN* in the first place—newcomers need entry-level help.) Thus, I view *WLN* as a journal for these fledgling directors, as well as a source for new ideas and approaches for experienced writing center administrators who want to stay current and/or are seeking ways to meet new institutional needs. I also continue to save space in every issue for the voices of tutors as they engage in the vital work of one-to-one writing instruction. Sharing what they learn while tutoring seems self-evidently important to the field. Many of those "Tutors' Column" essays have served as readings in tutor-training courses and sources for group discussion in staff meetings, thus allowing tutors in different writing centers to share experiences and reflections with each other. Similarly, articles by writing center specialists are reading matter for tutors, and we are particularly proud of having articles repeatedly selected for publication in some of Parlor Press's annual book collection, *Best of the Journals in Rhetoric and Composition*.

WLN's goals and readership were reinforced when I asked subscribers about their preferences for content and format. (Conferences are great venues for doing audience analysis, a topic dealt with later in this essay.) Uniformly, WLN readers wanted help in defining and keeping up with new developments in the field and in theory and praxis, as well as articles relevant to administrative concerns. There remains a generally emphatic agreement that articles in WLN should remain brief, as readers remind me how busy their lives are and how they appreciate being able, in a coffee break or two, to read a whole article that is short and focused. It is also rewarding to learn how gratified tutors are whose "Tutors' Column" essays are published. WLN has matured in many ways, but that initial comment I put in the first issue of WLN about including "brief, useful, and informative" content continues to shape the journal's philosophy many decades and volumes later. We continue to ask authors to limit the word count so articles are tightly focused and the page length of each issue is contained, and we ask that the writing style be accessible to all readers, thus warning prospective authors against the temptation to load their prose with jargon-laden strings of nouns and possibly obscure references. We also continue to recognize that many writing center directors who also have a heavy load of other teaching and administrative positions don't have the time to read widely in the field but want to keep informed and updated. On a more pragmatic note, I recognize it's important to keep the subscription cost as low as possible, so the word count for articles also keeps current page limits within the budget for printing and mailing issues. (More pages obviously raise printing and mailing costs.)

BRANCHING OUT

While I initiated WLN as an impromptu means to reach out and share ideas, resources, experiences, and reflections, I didn't think WLN continued to meet that goal when *it* morphed into a journal. With the new opportunities technology and the digital world afforded, we saw new opportunities for people to interact and connect. A member of our editorial staff, skilled in interacting in the digital world, created a Twitter feed and a Facebook page, and the Twenty Six Design staff uploaded to the website all previous volumes of WLN and made them open access and searchable. At some point, we realized that while WLN had some international subscribers, WLN wasn't getting submissions from outside the United States, but it seemed appropriate to try to connect with colleagues beyond our borders, to hear what people in other countries were doing, thinking about, and accomplishing. I hoped they would be interested in learning more about writing centers in the United States. However, though I knew writing center organizations were springing up across various geographical borders, there was no venue for writing center people to communicate around the globe other than traveling to conferences in far-flung places. Hoping to help foster conversations across these boundaries, we started a blog, envisioning it would attract multiple voices. We were mistaken because the silence was deafening. A few people asked questions or contributed other comments, but the blog has been successful mostly as our blog editors reach out to interview people, announce conferences, or introduce writing center professionals talking about their work. Somewhat unusual, though, was an outpouring of dozens of responses from tutors and directors in various countries when they were invited to offer their responses to the COVID-19 pandemic.[3]

WLN has been branching out in other ways. Because the editorial staff recognizes we have a mentoring responsibility to assist those writing for publication in *WLN*, and because we want to help ensure the quality of articles published in *WLN*, we started several programs designed to help prospective authors write those articles. One such program offered webinars on writing for publication in *WLN* (videos of past online sessions are available on the *WLN* website: wlnjournal.org/resources.php). In addition, we had a mentoring program in which writing center professionals volunteered to be online mentors to assist authors thinking about or in the process of writing for possible publication in *WLN*. Another way *WLN* can act as a resource and encourage sharing—in addition to our open-access collection of past volumes with an accompanying search engine—is a fairly new project we describe as open-access digital edited collections (DECs) on specific topics. The first DEC, openly available on the *WLN* website (wlnjournal.org/resources.php), was developed from submissions to a guest-edited *WLN* issue on tutor education. The chapters take advantage of the multimedia enhancements of visually effective formatting and links to digitally available resources to enrich each chapter. In addition to the DECs already uploaded or in preparation, we hope more DECs will continue to be proposed and eventually uploaded. *WLN*, a newsletter that became a journal, was initiated as a means for writing center specialists to collaborate and share, so with the advent of technology that allows such sharing and collaborating, I view the print journal as the platform or base upon which to expand our mission. What I offer here about the origins of *WLN* and how it has developed is a tale told from my perspective, but others have written about *WLN* as well. Listed in the "Archives" section of the *WLN* website (wlnjournal.org/archives.php) are links to studies of *WLN*: (a) a history by Kim Ballard and Rick Anderson that notes *WLN* is "grounded in the collaborative nature of writing lab tutoring"; (b) a history by Michael Pemberton that traces *WLN*'s contribution to the growth of a scholarly community; and (c) an analysis of the topics of *WLN* articles through the decades by Molly Phelan and Jessica Weber, who conclude that *WLN* is "always striving to unify and stimulate conversation within the writing center community" (2) and that *WLN* is "a valuable resource not only because of the information it shares, but also because it provides a supportive, inquisitive network of peers and colleagues to which one can turn" (10). A fourth study, by Elizabeth Kleinfeld, Sohui Lee, and Julie Prebel, examines the demographics of authors who publish in *WLN* (2021). In addition, as previously noted, Connors's 1984 review of composition journals included a short overview of *WLN*.

THE MOVE TOWARD BEING A REVIEWED JOURNAL

As *WLN* inched toward becoming a peer-reviewed journal, I tried to maintain the we're-here-to-help-not-judge mentality of a writing center interaction. For that reason, being a peer-reviewed journal is still a work in progress, as the submission process keeps shifting and changing to follow different paths toward potential publication. In an attempt to explain how we proceed, I try to suggest some paths different submissions travel. As the first reader for all submissions, I try to sort new submissions into various piles and send essays ready for review on to the others in the editorial staff, who then send them out for reader response. While there are no neat piles to sort submissions into, many tend to fall into the following categories:

- Not appropriate for WLN

    Some essays are clearly not intended for readers who focus on one-to-one interaction. For example, a submission about what teachers should be doing in the composition classroom is thus not relevant and should be sent to a general composition journal. My response to such authors is to suggest they seek more relevant publications.

- The wheel rediscovered

    Occasionally, someone offers an essay that, for example, extolls some exceedingly basic concept or practice that has long been a mainstay of the field but adds nothing more than repeating the need for or importance of whatever they are excitedly extolling. I respond by explaining that the essay is not appropriate because the topic has been extensively covered in the literature of the field and any new discussion should build on what is known or chart a different course. With the help of anyone else on the staff who has suggestions, I try to offer some way to revise by digging deeper into a topic mentioned in the submitted draft. (*Draft* is a very useful term in writing center practice because of the implication of being a work in progress that can be revised.)

- The essay with potential

    When submissions have promise but could be strengthened by some revision, we try to intercede before reviewers are likely to reject the current draft. Because of the editorial staff's perspective that editors should have some responsibility to be mentors, most of us on the current editorial staff read the essay and offer suggestions. Although we try not to overwhelm the author with too many suggestions, we attempt to include most of what has been suggested and offer the author a one-time opportunity to revise and resubmit. Authors who respond positively send back a revised draft that then goes out for review. This is the case for most, but not all, authors invited to revise. Some disappear and may never be heard from again, though our assistant editor sends an email to all authors who have not sent in a revision by the deadline, asking whether they are still interested in rewriting. Sometimes a reminder is needed to stir people into taking a project off the back burner. Sometimes an author puts the draft in a drawer, where it will gather dust.

- The not-ready-for-prime-time draft

    When an essay comes in that would clearly be rejected by a reviewer because it drifts around with no core to build on or lacks awareness of any scholarship that has previously appeared or is lost in clouds of vague generalities, and so on, we realize that because a flat-out rejection is so disheartening, especially to people first learning how to write for publication, we try to help the author become aware of problems and, perhaps, offer paths for revision. Again, because we have learned over the years that revisions can go on for draft after draft and never move towards major improvement—which is discouraging for the author and frustrating for the editor working with the author—we have come to realize we need to invoke the one-time-revision-before-review guideline and set a deadline for response. But even the single revision or deadline is malleable when the author explains some major life or work event is delaying a response or simply that the draft is progressing but still needs more work. And sometimes, that one-time limit for revision before review is put aside as the editor in charge of that submission works with the author through another draft or two. Unfortunately, it's not always clear as to when to cut the cord when revisions aren't making much headway.

- The essay that goes out for review

    When an essay comes in that is ready for review, one of the current editors oversees that submission and sends it out for review. When the review comes back, that editor sends the feedback to the author and is likely to continue to work with the author as revisions are made. It is here that we try to assist as mentors (or, more aptly, as tutors), helping the author move towards revision that can result in publication. Sometimes the reviewer gets involved, and sometimes, the reviewer considers the one-time review as having met the responsibility of a reviewer. Some authors require minimal interaction with a member of the editorial staff, but sometimes there are numerous back-and-forth comments and revisions and more comments and more revisions. Some authors have no doubt become exasperated by the requests for revision, but some express appreciation. Before a manuscript goes into the queue for future publication, all of us on the editorial staff read the essay to be sure it's ready for publication. Occasionally, this prompts requests for some minor last-minute revisions.

SOME *WLN* EDITORIAL PRACTICES

With some (well, a great deal) of trepidation, I offer an overview of some of the editorial practices of the *WLN* staff. I've already belabored the review and other guidelines in terms of how they mirror accepted principles in writing center theory, but practices are more malleable and no doubt vary from journal to journal.

- Do some audience analysis at conferences.

    An editor and fellow editorial-staff members may have a vision for a journal, but what that journal is, how it looks, and what it contains should also be shaped by its readers. I had (and continue to have) neither the funds nor the skills to conduct full-scale audience analysis and have relied instead on getting informal feedback at conferences. Rather than drawing up lists of questions, I started conversations with people I knew as they chatted in the hallways between sessions, asking them what they liked and disliked about *WLN*. When I was speaking at a session likely to attract writing center people, I invited attendees to stay after for a few minutes to help shape *WLN*. That tended to exclude people who needed to rush off to sessions in remote locations, but a few such people stopped me at other times to offer their thoughts. I also roamed around at publishers' parties in the evenings to hear what people had to offer. When *WLN* was about to change names, we agreed we needed a new format, perhaps changes in page size, different colors, and so on. Richard Hay's company, which manages *WLN*, mocked up samples of a few options, and I again roamed the halls of conferences and walked around hotel lobbies where people were networking or relaxing to ask them to look at the mock-ups and offer responses. I found this open-ended, informal approach inordinately useful as I heard people expressing whatever came to mind as they talked with me. I also heard some valuable suggestions we hadn't thought of. Since I had a few specific concerns, I tried to bring them into these short conversations and sometimes succeeded in doing so.

- Find someone with digital skills who can organize the work.

    A crucial addition to every journal's staff is someone who keeps track of the flow of manuscripts, the revisions, reviewers' responses, and so forth and watches that deadlines don't fly by unheeded. We realized the need for such a person when, at some point, we were delaying, pushing to the back burner, or possibly forgetting to move forward with some submissions and other projects we were involved with. Although I'm not a fan of or adept in creating Excel spreadsheets, I recognized the need for someone on the staff who maintains a spreadsheet, sends us weekly status updates about what's been done and what needs to be done, sends out reminders to authors about deadlines by which to send in revisions, and generally keeps us organized. That person, like the head secretary in an academic department, is a highly valued and absolutely necessary member of the editorial staff.

- Be prepared for knotty, messy questions.

There may be journals with standard procedures that work at least 99 percent of the time. *WLN* is not one of those journals. Our editorial staff seems to engage in long email discussions about numerous situations, and the time that work involves is part of the job description of an editor. It's also inordinately generative as we find new matters to clarify for ourselves. For example, What can we expect or ask for from reviewers? It would be beneficial if there are uniform policies all reviewers agree to, such as agreeing to respond within a specified deadline and agreeing to read revisions. But some reviewers, who are competent and whom we would like to continue calling upon, are not always amenable. Questions about reviewing and reviewers are never-ending. What do we do when one reviewer rejects a submission while another reviewer requests heavy revisions? Should we publish a submission that has been accepted by reviewers but that we think has serious discrepancies? What do we do when some of the editorial staff think a submission is ready for publication but others disagree? Should it be a majority decision? When is it time to pull the plug after an author has revised and revised but is only millimeters closer to an acceptable draft? Given the immutable connection between publishing and tenure, there are going to be authors desperate to get their writing published. What then do we do when someone whose article was recently accepted wants their article published NOW, despite a backlog of other articles waiting to be published? If the author truly needs publication rather than a *forthcoming* attached to their listing in a CV, we try to accommodate but aren't always able to. What should we do when one or more members of an editorial staff are besieged by other responsibilities and work is not moving forward as it should (there's that nagging reminder that authors should not be kept waiting too long for feedback)? The answers to such sticky questions vary with each case, so settled practices are not possible. As editor in chief, I try to keep us on track, but I'd rather not have to quantify or report percentages as to how successful I am in getting work done. But I hope other editors reading this are nodding as they recognize similar situations they deal with. I hope there is some nodding going on, and I find comfort in knowing that having to work our way through such difficulties is not unique to *WLN* and is not an indication of inept editing.

ADVICE TO AUTHORS WRITING FOR PUBLICATION

Any advice I have to offer about how to successfully write for publication is merely a repetition of the familiar advice tutors and classroom instructors offer students about improving writing skills. However, the validity of the advice is equally evident when writing center colleagues also write essays with the hope of getting them accepted in a peer-reviewed journal. It's easier to spot problems in other people's writing but far more difficult when reading our own prose. And for authors it's important to remember almost all of us profit from revision. Rarely does *WLN* get a submission that requires no revision.

- Ask yourself why others should read your essay.

    This of course seems obvious, but some authors are inclined to succumb to the lure of the narrative of their story. That is, an essay can lapse into an account of little use to others because it is so dependent on local context. There's also the temptation to write about, for example, the superb services a writing center offers and how its numbers have increased—without any hint or explanation as to why. Similarly, an author succumbs to describing a new service or tutor-training approach and claim great success with no proof other than that the author makes that claim. Too often such essays read like a promo for that writing center but add little or nothing to existing scholarship. Instead, the author can investigate the process of how the writing center improved its services or tutors' abilities, increased student usage, or whatever the narrative promotes about that writing center. Tutors writing essays intended for the "Tutors' Column" who focus on themselves as the reader of what they write might be inclined to write an essay about personal preferences, with little or no further reflection or insight. The result holds scant interest for readers if there are no attempts to enlighten other tutors, to reflect on and generalize beyond the immediate context and their own responses.

- Provide context within which to place your topic.

    While it's not necessary to start with an extensive lit review, authors need to help readers see how their focus fits within the context of how that subject has been researched and discussed. That may mean offering a few key articles or books that delve into the topic, which allows the author to help readers see what they are offering is new or expands on current knowledge.

- Explain instead of summarize.

    This basic adage of composition teaching seems unnecessary, but some authors don't realize they shouldn't merely state conclusions and outcomes, such as "we tried some outreach projects with faculty around campus that were highly successful." But what those "outreach projects" were remains a mystery. Similarly, an author might note tutors gained more confidence when they were able to observe experienced tutors working with students. Without some discussion of perhaps how the observations were structured or what the tutors did in terms of learning from the observation or how a judgment of success was determined, such a summary is of little use to a reader interested in gaining a more detailed understanding. While it's easy to identify problems when we read such examples in the writing of others, it's much, much harder to recognize the difficulty when we are the authors.

- Draw a substantive conclusion.

    Occasionally essays come in that go into extensive detail but fail to rise above the specifics to see the larger implications of what was done, surveyed, reflected upon, or studied. For example, an author might offer reports of what a number of students did or what tutors reported but stop short of making meaning out of all the data included. Sometimes this presentation of data takes the shape of graphics, such as tables with a lot of numbers and percentages but no meaningful conclusions.

- Become acquainted with the journal to which an essay will be submitted.

    More than learning whether the journal asks for citations in MLA or APA or other submission requirements, prospective authors who are not regular readers of the journal should browse through past issues, look at the writing style and topics discussed, get a sense of what reviewers for that journal are likely to respond to as appropriate for that journal. Read any advice or guidelines offered on the journal's website. Are there genre expectations? For example, does the journal focus on research reports normally written in a standard report format, or are articles more likely to be discursive essays? It's also important to recognize that a conference presentation is different from a publishable article, though the conference presentation may be the basis the article. But revision is necessary to turn that conference presentation into an article. For *WLN*'s "Tutors' Column," tutors need to learn that a paper written for a class should be revised for possible submission because an essay for "Tutors' Column" and a class paper are two different genres. It's also important to think about the designated readers of that journal and whether the essay to be submitted has those readers in mind. For *WLN*, whose intended audience ranges from people new to the field of writing centers looking to learn more about writing center studies to more experienced scholars, it's inappropriate to include passing references to obscure scholarship or to write in jargon-laden prose. In short, become familiar with the characteristics of published articles in that journal. Ted Roggenbuck, one of our *WLN* editors, captures our emphasis on readable prose well: "Nothing dazzles quite like clarity."

- Be prepared to revise.

    Accept the fact that submissions usually go through revisions before being accepted. Reader feedback and requests for revision from the editors or reviewers are intended to help improve the essay and are meant to show support for the author whose work seems promising.

Authors may be reluctant to delete some section of an essay they delighted in writing, but if that part doesn't work for others, it probably should disappear. Perhaps it's necessary to simply close one's eyes while hitting the delete button.

CONCLUSION

WLN has morphed from a few stapled sheets of names, comments, and announcements to a print journal with offshoots meant to help authors and readers continue to share and collaborate, and I hope there will be new additions and changes to *WLN* in the future. A mission can stay constant while the ways to implement it can vary. But to implement that mission, I found that gathering really talented, dedicated, and knowledgeable people to work on seeing that the mission guides our actions is an absolute must. It takes a village of highly skilled editorial staff, reviewers, readers, managers, and, most of all, authors to make a journal thrive. Or, in the case of *WLN*, it takes a village of writing center people to grow a journal and help grow a field of study.

NOTES

1. The panel for this 1977 CCCC session included Mary Croft, Joyce Stewart, Janice Neuleib, and me.
2. Those first and all succeeding issues of *WLN* (other than the volume currently being published) are available in *WLN*'s open and searchable archive: wlnjournal.org/archives.
3. Because so many people responded to our request for short pieces about dealing with the COVID-19 pandemic in their writing centers or as tutors, our blog editors created a separate COVID section of the blog: https://www.wlnjournal.org/blog/covid-19/.

REFERENCES

Connors, Robert J. 1984. "Journals in Composition Studies." *College English* 46 (4): 348–365. https://doi.org10.2307/376941.

Kleinfeld, Elizabeth, Sohui Lee, and Julie Prebel. 2021. "Whose Voices Are Heard? A Demographic Comparison of Authors Published in 2005–2017 and Writers Interested in Publishing." *WLN: A Journal of Writing Center Scholarship* 45 (7–8): 11–17.

4
PRE/TEXT

Victor J. Vitanza
Clemson University

Also known as . . .

Figure 4.1. PRE/TEXT Logo

The journal has a title that, I suspect, rings at the door by a person called OVID. And that Chicken Claw! Metamorphosis. Titles undergo, at a sublevel, different ways of thinking of the journal. The first volume (1980) is "An Inter-Disciplinary Journal of Rhetoric." In so many waves /\/\/\ it remains Mediterranean. The first called for thirst of *P/T*. The publisher/editor just did not know what is traditional in terms of rhetorics, which contributed unreadable for many in the field of rhetoric and composition, not until, the publication of the book *PRE/TEXT: The First Decade* (University of Pittsburgh Press, 1993).

How "the Event" in Pittsburgh started: I, with unknown others, applied and received a NEH Fellowship in Residence for nine months, 1978–1979: especially to work with **Richard Young** at Carnegie Mellon University on the topic of "Rhetorical Invention and the Composing Process." Other participants included **Sharon Bassett, James A. Berlin, Lisa Ede, David Fractenberg, Robert P. Inkster, Charles Kneupper, Sam**

Watson Jr., Vickie Winkler, and William Nelson. We were from literature (English departments), speech (communication studies), and philosophy. We were colleagues who helped each other, learning from each other.

During the opening months, we met twice a week, Mondays and Thursdays. What was so wonderful was the return to rhetorical invention: **Aristotle**'s twenty-eight topoi that **Cicero** cut down to sixteen, and a few centuries later then **KB**'s pentad. And yes, the event, **Young, Becker, and Pike** put forth the matrix of Contrast, Variation, Distribution together opening Particle, Wave, and Field. Yes, **Young** *et al.* put forth Tagmemics and Heuristics. There's so much more. But there are spin-offs: a few years later, I was invited to write a chapter **Maureen Daly Goggin**, as editor, wanted for a book: *Inventing a Discipline: Rhetorical scholarship in Honor of Richard E. Young* (2000). My title: "From Heuristic to Aleatory Procedures; or Toward 'Writing the Accident.'"

After the first NEH fall semester, the ten of us began to meet once a week, in the evenings, reading and discussing, yes, **Jacque Derrida's** early book (*Of Grammatology*), **Michel Foucault** (*The Order of Things*), **Michael Polanyi** (*Personal Knowledge: Towards a Post-Critical Philosophy*). And so many more! . . . I have to tell you, however, that during a break, **Sharon Bassett**, showed me this strange-looking book by **Paul Feyerabend**, *Against Method*. She pointed to the index: "rhetoric, 1 through 309" (1975) . . . What a Hoot.

When we all left Pittsburgh, at the end of the seminar, **Charles Kneupper** said he was going to start a biennial RSA conference. At that time, he had accepted a position at UT at Arlington, where I was. He developed three conferences and was working on the fourth when he passed away. **Michelle Ballif** and I followed through for the event.

When I left Pittsburgh, I announced to the seminarians I was going to start a journal that in no time became *PRE/TEXT: A Journal of Rhetoric Theory*. They said: "Yes, V, do it." The first volume appeared in spring-fall 1980, featuring articles on **Paul Feyerabend**. I sent him a copy: he was excited. **Samuel Ijsseling**, whom I met in Pittsburg at a conference, became my European associate editor. He is the one who wrote *Rhetoric and Philosophy In Conflict*. Etc.

As mentioned in the first paragraph, Victor J. Vitanza, the owner/editor, recommends reading and studying ***PRE/TEXT: The First Decade***. In it are opening two retrospectives: VJV and then James A. Berlin. And other retrospectives by Paul Kameen, "Rewording the Rhetoric of Composition"; Louise Wetherbee Phelps, "The Dance of Discourse"; Patricia Bizzell, "Cognition, Convention, and Certainty"; S. Michael Halloran, "Rhetoric in the American College Curriculum"; C. Jan Swearingen, "The Rhetor as *Eiron*"; William Covino, "Thomas De Quincey in a Revisionist Rhetoric"; Charles Bazerman, "The Writing of Scientific Non-Fiction"; Sharon Crowley, "Neo-Romanticism and the History of Rhetoric;" John Schilb, "The History of Rhetoric and the Rhetoric of History"; and Susan C. Jarratt, "Toward a Sophistic Historiography." And two afterwords: David Bartholomae and Steven Mailloux.

Officially put forth, and still in mind, **PRE/TEXT** has among its objectives:

1. to encourage the rediscovery of rhetorics as historically a transdisciplinary, "architechtonic productive art," informing such fields today as psychology, anthropology, art, linguistics, philosophy, music, mathematics, composition, economics, artificial intelligence, sociology, communications, and science in general;

2. to publish particularly exploratory articles and working papers on the transdisciplinary nature of rhetorical theories and rhetorical metatheories (which are concerned with describing/prescribing the properties of adequate theories);

3. to review all publications that contribute directly or indirectly to the understanding of rhetorics as transdisciplinary studies;

4. and to provide a transdisciplinary forum for the exchange of ideas and information about rhetorics.

And Yet from the Beginnings *PRE/TEXT* has followed **P. T.** Barnum's Selected Quotes.

And of course, **P/T** has published the very bestest Guest Editors and Writers who are quite liberal in thinking-writing rhetorics . . . And **OVIDian Clowns** . . . Of course, the traditional others made fun of our Clowns. Hence the card below announced, and gave copies of this card: But the best ways are to bring out the perverseness of *P/T* to the readers and other editors of other journals. For examples:

An Editor for *College English* announced she wanted to have a volume entitled "Queer" in front of a session at the Conference on College Composition and Communication. Of course, at that time, I and a guest editor, Margaret Morrison, for *P/T*, were preparing her volume of writing: "Laughing with Queers in My Eyes: Proposing 'Queer Rhetoric(s)' and Introducing a Queer Issue." The cover, of course, has the *P/T* chicken paw, which appears throughout the lives of *P/T*. With a smile.

Volume 13: 3-4 (1992)—Special Double Issue on Queer Rhetoric Guest Edited by Margaret Morrison, "Laughing with Queers in My Eyes: Proposing 'Queer Rhetoric(s)' and Introducing a Queer Issue"; Harriet Malinowitz, "Construing and Constructing Knowledge as a Lesbian

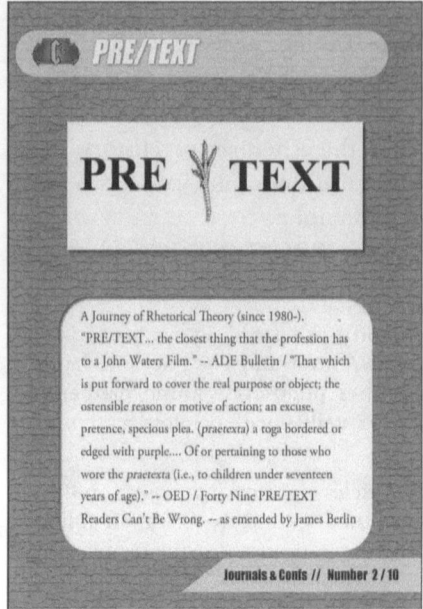 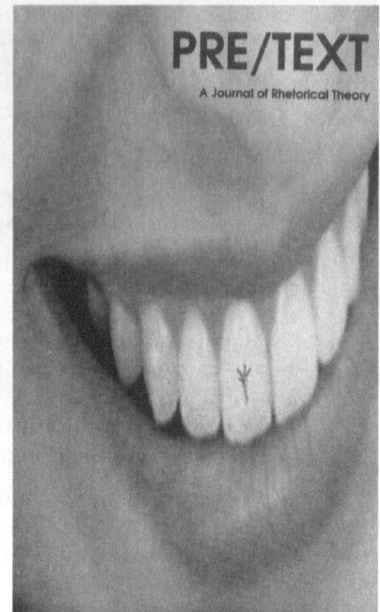

Figure 4.2. PRE/TEXT Cover 2.10   Figure 4.3. PRE/TEXT Cover 13.3

or Gay Student Writer"; David A. H. Hirsch, "De-Familiarizations, De-Monstrations"; Kate Cummings, "The Double Scene of Televised AIDS Campaigns"; Sarah Chinn, Mariod DiGangi, and Patrick Horrigan, "A Talk with Eve Kosofsky Sedgwick"; Fadi Abou-Rihan, "Being-Gay/ Becoming-Lesbian"; Roger Moss, "The Rhetoric That Dare Not Speak Its Name"; Karin M. Cope, " 'Publicity Is Our Pride': The Passionate Grammar of Gertrude Stein"; Shelton Waldrep, "Deleuzian Bodies: Not Thinking Straight in Capitalism and Schizophrenia"; Cindie Patton, "In Vogue: The 'Place' of 'Gay Theory.' " Recently, a guest editor gave us a second volume: Entitled "Special Issue: Queer Rhetorics."

The chicken shows up again and again in other forms, in this case, shooting the finger:

"CONSTRUCTING MASCULINITIES."

... And more ... Out of Order ...

Volume 14: 3–4 (1993)—edited by James E. Porter (posthumous publication), James A. Berlin, "Rhetoric and Citizenship: Notes and Essays on Emerson" Charles J. Stivale, "Pragmatic/Machinic: Discussion with Felix Guattari"; Deborah A. Covino, "Looking At (the) Logos: Hard Evidence,

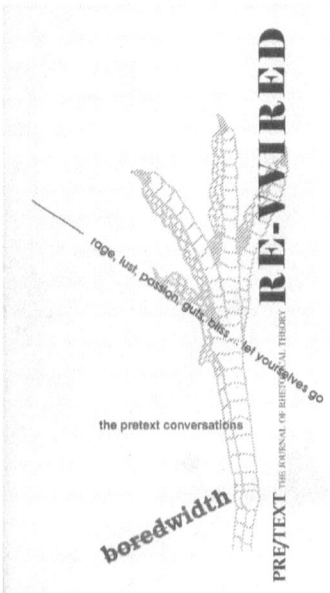

Figure 4.4. PRE/TEXT Cover 13.4

Figure 4.5. PRE/TEXT Cover 14.3

Gender Dialectics, and Intentional Phallacies"; Rosa A. Eberly, "Andrea Dworkin's Mercy: Pain, Ad Personam, and Silence in the 'War Zone'"; James J. Sosnoski and David B. Downing, "A Multivalent Pedagogy for a MultiCultural Time: A Diary of a Course"; Janet M. Atwill, "The Uses of Deception: Epistemological and Axiological Measurement in Aristotle and Ancient Thought."

And then, there is alongside the works of Feminists, by way of a *P/T*,

Vol. 16. 3–4 (1995)—"Constructing Masculinities." Special Issue Guest Edited by Robert Connors. Bruce Ballenger, "The Tuft of Flowers in a Leveled Field"; Steven D. Krause, "Cross-Dressing the 'New Rhetorics': A Modest Metaphor for the Teaching of Writing"; Lynn Alexander, "Heroic Creation: The Ambivalence of the Gendered Subject"; Michael Donnelly, "Male Instructor, Feminist Pedagogy: Interrogating Presence and Authority in the Classroom"; Ruth L. Smith and John Trimbur, "Teaching Tragedy: Norman Maclean and the Rhetoric of Masculinity"; John Ramirez, "The Chicano Homosocial Film: Mapping the Discourses of Sex and Gender in American Me"; Mary Murray, "I Want a Real Man: Teaching Masculinity Literature in First-Year Composition"; Michelle Ballif, "Mothers in the Classroom: Composing Masculinity via Fetal Pedagogies."

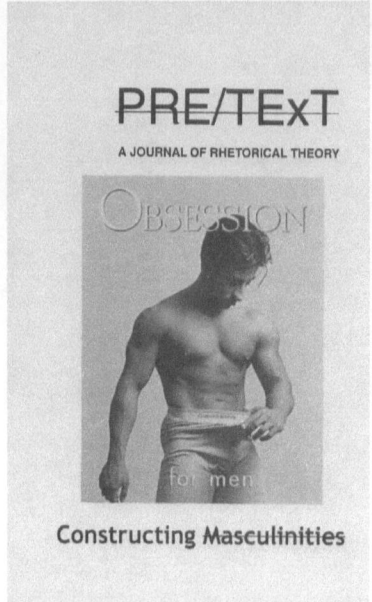 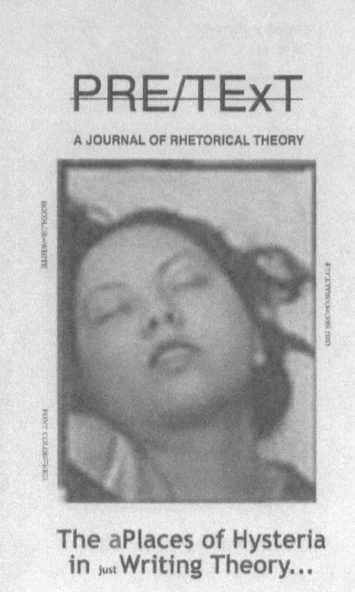

Figure 4.6. PRE/TEXT Cover 16.3   *Figure 4.7. PRE/TEXT Cover 17.1*

Of course, then, there is the issue **Vol. 17. 1–4 (1995)—"The Places of Hysteria in Just Writing Theory...."** Jane Love, "Justeria: Innocence as hysteria in the Justice System"; Marshall Alcorn, "Desire as Agency in Composition: The Ethics and Politics of Writing Instruction"; Robert Samuels, "The Rhetoric of Self-Composition: The Modern Subject and Lacan's Critique of Postmodern Discourse"; Brenda Jo Brueggemann, "Diagnosing Deafness: Rhetoric and the (Female) Audiogist's Authority"; Jane E. Hindeman, "[Mis]Recognizing Awesome Bodies: Gender and Publishing in Rhetoric and Composition Studies." Response: Theresa Enos.

Of course, then, there is the issue of "The SwimSuit Issue" in **Volume 15: 3–4 (1994)—**

"The Swimsuit Issue." Lynda Haas, "The Daughter's Seduction; or, Writing with the Rhetors"; Daniel Mahala and Jody Swilky, "Constructing the Multicultural Subject: Colonization, Persuasion, and Difference in the Writing Classroom"; Derek Pell, "The Elements of Style"; John Scenters-Zapico, "The Function of Enthymemes in a Print Culture: An Enthymematic Examination of the Discourses of the French Government and the Paris Communards of 1871"; Geoffrey Sirc, "English Composition as a Happening II" Part One.

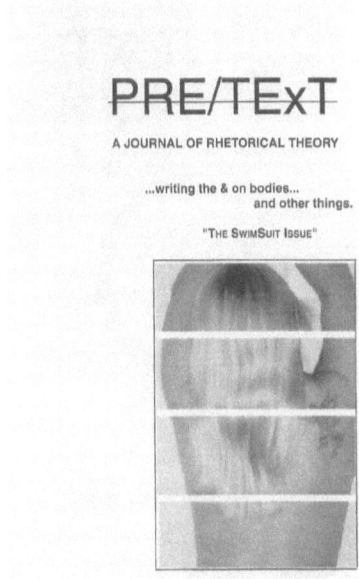

Figure 4.8. PRE/TEXT Cover 15.3

Figure 4.9. PRE/TEXT Cover 18.1

Vol. 18. 1–4 (1995)—"Prison. Literacy. Cultures," Guest Edited by Daniel Moshenberg. Daniel Moshenberg, "Stepping Out: Of Prison Literacy Culture(s)"; Kathleen Kelly, "'Authoratative Disorders': Contradictory Bakhtin and Contrary Literacies"; Rajeswari Sunder Rajan, "Beyond the Hysterectomies Scandal: Women, the Institution, Family, and the State in India"; Christine Shearer-Cremean, "Women as Text: Depictions of Abused Women in Conjugal Violence Police Reports"; Patricia O'Connor, "'If You're Afraid to Die, This is the Wrong Place to Be': Necessary Literacies in Prison Discourse"; Dorinda Welle and Gregory Falkin, "Women Inmates in Drug Treatment: 'Bio' Power and Bodies of Righting"; Varvara Rao/Venkat Rao, "Portrait of the Future/Voices of Unity"; Susan Ross, "'Did I ever say yes'? I said only 'let's just say': Rhetoric and Interrogation"; You-me Park, "'A Woman Guerrilla, Bound': Sexuality, Violence, and the Shadow of Prison"; David Staples, "Las luchas continuan."

And the beat goes on focusing on French philosophers and politicians and historiographies:

Volume 15: 1–2 (1994)—Special Issue on Jacques Lacan. David Metzger, "Let's Give Them Something to Talk About: (Guest Editor's Introduction to) 'Lacan and the Question of Writing'"; Russell Griff,

Figure 4.10. PRE/TEXT Cover 15.1   *Figure 4.11. PRE/TEXT Cover 13.1*

"Metaphor and Metonymy"; Ellie Ragland, "Psychoanalysis and Pedagogy: What Are Mastery and Love Doing in the Classroom?"; Tim Dean, "Bodies That Mutter: Rhetoric and Sexuality."

Volume 13:1–2 (1992)—Special Double Issue on Marxism and Rhetoric. Guest Edited by James Berlin and John Trimbur, "Introduction"; Victor Villanueva Jr., "Hegemony: From an Organically Grown Intellectual"; Lester Faigley, "The Left in New Times"; C. Mark Hurlbert and Michael Blitz, "The Institution('s) Lives!": Nancy Mack and James Thomas Zebroski, "Remedial Critical Consciousness?"; Karyn Hollis, "Literacy Theory, Teaching Composition, and Feminist Response"; William J. Rouster, "Social Construction, the Dominant Classes, and Cultural Criticism"; John Trimbur, " 'In the Beginning Was the Sixties': A Conversation with Richard Ohmann."

Volume 6:3–4 (1985)—Special double issue devoted to Kenneth Burke. Reviews: Hank Lazer, "Thinking of Kenneth Burke" (KB at Univ. of Alabama); Michael Feehan, "Three Days and Three Terms" (KB at Univ. of Texas at Arlington); Victor J. Vitanza, "A Mal-Lingering Thought (Tragic-Comedic) about KB's Visit" (KB at UTA); Gregory S. Jay, "Burke Re-Marx" (South Atlantic MLA panel on KB and Marx); Gerald A. Hauser, "An Afternoon with Burke and Cowley" (KB at

Figure 4.12. PRE/TEXT Cover 6.3   Figure 4.13. PRE/TEXT Cover 11.3

The Pennsylvania State Univ.); Kenneth Burke and Malcom Cowley, "A Conversation" (KB at Penn State); Tilly Warnock, "Anecdotes on Accessibility: KB in Wyoming" (KB at the Wyoming Conference on Freshman and Sophomore Literature). Articles: Paul Jay, "Kenneth Burke: A Man of Letters"; Denise M. Bostdorff and Phillip K. Tompkins, "Musical Form and Rhetorical Form: Kenneth Burke's Dial Reviews as Counterpart to Counter-Statement"; Don M. Burks, "Dramatic Irony, Collaboration, and Kenneth Burke's Theory of Form"; Bob Heath, "Kenneth Burke's Perspective on Perspectives." Photographs/Sculpture: Don and Virginia Burks, "KB at Home and Bust of KB." Notes: Lewis Baker, "Some Manuscript Collections Containing Kenneth Burke Materials"; Charles W. Mann, "The KB Collection: The Penn State Library." Statement/Counterstatement: "Oscillation as Assimilation: Burke's Latest Self-Revisions"; Kenneth Burke, "In Haste." A pre/text: Lewis Baker, from "A Biography of Kenneth Burke (in progress)."

Volume 11:3-4 (1990)—Issue devoted to Historiography and the Histories of Rhetorics II: Revisionary Histories and Ethics: James A. Berlin, "Postmodernism, Politics, and Histories of Rhetoric"; Susan C. Jarratt, "Speaking to the Past: Feminist Historiography in Rhetoric"; John Schilb, "The Role of Ethos: Ethics, Rhetoric, and Politics in

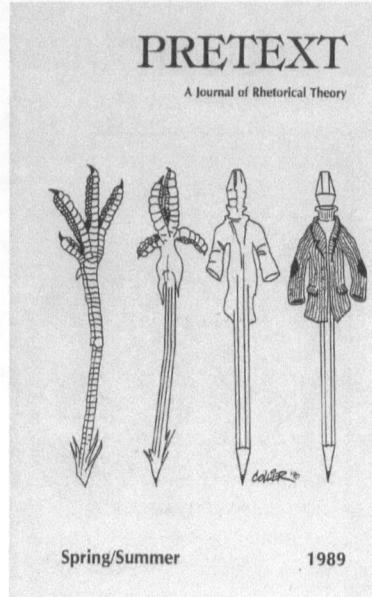

Figure 4.14. PRE/TEXT *Cover 10.1*

Figure 4.15. PRE/TEXT *Cover 6.1*

Contemporary Feminist Theory"; Victor J. Vitanza, "An Open Letter to My 'Colligs': On Paraethics, Pararhetorics, and the Hysterical Turn." Additional articles by Cynthia Haynes-Burton, "The Ethico-Political Agon of Other Criticisms: Toward a Nietzschean Counter-Ethic"; Theresa Enos, "Gender and Publishing." And the "Burpean" Corner.

Volume 10:1–2 (1989)—Paul Jude Beauvais, "Sartre's Pleas and the Purposes of Writing"; James J. Sosnoski, "The Psycho-Politics of Error"; Patricia Harkin, "Bringing Lore to Light." **A Polylog on Presocratic fragments**, with Dilip Gaonkar, Susan C. Jarratt, Henry Johnstone Jr., Takis Poulakos, Jane Sutton, and Victor J. Vitanza.

Volume 6: 1–2 (1985)—James P. Zappen, "Historical Perspectives on the Philosophy and the Rhetoric of Science: Sources for a Pluralistic Rhetoric"; Brian G. Caraher, "A Grammar of Actions and Attitudes: Unfolding a Humanist Theory of Literary Studies" (review of Charles Altieri's Act and Quality); Richard Leo Enos and Elizabeth Odoroff, "The Orality of the 'Paragraph' in Greek Literature"; R. J. Reddick, "The Grammar of Logic" (review/article of Beau^{a}ze's article on grammar, originally published in Diderot's *Encyclopedie*); Ralph Flores, "The Rhetoric of the Buddha: Selfless Selves, the Theatre of Persuasion."

Figure 4.16. PRE/TEXT Cover 4.3

Figure 4.17. PRE/TEXT Advertisement

Volume 4: 3–4 (1983)—Special issue on Paul Ricoeur, guest edited by Louise Wetherbee Phelps and featuring articles by Charles Regan, "Hermeneutics and the Semantics of Action"; Mary Gerhart, "Genre as Praxis: An Inquiry"; Stephen William Foster, "Deconstructing a Text on North Africa: Ricoeur and Post-Structuralism." With additional articles by Louise Wetherbee Phelps, "Possibilities for a Post-Critical Rhetoric: A Parasitical Preface 6"; Robert D. Sweeney and Louise Wetherbee Phelps, "Rhetorical Themes in the Work of Paul Ricoeur's Interpretation Theory: A Beginner's Guide"; C. Jan Swearingen, "Between Intention and Inscription: Toward a Dialogical Rhetoric"; Stuart L. Charm, "Paul Ricoeur as Teacher: A Reminiscence"; Leonard Lawlor, "Event and Repeatability: Ricoeur and Derrida in Debate."

***

And the beat goes on and on and on . . . out of order . . . a throw of the dice . . .

For the fun of it, here is an advertisement I distributed to virtually everyone at a conference who attended. Pictures/Images tell a story. Here is the dream for this resume . . .

***

I recommend to Researchers, Authors, Potential Editors who may have questions or concerns about what I have discussed, understand what I have done from the beginning is to [keep perpetually in interests in what might be the traditional journals (published in press and digital online)]. Also, however, for sure you and I should take interest in the various other journals in different disciplines but especially [indifferent] transdisciplines. All genres. As cartoonist, as demonstrated above. For example, instead of simply using the genre of reviews for books, [establish for your journals interviews and discussions online books or whatever]. One example, I established *Pretext Conversation* (an electronic discussion group on theoretical theory and interviews/reviews of work in rhetorics, broadly defined). For example, we had conversations for weeks and even months with Jane Gallop, Noam Chomsky, Sharon Crowley, Geoffrey Sirc, and so many others.

***

Okay, Search on Google for *journals on line.* Study them.

PRE/TEXT has a home at *PRE/TEXT: A Journal of Rhetorical Theory.*

I'm, along with p/t Barnum, also available at sophist@clemson.edu . . .

5
GETTING UP FROM A FALL
Five Years as Editor of WPA: Writing Program Administration

Alice S. Horning
Oakland University (retired)

In the course of preparing this chapter, I had conversations with two other journal editors that made me think carefully about the ways editing a journal entails providing sponsorship of several different kinds. I'm using "sponsor" in Deborah Brandt's (2001) sense of the term, meaning people who provide support for literacy activity that results in the achievement of personal or professional goals. She provided this definition: "Sponsors, as I have come to think of them, are any agents, local or distant, concrete or abstract, who enable, support, teach, and model, as well as recruit, regulate, suppress, or withhold, literacy—and gain advantage by it in some way" (19). Underlying my work for five years as the editor of *WPA: Writing Program Administration* was an effort to sponsor authors and readers, of course, but it turned out to offer opportunities to sponsor my coeditors and staff, members of the editorial board, and various others. I absolutely benefited personally from my role as editor by virtue of a reduced teaching load, by virtue of taking on work I liked and felt capable of doing effectively, and by virtue of gaining friends and colleagues I would have for the rest of my career and beyond. But my personal satisfaction from the editing work is somewhat beside the point for the purposes of this chapter. The myriad aspects of sponsorship involved in serving as a journal editor offer a chance to see how this work supports the discipline and those working in it.

HOW I GOT THE JOB
Well, yes, I had applied to edit *WPA: Writing Program Administration* with the support and agreement of colleagues Deb Dew, Glenn Blalock, and Ed White, but I was still surprised when Shirley Rose called me in January of 2009 to offer me the job. I was lying on the sofa, nursing my fractured

right wrist, broken in a fall on black ice on Christmas Day, 2008, and still leaning on Vicodin for the pain. She said she hoped the position offer would make me feel better, and it definitely did. My department had been restructured so the rhetoric program, formerly in a marriage of administrative convenience with communication and journalism, was going to become an independent department, and someone else had been chosen to be the founding chair. I was about to lose the administrative role I had mostly really enjoyed for ten years, which is when I saw the call for new editors for *WPA* and thought that would solve my problem. And it did.

Among other things, the editorship allowed me to keep the reduced teaching load I had as WPA. And it put me in frequent touch with people around the country on the editorial board, whom I regularly saw at meetings and talked with now and then by phone. I was also in constant touch with Deb (at the time WPA at the University of Colorado Colorado Springs), Glenn (WPA at a small college in Louisiana I think, but later at Texas A&M Corpus Christi), and Ed (who had run the writing program at Cal State and was the field's assessment guru, among many other professional roles), all of whom were thoroughly experienced WPAs themselves, as well as expert writers and editors. Deb Dew and I had known each other professionally via the WPA list, via a chance visit to her campus for an unrelated reason, and as a by-product of joint work on an edited collection about nontenured faculty serving as WPAs (Dew and Horning 2007). The book arose from our vehement disagreement about this issue. I knew Ed because he and Kristine Hansen had done a WPA consultant evaluator visit at Oakland, and as anyone who knows him knows, once you've met him, you feel as though you've known him forever. And I got to know Glenn through our mutual friend Rich Haswell, another WPA I had connected with through the WPA list. Ed agreed, since he was already retired but still professionally active, to be book-review editor, and Deb, Glenn, and I took up the rest of the work, with me as managing editor.

We were, if I do say so myself, a great team. We were also lucky to have the support of assistant editors Lori Ostergaard and Jim Nugent, who have lately become the editors of *WPA* themselves, and Greg Giberson, now the managing editor of *Composition Forum*, as well as student assistants who made a meaningful contribution to the journal. I *invited* my three younger colleagues to become assistant editors, despite Greg's claim in the opening chapter of this collection that I *told* him he would be joining the team. Really! I did want and need help, and the department chair at the time thought it would be good for all three of them, as their own happy outcomes demonstrate. Thus, my path to the editorship of *WPA* was more direct and a result of specific application, unlike Kelly Ritter's route to the leadership of *College English* (see her chapter in this volume).

While Glenn would leave us part way through our first term, we did a good enough job to get renewed for two additional years, so I served as managing editor from July 2009 to 2014. We were lucky to have Ed with us since he knows everyone and is among the most highly respected scholars in the field. The job was an on-going challenge for me personally at times, particularly as we were finishing an issue, but I mostly really loved editing the journal, working with authors, consulting with David Blakesley at Parlor Press, who handled all the production stuff and knows everything, and talking over submissions with Deb and Glenn. I found deep satisfaction in being able to support the presentation of solid research while setting high ethical standards for running a professional publication. I also built great friendships that persist to this day. I freely confess I have very odd ideas of what constitutes fun, but to me, this job was some of the best fun I had in my career. Being a sponsor, as Brandt's term suggests, is a highly rewarding role.

SPONSOR AS SUPPORTER

There were five key principles that drove my approach to the management of the journal: the golden rule, integrity of process, respect for everyone's time, fairness, and the publication schedule. My goal was to shape the journal to function in an ethical and professionally appropriate way; I hope my principles set a model for others, something sponsors often try to achieve. My desire/intention to run the journal consistent with "do unto others" related to my own experience as the author of a few dozen journal articles, including one in *WPA* when it was edited by Greg Glau and Duane Roen. Far too often, my submissions sat with editors for some extended period of time and then came back rejected with or without much rationale. Sometimes I got to revise and resubmit and then occasionally got rejected on the second try. Like most writers, I hated getting rejections, but as an editor/sponsor, I hated sending rejections! My own experiences, though, made me want to treat our authors the way I would have preferred to be treated myself. So, I tried hard to respond promptly to every submission to let authors know their work had been received and to make sure our editorial-board members reviewed articles by the deadlines we set. I think these are fair expectations authors should have if editors are serving as sponsors.

To meet these rather high standards, we were indebted to our Oakland University undergraduate student assistant, writing and rhetoric major

Jason Carabelli. Jason rather expertly designed a spreadsheet we kept in Google Docs so we could all access it. We logged the submissions as they came in and noted our collective editorial appraisal, and if we sent the piece out to members of the editorial board, we could see in the spreadsheet who got it and their assigned deadlines. This way, if an author contacted me about status, I could say exactly where every article was at any given moment. It was a great system, thanks to Jason's genius in creating it. After Jason graduated, several other student assistants helped us maintain the spreadsheet to ensure it functioned to keep us all on track. We benefited as well from editorial help from assistant editors. These staff folks also benefited from our sponsorship since we provided opportunities for them to learn journal editing from the inside. Authors of journal articles should be aware there are probably staffers working with editors to ensure the integrity of the process of article submission and review.

Once an article was in our system, we tried to respect both our authors and the board members reviewing articles, a third general principle of my sponsor role. This respect was reflected in our prompt handling of the articles, of course, with an attempt to keep authors updated on the status of their submissions. It was also reflected in the fact that our peer-review system was anonymous for authors and reviewers. I felt this approach insured a high degree of fairness and integrity in the review process. I was keenly aware some pieces came from younger faculty needing to build records of scholarly work, for whom delays had important implications. For them in particular, an anonymous peer-review approach could assure promotion and tenure committees that younger scholars' work had been rigorously reviewed. I was also keenly aware members of our editorial board were themselves busy WPAs whose time was at a premium. Generally, their rich, full responses (some of which I shared in a recent study of editorial expertise—see Elliot, Horning, and Haller 2018) reflected their generous willingness to put their time, knowledge, and skill into support for our authors. Thus, we tried to respect everyone's time-based needs. While the editorial board members mostly did not need much support, the goal was to make sure everyone's time was respected.

There were, of course, cases of people who could not meet a deadline or promised to review a piece and never did the work. We did not ask people to resign when this kind of thing happened; we were simply more selective about where we sent articles to be read. We quickly learned whom we could count on to do a timely and thorough reading of an article. While we tried hard not to overimpose on our most effective and efficient board members, if the number of articles anyone got to review had been tracked, our favorites would have been obvious. We were also often surprised by articles and reviews by senior scholars that needed extensive editing, both for MLA format and for clarity, organization, and other editorial issues. We tried in all cases, whether with editorial-board members or with writers, to operate in a fair and professional way, respecting people's time and effort and forgiving weaknesses as needed.

When we sent articles to the editorial board, we gave them a list of guide questions to respond to in their reviews. We inherited these questions from the previous editors, I think, but may have modified them over time. The intention was both to provide clear criteria for evaluation and to help readers shape their responses to authors. Some editorial-board members followed the guide explicitly and some did not. We also gave readers the opportunity to share their reviews with one another, and as I recall, most readers did want to see how another person responded to the paper. Some reviewers sent annotated manuscripts, but some just wrote notes, generally fairly detailed, to support their recommendations to accept, revise and resubmit, or reject. We allowed reviewers to write to us directly and confidentially in addition to their notes for the writer. And we asked for specific, constructive feedback to the writer, including comments on the substance of the discussion, lit review, methodology, organization, editorial issues, and related matters. It would be fair to say, I think, that we sponsored thorough and careful reviews for our authors. As I recall, most reviewers tried hard to be sponsors themselves for our authors. The reviews were commonly generous and supportive, even when they called for extensive revision of a piece.

Mostly, the point of the questions was to keep editorial-board members focused on the needs of readers of the journal. WPAs do not have a lot of time to spare, and I wanted to be sure the journal offered articles that could help everyone do a better job of running writing programs all over the country. One innovation toward this goal was to include an abstract with each article; when we took over the journal, abstracts were not routinely presented. Another innovation Ed introduced was review essays so multiple books could be reviewed within each issue. This approach made the job of the reviewers a little more challenging since they had to read more than one book for the review, but it allowed us to consider more books and provide readers with more information about work being published in the field. While abstracts and review essays became features in *CCC*, begun at more or less the same time under Kathi Yancey's leadership (around 2009, according to her recall; pers. comm., and see her chapter in this volume), *WPA* had not previously had either one, so they were new for us.

Finally, one of the challenges we had been given with the job was to put the journal on a regular publication schedule, ensuring consistent issues at predictable times in the spring and fall of the year. A regular schedule sends a message about professionalism and consistency. I've lately learned that consolidators like JSTOR are more willing to include journals that publish on a regular schedule. We worked hard with David Blakesley and his crew at Parlor Press to make sure our issues appeared more or less on time. We competed often on the spring issue with Dave's "mandatory" attendance at South by Southwest, which frequently took place back to back or overlapping with CCCC in an infuriating way that delayed the appearance of an issue after we'd long since finished the editing. We also proofread everything multiple times. I know errors persisted despite all the efforts we made to be consistent, accurate, and error free, with proofing by authors, by us, and by Dave and his team. Most of the time, I think the issues came out on time and looked pretty good, albeit not flawless. If substantive corrections were needed, we provided them in the very next issue and certainly never left errors by intention. I don't think our efforts were particularly out of the ordinary—readers and authors should see that editors do intend to work as sponsors as they read, review, and publish journal articles.

TEAM SUPPORT: JOURNAL EDITOR AS SPONSOR TO THE FIELD

In the general running of the journal, I was lucky to have the support of a very good team of coeditors, assistant editors, and student assistants, as well as backup from an assortment of ad managers (including Donna Scheidt) and the Parlor Press gang. So, if *WPA* was a successful journal under my leadership, it was absolutely, positively a result of team effort. Kathi Yancey saw her work at *CCC* in the same way, as noted in her chapter, which ends with the observation that journal editing is "an act of supporting community." And that's not even including all the people on the editorial board over the five years I was in charge, a mostly stable group of committed scholar-teacher-WPAs. The team effort was reflected in two specific features that were by-products of the collaborative work we did to provide sponsorship to the field at large.

First, at both the summer WPA Conference and at CCCC in the spring, I held a meeting for the members of the editorial board. Especially at CCCC, no matter when I set the meeting, some people were unable to attend due to conflicts, but it was often true that half or more of the board attended. Prior to these meetings, with permission from the author, I sent out an article we had under review or in production.

Everyone coming to the meeting read the article so we could discuss it to address the challenges of our review process. Often, a group consensus emerged after inevitably lively discussion of the piece. If the author was still working on it, I summarized the comments and shared them with the author. And I did summarize the meeting and share that with ALL members of the editorial board so even those who did not come to the meeting were aware of the discussion and ideas. I also used those meetings to discuss more general issues in the running of the journal, sponsoring a more cohesive view of our collaborative work as editors and reviewers.

A second outcome of the meetings beyond the sense of teamwork and camaraderie was an important discussion of the kinds of research being conducted and reported by authors. It was pretty clear to members of the editorial board that many WPAs writing for the journal had no background in empirical research and no idea how to conduct that kind of research study. It was also, as Michael Pemberton notes in his chapter in this collection, sometimes a challenge to find appropriate reviewers for articles reporting research results with statistics and analysis. The editorial board, then, was thinking collectively about how the journal or the organization might sponsor additional "inservice training" in effect, especially for younger scholars in the field. What emerged from this discussion was the Dartmouth Summer Seminar for Writing Research, an idea already floating among Christiane Donahue, Chuck Bazerman, and others, according to Donahue (pers. comm. Sept. 9, 2019). The idea for that program came in part from *WPA* editorial-board-meeting discussion. We agreed that most people with PhDs in English had no training in research procedures and statistics but that there were plenty of people on and off the editorial board who did have that kind of background and could teach it to anyone who wanted to learn. The Dartmouth program has been in existence for about ten years now and each year draws a group of younger scholars to learn how to do the kinds of studies administrators find persuasive on perennial issues like class size that can make a difference to the field and to student success. This outcome is a key contribution to the field that arose in part from the editorial board on my watch.

We added two other regular elements to the journal's content as well with the goal of making the journal a sponsoring resource for everyone in the field. First, we added a regular travelogue component that promoted the summer conference venue. Shirley Rose volunteered to take on the role of WPA interviewer at the host institution. She explored the general situation of writing programs in the area, as well as the particular program that was hosting the meeting. We also regularly published the keynote talks from the conference in the fall issue for those unable to attend the meeting. Both features were an attempt to make the journal more useful to everyone. In these ways, *WPA* served as sponsor/resource for the field in general.

WHAT EDITOR/SPONSORS WANT YOUNGER SCHOLARS TO KNOW

A few years ago, Kathi Yancey and I were both at the Research Network Forum Editors' Roundtable, held annually at CCCC. All the editors had a chance to say a few things to the participants in the session before individual conversations got underway. One of the things she said that made me (and I am betting every other editor) want to stand on my chair and yell "YES!" was that potential contributors should read the journal carefully. It seems obvious to anyone who has been a journal editor but evidently not to authors. So, this point is the first key piece of advice I'd offer. It is quite clear to an editor if an author submits an article and has no idea what the journal is or who reads it.

And while looking, authors should take note of the journal's style requirements and follow them. I would be a rich woman if I had a nickel for every time a piece came in that did not follow MLA format for *WPA*. We were very clear about our style in the journal itself in the information for authors, as well as on our website. Now, I am confident most journals have a website even if they still publish on paper the old-fashioned way, and the style requirements are stated there quite explicitly. Is it a pain in the neck to change the style of an article for a different journal? Sure. In my own work, because it might appear in a journal using APA or one using MLA or Chicago, I have had to change the style a number of times on different pieces. Still, it is quite annoying to editors, especially if a piece seems appropriate to the journal and potentially publishable, if it does not meet the journal's style requirements. A perfectly good article can get screened out on style if the editor is feeling cranky, so it is important to meet the style requirements, whatever they are.

New scholars should have a fair expectation about review processes. The procedures I've described here and put into place for *WPA* are, I believe, appropriate and ethical standards all journals should be adhering to in the handling of articles if editors see themselves as sponsors in all the various ways I have discussed. But that's just my opinion. I've had plenty of my own work mishandled by journals that do not follow the standards I set for *WPA* and have heard from younger scholars about similar mistreatment. I generally advise young scholars to expect an acknowledgment of a submission within a day or two. After a month from the time of acknowledgment, an author should contact the editor for a status update. If there's no response after two weeks, I'd suggest writing again to say that if there's no status update in two weeks, the article will be submitted elsewhere. And if there is no response, the article should be sent to another journal, with notification to the editor of this action. If the editor wants to end consideration of the article, fair enough. But young scholars do not have the time to wait for inconsiderate editors to respond to their work. Again, these guidelines are just my opinion and should be taken with an awareness that they come from someone with high standards who sees the role of sponsor as a key component of journal editing.

CONCLUSION

Recently, I had a conversation with Michael Pemberton, as mentioned at the outset of this chapter, who is also an editor of a journal and a book series. He is someone I have a great deal of respect for, and not only because he has published a fair amount of my work. He also has a great deal of integrity and is the person I turn to for advice on editorial matters of various kinds. He has wide experience and great common sense, as well as little patience with academic nitpicking and silliness. We were talking about the fact that as editors we serve as gatekeepers, playing a role in the future of younger colleagues by virtue of our acceptance or rejection of their work for publication—a topic he explores in his chapter in this volume. As he indicates, he feels a bit uncomfortable with this role, but I do not. I believe I have used my own experience as a writer and researcher to serve as a sponsoring editor in accordance with an ethical golden rule. In general, my editorial-board colleagues have not only accepted but have also supported my standards and goals. In setting high standards, I hope it's true that I've helped raise the expectations of authors, reviewers, and readers about the work we do together. Ultimately, younger colleagues should see that editors' collective goal is to sponsor, publish, and support the important work being done by scholars and researchers in our field.

REFERENCES

Brandt, Deborah L. 2001. *Literacy in American Lives*. New York: Cambridge University Press.
Dew, Debra Frank, and Alice Horning, eds. 2007. *Untenured Faculty as Writing Program Administrators: Institutional Practices and Politics*. West Lafayette, IN: Parlor.
Elliot, Norbert, Alice Horning, and Cynthia Haller. 2018. "Message in a Bottle: Expert Readers, English Language Arts, and New Directions for Writing Studies." *Composition Forum* 40. https://compositionforum.com/issue/40/message-bottle.php.

6
OPENING SPACES IN WRITING STUDIES
An Impetus for Change at Composition Forum

Christian Weisser
Penn State Berks

I've served as editor of *Composition Forum* (*CF*) for about fifteen years. During that time, I've worked with a tremendous editorial team that has implemented some fundamental changes and additions to the journal, including the addition of new sections of the journal like "Interviews," "Program Profiles," and "Retrospectives"; the development of a special-topics series within the journal that has become a regular feature; and various changes in the format and delivery of the journal. Yet despite the extensive structural changes we've implemented at *CF* over the years, the most significant contribution we've made—and one I argue is the essence of scholarly editing—is much more subtle and inconspicuous: the gradual and fragmentary shaping of the scholarly conversations in writing studies.

Journal editors play a fundamental role in shaping, guiding, and influencing the conversations in writing studies, as in any field. The choices they make have far-reaching implications for the scope and direction of present and future scholarship. Drawing upon the Burkean parlor metaphor, I believe journal editors not only contribute to scholarly conversations but also arrange the chairs, set the lighting, choose the background music—all subtle yet profound acts that help shape how and what the participants discuss in these academic parlors. Understanding the importance of this role is vital to success as a journal editor, and the responsibility editors have in guiding the direction of the field is palpable. It would be difficult to describe or categorize the many incremental internal decisions journal editors make on a regular basis, all of which culminate in large-scale changes in scholarship. Instead, in this article I focus on one specific change in scholarly

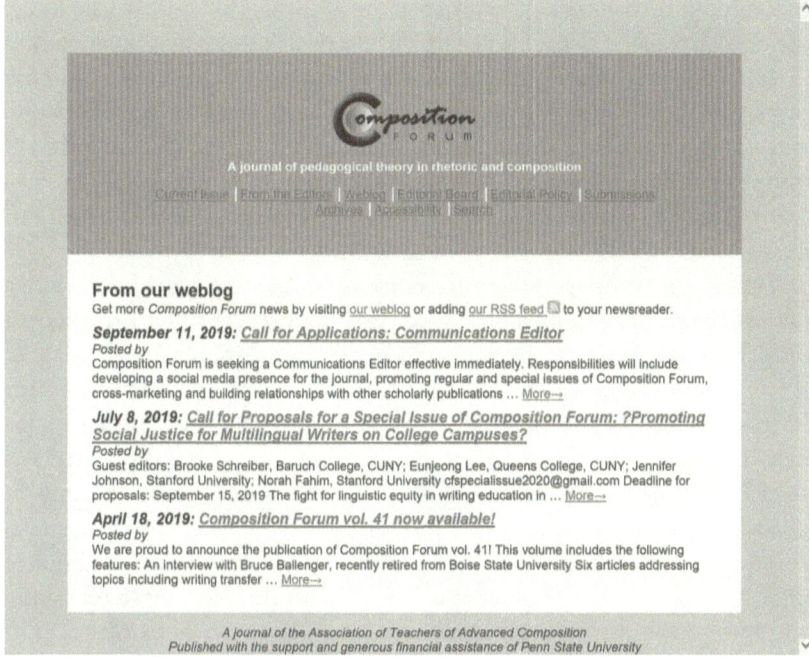

Figure 6.1. Composition Forum *Homepage*

production that has recently impacted scholarly publishing—the move to open access.

Open access refers to a process whereby scholarly research is published and made available via the internet to the end user at no cost. In contrast to traditional academic publishing, sometimes called *toll access*, open-access readers do not pay fees of any type, nor do they face other subscription limitations in retrieving, reading, downloading, citing, and sharing scholarly research. Open-access publication was enmeshed with the development and expansion of the internet in the late 1990s for a number of technological, economic, and logistical reasons.[1] The Budapest Open Access Initiative of 2002 (n.d.) put forth one of the first formal explications of the term, and it remains a central definition today:

Open access refers to peer-reviewed journal literature with free availability on the public internet, permitting any users to read, download, copy, distribute, print, search, or link to the full texts of these articles, crawl them for indexing, pass them as data to software, or use them for any other lawful purpose without financial, legal, or technical barriers other than those inseparable from gaining access to the internet itself. The only constraint on reproduction and distribution, and the only role for copyright in this domain, should be to give authors control over the integrity of their work and the right to be properly acknowledged and cited.

To summarize, then, open-access publication hinges upon two concepts: first, providing research and scholarship to readers free of charge, and second, utilizing the internet, rather than print, as the primary means of producing and distributing scholarship. Open-access publication has had a significant impact on scholarly journals over the past two decades, and publications in writing studies are no exception.

The timing and opportunities afforded by this worldwide move toward open-access publishing have played a central role in the recent history of *Composition Forum*, a peer-reviewed scholarly journal in rhetoric and composition, as well as in my role as the current editor of the journal. This article begins with a description of the early history of *Composition Forum* and the challenges and obstacles it faced as a traditional print publication. It then describes a fundamental shift in *Composition Forum*'s format, distribution, and structure, which was triggered by the growth of open-access publication and the development of internet technologies. The chapter reflects on the ways these technologies have not only granted easier access to *CF*'s material to readers but also have expanded the capabilities and possibilities of the journal over the past eighteen years or so. The article concludes with reflections on the future of *Composition Forum* and the ways open-access and online publication create further opportunities for new and innovative forms of scholarship in the field.

A BRIEF HISTORY OF *COMPOSITION FORUM*

Composition Forum began as an offshoot of *JAC: The Journal for Advanced Composition* (later renamed *JAC: A Journal of Rhetoric, Culture, and Politics*). *JAC* was first published in 1980 under the guidance of *ATAC: The Association of Teachers of Advanced Composition*. Many of the articles published in the early years of *JAC* focused on advanced composition pedagogy; that is, issues relating to the teaching of composition to advanced undergraduate students. However, when Gary A. Olson became editor of *JAC* in 1987, the journal began to publish more articles based in composition theory, reducing the number of articles with a pedagogical emphasis. This theory-centered approach seemed to be Olson's focus from the start, as his inaugural "From the Editors" column (a genre feature still present in *Composition Forum*) in volume 7.1 points out *JAC* is "not interested in articles that simply describe classroom techniques divorced from their theoretical underpinnings" and then references *theory* six times in regard to the topics of interest for prospective publications. Equally interesting is Olson's note that *JAC* had previously encountered delays and difficulties in publication and that "the high cost of printing is one contributing factor"—an issue prevalent in traditional print journals and one this article addresses in greater detail in describing *Composition Forum's* move to an open-access format. *JAC* quickly emerged as one of the premier theoretical journals in rhetoric and composition, and with that emergence came both a more exclusive focus on theory and a growing number of submissions.

In response to *JAC*'s shift toward composition theory and an increase in submissions, ATAC created *Composition Forum* in 1989 as a sister publication to *JAC*. This new journal, in its print incarnation from 1989 until 2005, was funded by ATAC and distributed at no additional cost to *JAC* subscribers. The initial goal of *Composition Forum* was to publish articles that focused on pedagogical theory in rhetoric and composition. ATAC recognized the need for an academic space for high-quality articles that integrated theory and pedagogy in rhetoric and composition; while *JAC* focused on theoretical scholarship, *Composition Forum* focused on scholarship that merged theory and pedagogy. The focus of *Composition Forum* has not changed much in nearly thirty years. In the "From the Editors" column in volume 12, issue 1, incoming editor Joe Hardin (2001) writes that *Composition Forum* will continue to publish "provocative articles on pedagogical theory and practice . . . as the field has embraced pedagogy that is increasingly guided by sophisticated and inter-disciplinary theory" (iii). This description is quite similar to *Composition Forum's* current editorial mission statement, now found on our website: "The journal features articles that explore the intersections of composition theory and pedagogy, including essays that examine specific pedagogical theories or that examine how theory could or should inform classroom practices, methodology, and research into multiple literacies" ("Editorial Policy" 2019).

Composition Forum continues to provide a space for scholarship at the intersections of composition theory and pedagogy. This area of praxis, to my thinking, is among the most fundamentally important areas of inquiry in our field. Many scholars have recognized composition's deep ties to writing classrooms and instruction, and the field would be remiss in removing itself entirely from pedagogical work. At the same time, composition's continued development as a separate and legitimate field of scholarly inquiry is dependent upon critical and sophisticated theories about writing as a subject itself. Consequently, scholarly spaces like *Composition Forum* and others like it that bring together theory and pedagogy in rhetoric and composition serve a vital role in advancing the work of writing instruction while at the same time developing theories and concepts that expand our understandings of composition as a scholarly subject. The journal's thirty-year history of praxis-oriented scholarship has resulted in an extensive body of work by a wide range of scholars, and I hope *Composition Forum* will continue to highlight work at the intersections of composition theory and practice for years to come.

While *Composition Forum's* emergence provided (and continues to provide) a much-needed space for praxis-oriented scholarship, the journal was faced with some of the economic and logistical constraints of traditional print publication from the outset. As a sister publication of *JAC*, the journal was dependent upon funding from ATAC, with supplemental funding provided by various supporting institutions—typically the home universities of one or more of the journal's editors. This funding was limited, not just because *Composition Forum* was a sister publication to *JAC* but also because nearly all journals face limited financial support—the funding issue is addressed in other chapters in this book and is a consistent challenge in scholarly publishing. The cost of print publication limits what a journal can accomplish in a number of ways—it influences how many volumes can be produced in a given financial cycle; it affects the length of volumes and the number of articles and other features that can be included since more print pages mean a higher cost per volume; and it dictates the overall quality of printing and production, including paper and cover type, binding methods, and so forth. In addition, distribution costs can place a significant strain on tight budgets, and the steady rise of mailing fees often limits the number and speed of delivery of outgoing publications. Such issues are particularly cogent for smaller independent journals (especially those outside the sciences, where funding is more readily available). In my conversations with Joe Hardin and Julie Drew, the two *Composition Forum* editors who directly preceded me, they were quick to note the financial challenges they faced during their editorship in the early 2000s. Hardin (pers. comm. Oct. 28, 2019) writes that "time and money were the biggest obstacles we faced as editors of *Composition Forum*. If you are doing it right, there are never enough resources. ATAC mostly supported us in those days, but print publication was costly and sometimes difficult to manage."

Along with the financial limitations of print publication, the traditional model also placed constraints on the logistics of running a journal. I served as *Composition Forum's* book review editor from 2000 to 2005, during which the journal still appeared in print, and I remember a number of ongoing logistical challenges related to the traditional print format. Print deadlines were often firmly set in advance, and late changes or revisions to articles often meant a last-minute scramble to get everything print ready before it was sent to a publisher. Likewise, errors and typos were a constant source of worry—it's remarkable how easy it is to spot mistakes after a volume has been sent to print, but of course by that time it is too late to correct them. In addition, print format restricts or prohibits the use of some types of multimedia, including limits on the number and quality of images, as well as the inability to include audio or video. Printing was in black and white, and like most journals in rhetoric and composition at that time, visuals and graphics were limited and often poorly reproduced. With the expansion of the internet in the 2000s, more scholars were proficient and interested in incorporating multimedia (and often focusing on multimedia as a scholarly topic), yet print publication restricted what could be done. My service as book review editor with the traditional print version of the journal placed me in a unique position to make informed decisions about the format of *Composition Forum* when I became editor.

OPEN ACCESS AND THE EXPANSION OF *COMPOSITION FORUM*

When I was invited to serve as editor of *Composition Forum* in 2005, my primary objectives for it revolved around diversifying the journal and expanding access. I saw these two concepts as interrelated, and I used them as the basis for much of the decision-making in the journal's development in my early tenure. Quite simply, I wanted to make the journal more diverse in its offerings and more accessible to a wider range of readers. Diversity is typically associated with the inclusiveness of subject positions like race, class, and gender, and that type of diversity has always been important in publication decisions at *Composition Forum*. At the same time, though, I thought of diversity in broader terms encompassing not just the representation of diverse and marginalized voices in rhetoric and composition but also an expansion of genres, formats, topics of conversation, editorial roles, and means of distribution of *CF*'s content. The traditional print format, to my thinking, limited the diversity of what we could include in the journal, as well as access to a paid subscription list of readers.

The first step in *Composition Forum*'s expansion was probably the most fundamental: converting from a traditional print subscription-based format to an online, open-access format. In 2005 there were several recently developed "digital-native" journals in rhetoric and composition (such as *Kairos* and *enculturation*), as well as one or two journals, like

Computers and Composition, that were supplementing their print-based journals with an online companion to offer readers new and emerging forms of media. But the vast majority of the peer-reviewed journals at the time were still entirely print based. To my knowledge, *Composition Forum* was the first peer-reviewed journal in the field to execute a complete transition from print to digital—what David Solomon, Mikael Laakso, and Bo-Christer Björk (2016) refer to as "flipping" a journal from print-subscription based to online open access (29). At the time, there was much discussion about the risks of publishing online, including being stigmatized by authors, and perhaps more important, tenure committees, in terms of the rigor of peer review in an online format; concerns about maintaining a high rate of quality submissions; and the technological challenges of offering new forms and formats of scholarship through the internet (Hahn et al. 1999). However, I was encouraged by the growing number of journals outside rhetoric and composition that were transitioning from print to online. In "A Study of Innovative Features in Scholarly Open Access Journals," author Bo-Christer Bjork (2011) estimates that "the number of OA journals increased by 500% during the decade of 2000–2009 . . . resulting in nearly 5000 OA journals by the end of the decade." In consultation with other editors, scholars, and executive-board members, we became increasingly interested in joining this new wave of scholarly publishing and taking advantage of the opportunities it offered.

Creating the position of website editor and inviting Bradley Dilger to serve in that post was an essential first step. Dilger's expertise in online publishing, HTML coding, and open-access scholarship made him an indispensable part of *Composition Forum's* transition from print to digital. He quickly convinced the rest of the editorial team we should adopt the highly flexible CC-BY-SA open-access license (Creative Commons, Attribution, Share-Alike) to enable widespread sharing and to give authors control over their content. Dilger (pers. comm., Sep. 10, 2019) writes, "Hey, we'll share with you, but only if you share too."

To facilitate this form of open access, Dilger designed a set of simple web templates to be forward compatible. Rather than pick a platform that could become outdated, he created a semiautomated process for converting manuscripts from word-processor files to standards-compliant web code designed for broad compatibility. So, *CF* code written in 2005, 2008, or 2011 still looks pretty good today. Dilger (and his predecessor Kevin Brock) also set a high bar for web accessibility. Both website editors have worked closely with authors to get captions for videos, to include long descriptions for text elements, and to recast graphics when necessary. Dilger suggests that most authors were eager to collaborate on accessibility, and the result made their work better for everyone. In keeping with the move toward accessibility, the website editors use print-friendly pages without having separate versions or using PDFs, which makes their workflow much less complicated and allows readers to view and share content more easily. That has helped the journal build citations as well; rather than two or more web addresses to cite, there is just one, and linking to and from the journal becomes easier.

The conversion from print subscription to online open access has been mostly positive for *Composition Forum*. Some of the advantages were immediate and tangible within the first year of online publication in 2005 while others emerged more slowly over time. It is impossible to address all the benefits of open access, though several are worth noting.

Financial Advantages

Converting to open access had an immediate positive impact on the financial challenges associated with print publication. After switching to the online format, *Composition Forum* was no longer faced with the costs of printing, binding, and mailing physical copies of the journal to subscribers and libraries. Though there are costs associated with the development and maintenance of the journal, such as costs for hardware and software, as well as website-hosting fees, these are negligible in comparison to the repeated costs of print. *Subscribers* became *readers* or *viewers*, and they no longer had to pay for access to published content in the open-access version of *Composition Forum*. Some open-access journals require a publication or formatting fee from authors, but we were wary of any association with a "pay-for-play" model, so *Composition Forum* has never assigned a cost to authors for publication. In short, the move online eliminated the majority of the costs to the journal, to authors, and to readers.

Increased Access

We envisioned increased access, greater visibility, and an expanded readership as major benefits in converting to open access. Through this model, authors are thus granted the ability to address a wider audience without the corresponding expenditure. Readers are free to browse the journal without paying for a subscription or searching a library database since all volumes and articles are available at no cost. As a result, the number of readers expanded from a few hundred paid subscribers to many more readers, on average. *Composition Forum*'s current website editor Kevin Brock has been tracking the number of views for each volume and article published online (detailed analytics are another benefit of the online format), and Brock (pers. comm., Dec. 3, 2019) notes that "based on Google Analytics data, which goes back to 2011, the most viewed article is John Swales's retrospective piece entitled 'The Concept of Discourse Community: Some Recent Personal History,'" which was published in *CF* 37 in fall 2017. As of December 2019, that article had 19,826 unique page views—far exceeding the number of subscriptions, and presumably the number of "views" of any print-based article in *Composition Forum's* history.

Open access has also expanded the geographic range of *Composition Forum*. We regularly receive inquiries, questions, and submissions from scholars around the world, which was not the case in print. The Enago Academy (2019), an academic-publishing support association, suggests that with open access, the "reach of articles or materials increases tremendously since readers can retrieve it regardless of their economic status or geographical location." The online format of the journal has been central to *Composition Forum*'s reader-based and geographic development as a medium for scholarship in rhetoric and composition.

Immediacy and Flexibility

Another benefit of open access is the ability to publish, update, or revise material at times most convenient and opportune for authors, editors, and readers. As noted earlier in this article, print versions of *Composition Forum* were often based around set schedules, with little flexibility to delay publication and no ability to revise submissions after they had been printed. The online format has enabled us to publish content as soon as it is ready. Though we still follow a biannual publication format, the ability to publish a volume earlier or later in the schedule has been a distinct editorial advantage. Authors occasionally need more time to complete revisions or to make corrections to accepted articles, and the online format allows us to delay publication (within reason) to accommodate those authors. Similarly, we have the ability to revise or edit a piece after it has been released; it is not uncommon to find small typos and formatting issues in a published piece, and those are easy to fix.

The flexibility of the open-access format also allows *Composition Forum* to include more content than it did in the past. Print versions of the journal were typically limited to three to five articles, a few book reviews, and later, one or two program profiles. The number of published articles has essentially doubled since the journal moved to open access, largely for two reasons: first, increased access and visibility have led to an increase in submissions; and second, there are no additional printing or publishing costs associated with more content in open access, so the journal is not limited to a page count. This has actually led to a more fair and egalitarian review process. Print journals are often faced with difficult decisions about which articles to accept or reject due to page limitations, whereas online journals can simply accept and publish articles based solely on quality of content. This expansion of publishing space has also enabled the journal to add new categories and sections of material over the past decade—along with new editors to develop those sections—including "Retrospectives," "Interviews," an expanded "Program Profiles" section, an increased number of "Reviews" of different types, and an additional volume per year focused on a special topic (usually appearing in summer). In addition, the flexibility of the online format allows *CF* to regularly post announcements, calls for papers, and other timely news items on our weblog. This information is no longer bound by the time and space constraints of print and can be added or updated immediately. We believe this flexibility creates a more dialogic environment, where readers can easily contribute news and information they believe will benefit others in the field. Generally speaking, new ideas can be dispersed more rapidly, more widely, and through a greater diversity of formats, which in turn triggers new research; the immediacy and flexibility of open access serves as an impetus for knowledge.

Expanding Media Formats

The print version of *Composition Forum* in the 1980s and 1990s reflected the traditional generic features of the time: a predominance of text, a linear structure, few images or tables (none in color), and of course nothing in the way of multimedia. Moving online allowed the journal to expand into hypertextual and multimedia formats. Though *Composition Forum* was not the first journal in the field to publish multimedia content, it benefitted from the increased interest and proficiency in digital publishing that emerged in the early 2000s, along with the development of new tools that made it easier for authors to create media-rich content. It was, as Cheryl Ball (2017) notes in "Building a Scholarly Multimedia Publishing Infrastructure," a rhetorically opportune and timely moment for scholars and publishers, a "crossroads of easily available, professional-grade production technologies for digital media;

feasible technological implementation of online journals; and the exciting hype of digital culture" (99).

Though many of the articles in *Composition Forum* are still text driven and maintain a linear structure, various authors have published creative and interesting multimedia projects, including interactive articles with animations, video and/or audio files, extensive data sets published as hypertextual appendices, and some stand-alone media projects. As an example, one of the most interesting multimedia pieces we've published was not an article per se—it was a sonic review of a book. Kyle Stedman and Jonathan Stone's "Experiencing Ambience Together: A Sonic Review of Thomas Rickert's Ambient Rhetoric: The Attunements of Rhetorical Being" was published in volume 30, fall 2014. Unlike the typical book review, Stedman and Stone's piece is a fifty-one-minute audio file divided into five parts that can be easily found in *Composition Forum's* archives. The review is stylized in podcast format, and it merges interpersonal dialogue, background music and sound effects (including clips from a Pearl Jam concert), and careful reflective scholarship on ambient rhetorics. It remains one of the most widely accessed pieces published in *Composition Forum*, and it stands as one model for the kind of innovative work that can be done in an open-access publication. Personally, I've listened to the piece half a dozen times, and I pick up something new from it each time.

Searching and Citing

The increased ease of navigating, searching, and citing are universally positive features of an online journal. The retrieval capabilities of journals in electronic form are far better than those in print. This has been beneficial to *Composition Forum* in a number of ways. Search engines have become a primary form of research discovery; students and faculty alike often begin their research by looking online, then using library databases as secondary sources of information. *Composition Forum* and journals like it are searchable in both formats, leading to greater access and higher visibility. Similarly, searches of online journals like *Composition Forum* allow for greater specificity since individual words, phrases, or authors can be investigated through internet search engines or through the journal's internal search engine. Searches based on title, keywords, author, subject, abstract, article, and full text can be executed to identify the journals and articles of interest to the reader. This allows readers to find new information or to search within a body of text for something specific. Every word in the article is a potential retrieval point, so even a caption of a figure can be used to find a half-remembered article.

In spring of 2009, four years after moving the journal online, we began including embedded tags and keywords, as well as author-generated abstracts (typically one to two paragraphs) at the beginning of each article, which allow for even greater flexibility and ease in finding information. The *Composition Forum* website also features a searchable and fully accessible archive of previous work, dating back to the first online volume of the journal, published in fall 2005. As a result of the increased ease and specificity of navigating and searching in *Composition Forum*, there has been a steady increase in the number of citations from the journal over the past decade. Using Google Scholar analytics, we can see an H5 index of 12 for *Composition Forum*, which means that over the past five years, twelve *CF* articles have garnered at least twelve citations in archived and searchable publications (Google). We see this as an indicator of strength and growth in the distribution of *Composition Forum's* content.

CONTINUING TRENDS

As should be clear, we see a decrease in cost, quicker and more flexible publication times, the ability to publish innovative multimedia content, the ease of navigating and indexing articles, and an increased visibility and greater citation count as the primary strengths of the open-access format of *Composition Forum*. The transition to open access and its aftermath have resulted in a few minor hiccups, mostly technological and mostly addressed by *Composition Forum's* two outstanding website editors Bradley Dilger (2005–2011) and Kevin Brock (2011–present), but we believe the benefits have far outweighed the challenges.

While the move to open access has allowed us to accomplish a lot at *Composition Forum*, there is still room for further diversification and expansion of the journal and its contents. Newer sections like "Interviews," "Retrospectives," "Program Profiles," and a wider variety of "Reviews" have enabled different types of scholarship, but we seek even more diversity of genres in the journal's future. As authors and readers gain interest in exploring innovative approaches to exploring the field, we hope to keep pace by offering a literal forum for genre exploration in rhetoric and composition. Frequent readers of *Composition Forum* are aware of the special issues we publish each summer—such as the summer 2019 issue devoted to "*Composition in the Presence of Disability*"—and we are always looking for guest editors with expertise and knowledge to assemble new collections devoted to evolving and important topics in writing studies. And while the online format of the journal has enabled more dynamic texts that incorporate images, audio, video, and other forms of multimedia, we believe there is room for new developments in scholarship as technology and scholars' fluency with it advances. We are particularly interested in scholarship that both addresses and utilizes social media—in fact, in 2019 we appointed a communications editor who will not only raise *Composition Forum*'s profile through social media integration but will also help us cultivate scholarship that examines and critiques emerging social platforms of communication.

So, while much of this chapter focuses on things the editors have done to open up and expand the journal, I want to close with a plea to our readers: send us innovative articles, reviews, and other features. Send us ideas for pioneering special issues. Send us material that utilizes new technologies and diverse mediums. Because ultimately, innovation and the progression of scholarship are not driven by editorial choices but by the scholars who create content and meaning.

Acknowledgments. *Composition Forum* would not exist without the expertise, effort, and insights of the many editors I've worked alongside since 2000. My deepest thanks to Brian Bailie, Michelle Ballif, Anis Bawarshi, Kevin Brock, Bradley Dilger, Julie Drew, Greg Giberson, Joe Hardin, Faith Kurtyka, Ashley Holmes, Sean Morey, Derek Owens, Mary Jo Reiff, Jacqueline Rhodes, Jeanne Rose, Lori Salem, Jody Shipka, Elizabeth Wardle, and Shane Wood.

NOTE

1. To be clear, there is some distinction between online journals, which are available on the internet and may or may not charge a fee, and open-access journals, which are also available on the internet but are by definition free of cost to readers. For the purposes of this article, I use the terms somewhat interchangeably, since *Composition Forum* meets both criteria. To be more specific, *CF* could be categorized as an online publication and an open-access publication.

REFERENCES

Ball, Cheryl. 2017. "Building a Scholarly Multimedia Publishing Infrastructure." *Journal of Scholarly Publishing* 48 (2): 99–115.

Björk, Bo-Christer. 2011. "A Study of Innovative Features in Scholarly Open Access Journals." *Journal of Medical Internet Research* 13 (4): e115. https://doi:10.2196/jmir.1802.

Budapest Open Access Initiative. n.d. Accessed November 1, 2019. http://www.budapestopenaccessinitiative.org/read.

"Editorial Policy." n.d. *Composition Forum*. Accessed November 4, 2019. https://compositionforum.com/editorial-policy.php.

Enago Academy. 2019. "The Benefits of Open Access Publications." https://www.enago.com/academy/benefits-of-open-access-publications/.
Google Scholar Citations. n.d. Accessed October 16, 2019. https://scholar.google.com.
Hahn, Susan, Cheri Speier, Jonathan Palmer, and Daniel Wren. 1999. "Advantages and Disadvantages of Electronic Journals." *Journal of Business and Finance Librarianship* 5 (1): 19–33.
Hardin, Joe Marshal. 2001. "From the Editors" *Composition Forum* 12 (1): i–iv.
Solomon, David J., Mikael Laakso, and Bo-Christer Björk. 2016. "Converting Scholarly Journals to Open Access: A Review of Approaches and Experiences." Digital Access to Scholarship at Harvard. https://dash.harvard.edu/handle/1/27803834.
Swales, John. 2017. "The Concept of Discourse Community: Some Recent Personal History." *Composition Forum* 37. http://compositionforum.com/issue/37/swales-retrospective.php.

7
GREATER THAN THE SUM OF ITS PARTS
Enacting an Editorial Philosophy at College Composition and Communication

Kathleen Blake Yancey
Florida State University

> "Elsewhere in this issue you will find a statement by the chairman of the CCCC regarding the objectives of our organization. This bulletin is designed to contribute to the achievement of those objectives, to provide a 'systematic way of exchanging views and information quickly' and a 'means of developing a coordinated research program,' and to preserve and disseminate to wider audiences the valuable papers and reports given at the fall and spring meetings."
>
> —Chas W. Roberts

In the December 2014 issue of *College Composition and Communication* (*CCC*), volume 66, number 2, the last I edited before turning it over to the next editor, I provided a quick accounting of what we had published during my five years as editor. Perhaps not surprisingly, we published a large number of articles: eighty-eight of them, to be exact. But we published a host of other genres as well, some institutionally oriented, among them six CCCC chair's addresses and five CCCC exemplar remarks; other texts representing a wide diversity of genres, among them eleven symposia texts; three round-robin book reviews; over thirty vignettes; several "Interchanges"; and twenty "Editor's Introductions." In each issue, we also published a new genre for *CCC*, a poster page identifying and defining a key term for rhetoric and composition, and in every issue we also included a review essay authored by a senior scholar addressing multiple books: during the five years of my editorship, review essays considered ninety-one books.

From the beginning of my *CCC* editorship, I understood editing *CCC* as an opportunity to contribute to the field in very specific ways, among them vetting and then publishing articles updating earlier research, sharing innovative methods or findings or theories, and articulating some provocations. And I also understood that by offering a suite of special issues, I could focus the field's attention on topics important to the discipline; the plan for one special issue a year was part of my application to become editor of *CCC*. In addition, I thought it important to design an editor's introduction to each issue that consistently provided at least two contexts for those articles and issues: the first context a disciplinary one, of course; the second context that of higher education more generally. Not least, I also hoped the predictable appearance of specific features—for instance, one poster page and one review essay in each issue—would encourage readers to read *CCC* regularly, and toward this end, my editor's introductions often shared with readers what they could expect in forthcoming issues. Put another way, the intended effect of these predictable offerings was to establish a rhythm habituating readers to the pages of *CCC*.

This is what I hoped; below is part of how I got there and some of what actually happened.

***

I came to editing initially as someone who wasn't confident in her writing ability but who thought she could edit reasonably well: edited collections, which account for some of my earliest publications (e.g., *Portfolios in the Writing Classroom*; *Voices on Voice*), as well as some of my most recent (e.g., *Assembling Composition*; *ePortfolios-as-Curriculum*), seemed a genre I should explore. In fact, the genre seemed a perfect solution for my writing insecurity: I wouldn't need to write too much at the same time I contributed something worthwhile. Of course, editing a collection isn't precisely the same as editing, an observation that several authors in this volume make and that became all too obvious to me as I embarked on editing my first collection. As I began that effort, I thought the editorial activity would consist chiefly of copyediting, helping authors sharpen their prose at the word or sentence level. But as it turned out (who knew?!), the publisher had a copyeditor—a good one. Instead, editing seemed to be a set of almost sequential, unfolding activities that then sometimes became recursive: imagining the edited collection; inviting authors or issuing a call for proposals; reviewing proposals and chapter drafts; providing response; tidying up the chapters, assembling them into a collection, and sending it to the publisher for review; reading reviews once they arrived and trying to make sense of them; interpreting them with contributors to determine the way forward—assuming fairly good news from the reviewers; working with contributors to revise accordingly and appropriately; engaging in the same practices for my own chapters, especially if major revisions were required; and sometimes having to return to the original vision for the project to reimagine it entirely. All *this* editorial activity was more and other than what I'd anticipated. Still, I liked it, especially the opportunity to bring together multiple voices around a given topic, especially when the topic was new, especially when the research on it was relatively nascent. Moreover, although I didn't know it then, these editorial practices began preparing me, at least in part, for editing *CCC*.

A second experience I brought with me to the *CCC* editorial work was cofounding and coediting another journal. At the same time I was developing edited collections, I was also collaborating with Brian Huot to create *Assessing Writing*, a new journal focused on writing assessment published twice yearly. This editing experience differed from editing collections in several ways. For one thing, it was a collaborative effort, so we had the benefit of two minds. For another, writing assessment at that time was still new, already interdisciplinary, with one foot in more qualitative forms of evaluation and a second foot in statistically driven quantitative measurement, which meant that while the journal was topically focused, it was important to effect some balance, to include articles with diverse ideologies, epistemologies, and methodologies. For yet another, unlike editing a book—a task completed when the final page proofs and index are submitted to the publisher—editing a journal is continuous: as editors, we were engaged year round. Learning to create balance over an extended period when manuscripts you don't anticipate come over the transom was also part of my preparation for editing *CCC*.

Some of this experience explains my interest in editorial work, but why *CCC*? I think four reasons. One, although I'm not sure I was more than tacitly aware of it at the time I applied for the *CCC* editorial position, I was influenced in my thinking by seeing early on in my career how a prospective editor for *CCC* might shape the field. My major professor, Tom Gaston, was an applicant for the *CCC* editorship at the same time as Richard Larson, in 1979. The rest is (an untold) history, as they say, but Tom shared with me his thinking about what he might do as editor of *CCC* as part of his application preparation: with a commitment to composition and English education more than to rhetoric, he would have taken the journal in a different direction than Larson did. Watching that process play out—Tom's thinking about the application process and developing his vision for the journal, contrasted with the direction Larson took—taught me about the importance of having an editorial vision and philosophy, about the opportunity such an editorship could endow. Two, editing *CCC* specifically might allow me to help others as I have been helped. Although this will probably sound amusing, during his editorship Rick Gebhardt did me an enormous favor by *rejecting* a manuscript I had submitted to the journal. The reviewers helped him in this task, to be sure, but while the article was sincerely written, its argument was badly theorized, and I'm (still) relieved that its wider circulation was precluded. During his editorship, Joe Harris encouraged the article I wrote historicizing writing assessment for the fiftieth anniversary double issue, an article that I have returned to more than once, that I have updated, and that has also informed others' thinking. During her editorship, Marilyn Cooper helped me with the page layout for my CCCC chair's address, another text I have revisited. In sum, as editor of *CCC*, I might have the opportunity to pay forward at least some of this generosity, which also functions as a kind of mentorship, a point made in this volume by Douglas Eyman and Cheryl Ball, by Paul Matsuda, and by Malea Powell, and one to which I'll return. Three, I was, and am, committed to CCCC: I've served as member of several CCCC task forces (e.g., Digital Teaching, Learning, and Assessing; Online *CCC*), as a member/chair of committees (e.g., Assessment, Nominating), and as chair of the organization itself. Serving as editor was, not surprisingly, another way to serve the organization that also tapped the institutional knowledge I had developed. And fourth, I did have a vision for the journal, which I outlined in my application: I wanted to focus the journal on research, which included scholarship made available to the field through the journal but also through review essays, written by leading scholars, of other research published in books. In this sense, the journal would function as a research hub, much like Byron Hawk's network coordination (this volume), circulating new research findings in the context of larger research activity. Moreover, in articulating this vision, I didn't advocate abandoning *CCC*'s commitment to teaching: I thought the journal could speak to both, often at the same time.

This, then, was some of the context for my editorship of *CCC*.

***

The reality of editing *CCC* day to day felt a bit dizzying. A continuing exercise of multitasking, it involved completing multiple tasks of different kinds, from writing to authors and contacting reviewers to choosing pull-out quotes for articles and, yes, copyediting, always inside a given rhythm, which itself interfaced and was rhythmically in dialogue with my day job of teaching and administering and working with doctoral students. The journal production schedule provided one tempo: there are dates for submitting the complete copy for the issue so it is published on time, for example, and for sending pages to authors and for returning corrected pages back to NCTE. A second rhythm was required for the review essays: with the help of a *CCC* editorial assistant—Kara Taczak, Matt Davis, Jenn O'Malley, and Bret Zawilski each ably filled that role—I identified books for possible review, considered how a set of four or five might be usefully assembled, assured that collectively and over time review essays spoke to a diversity of topics, and invited a colleague to take up the reviewing task. A third rhythm and set of practices was required for the special issues: each of them involved an open invitation for proposals; a review of those by editorial-board members and other reviewers to decide which proposals to encourage; then a review of the manuscripts; and so on. For some CFPs there were well over one hundred proposals; coordinating the proposal process while also managing the routine work of the journal required more than two hands. Put another way, this special-issue process was, in effect, overlaid palimpsest-like on the typical *CCC* process. And because it involved the extra step of inviting and reviewing proposals, we began the special-issue-development process by issuing the CFP for each special issue eighteen months in advance of the publication date. In addition, other *CCC*-related events contributed to the *CCC* portfolio: two webinars, for instance, extending the conversation begun in the pages of the journal. In sum, multiple interacting tempos structured our work.

All this—a continuing act of juggling requiring many hands—is how it felt to me. At the same time, the practice was also always about how the journal, how each issue, would appear to others, how it could inform them, could engage them, could motivate them to write back or teach differently or take up a new research question. Toward those ends, special attention was given to the editor's introductions, with titles signaling themes cutting across articles, with comments on trends in higher education, and with articulation of contexts for articles and often linking articles, even if in different issues. Symposia also served this purpose, focusing on topics ranging from NCTE's centennial and the multiple practices of peer review to MOOCs.

The context of the journal itself also played a role in the way *CCC* operated during my editorship. Editors differ, of course, in philosophy, in temperament, in practices, even when the journal is institutionally sponsored, as *CCC* is. Some *CCC* practices are required regardless of editorial disposition: *CCC* editorial-board members, for example, are nominated by the editor, but they must be approved by the CCCC executive committee. Other areas are more ambiguous, among them how much editorial discretion one exercises, and even here it can vary. On the one hand, I exercised considerable discretion as I invited symposia authors and review essayists and reviewers. On the other hand, more than once I published an article I wasn't sure met the standards of the journal, but reviewers had supported publication, and I supported their decision. In part, my support was a function of my definition of and attitude toward peer review. Peer review, entailing the reading and evaluation of a text to assure its claims are situated, valid, and evidenced, is intended to assure scholarship meets community standards. The scholars I had invited to make informed, thoughtful recommendations had spoken: when they speak in chorus, that's a decision to be respected. But in some ways even more fundamentally, and as I explain more fully below, I supported their decision because of a belief in our scholarly community: the editor of *CCC* has a voice that is amplified, no doubt, but it is nonetheless one voice among many.

It goes without saying, of course, that overall, this editorial work might be characterized more negatively, perhaps as the result of an Adam Smith-like Editor-as-Invisible Hand pulling strings and adjusting pulleys to achieve an individual vision. Admittedly, as indicated above, considerable editorial work is carried out behind the scenes. Even if not wholly visible, however, a good deal, perhaps most, of my editorial work wasn't so much a function of an Invisible Hand as it was a kind of purposeful collective intelligence, created through interactions with others, that I helped orchestrate through facilitating conversations between and among a dynamic network of prospective authors, thoughtful editorial-board (EB) members, generous reviewers, and active readers. A journal, in other words, can act intentionally as a nexus, bringing together writers, EB members, reviewers, and readers through multiple enactments, including letters of inquiry, proposals for special issues, anonymous submissions, signed reviews, letters to and from the editor, revisions, and interchanges.

For *CCC*, with its multiple research traditions and purposes, creating this nexus was tricky. Journals, like fields, vary. As Charles Bazerman (2000) explains, letters in science morphed into newsletters and then into scientific journals whose purposes are twofold: (1) validating the research they (2) disseminate.[1] In other fields, journals highlight new scholarly approaches and raise questions about their value: a 2017 issue of *PMLA*, for example, took up issues raised by Franco Moretti's provocative theory and practice of distant reading that, in effect, called into question the practice of close reading defining literary studies. In still other fields—especially medicine, architecture, education, and social work—journals publish research intended to forward best professional practices. Under my editorship, *CCC* tried to do all the above: present and disseminate research findings; explore provocative theories; forward best practices. A practical implication of such diverse aims is that *CCC* speaks to an interestingly distributed community whose members are teachers and scholars and researchers and theorists and critics and advocates.[2] Put another way, I see the field as a large, diverse, pluralistic community, one initially founded on the teaching of writing in a time of increasingly open college admissions, then widening its field of inquiry in response to new understandings, practices, texts, and contexts. As members of that community and in relationship with and to each other, we continue our historic understanding of ourselves as welcoming students, helping them acclimate to the academy, and developing writing knowledge and practices supporting college success, civic participation, and personal and intellectual agency. Early on, our focus was on that first field of activity, college writing; over time, we've theorized and studied students as they have composed in contexts other than school—in co-curriculars, workplaces, "self-motivated" contexts (Holmes et al. 2019)—and as they have graduated from school and moved into the workplace. Furthermore, we now study *writers*, and their multiple, layered, textured contexts, in the United States and around the world. The journal's focus, in other words, has both widened and deepened. My overriding editorial task, as I defined it, was both/and: include as many different voices and methods and genres as possible while also invoking our community—one created through multiple interactions—via multiple texts, both in the journals and behind the scene; via multiple kinds of texts; and thus via multiple textual conversations constituting the community and contributing to its vibrancy.

To enact this philosophy, what I did as editor—pretty much day in and day out during the term and the summer and the sabbatical—was to facilitate such conversations and thus foster relationships between and among all these participants in the field. This editorial task thus provided a different kind of opportunity to contribute to, construct, and represent the field.

In retrospect, a good question is what field or discipline *CCC* at that time constructed. My own sense, which is clearly not without interest but which is tempered by the gift of time, is that in substance the field constructed through *CCC* was variegated in interests, rigorous in method, innovative in insights, capacious in genres, generous and thoughtful in disposition. And if this is so, a good deal of credit goes to the *CCC* editorial boards that served during my editorship. On their recommendations, special issues fostered interest in research methods (September

2012); in the profession (September 2013); and in locations of writing (September and December 2014). And they supported capacious genres, specifically by encouraging genres like the vignettes—as examples of lived experience—that fronted the 2013 and 2014 special issues. My own sense is also that the editorial practices *CCC* constructed were made more transparent; for example, the names of reviewers were published annually, a practice that continues today. Perhaps most important, *CCC* intended to help *everyone* who submitted, regardless of whether the submission resulted in publication in *CCC* or not. Toward that end, over 95 percent of the manuscripts went to reviewers; reviewer responses were typically gracious, generous, and helpful; and where the manuscript was not recommended for revision or publication, as most are not, I tried to serve as a kind of mentor, providing comments to situate the reviews, to make sense of them, and often, to help the author(s) consider other venues that might offer appropriate publication hosts for their manuscripts. In doing so, I often thought—oddly enough, I admit—about the movie *Miracle on 34th Street*. In that movie, Macy's sends customers to other stores when they do not have the item the customer is seeking; although the analogy is imperfect, the point of helping others is not. I heard from many authors how helpful such collective intelligence and advice was, which was enormously gratifying. And over time I recognized manuscripts I'd seen in the review process when they were later published in other journals. In serving *CCC*, I believed I was serving not only those published in *CCC*, but also the community at large, writers as well as readers.

At the same time, it's worth noting that this articulation, while representing my aspiration and experience, doesn't pretend to comprehension. The review process is by definition exclusionary; potential authors, often the most vulnerable and marginalized among us, can be harmed by such gatekeeping, a topic of concern to many (see, for example, Alice Horning's comments and chapters by Michael Pemberton and Victor Villanueva in this collection); my goal, among others, was to minimize if not completely eliminate such harm.

This, then, is something of an account of what I did as editor and of some editorial enactments and effects.

***

WHAT DOES THIS EDITORIAL PRACTICE MEAN NOW?

For me: During my editorship and afterwards, I took and have taken (renewed) pleasure in looking up articles published during my editorship, re-reading them, and thinking about them again; in seeing articles we published in *CCC* informing new research, theory, and pedagogy; in recognizing articles we published expanded into books, some of them award winning; in advising former graduate students who are now journal editors themselves; in consulting with many scholars, most of them new and welcomed colleagues, on article manuscripts, book proposals, and research grants; in returning to my own writing and editing projects, among them four edited collections in as many years—and one special issue of a journal.

For others: During my editorship, I was asked several times to share editorial advice at conferences, and I often did so. For my own contribution to these conference sessions, I thought a collective-intelligence approach might be helpful, so I asked several editorial colleagues to provide one important piece of advice each, and I collected those into the list below. The contributors, speaking on behalf of a wide range of journals in the field, include Jeff Sommers, then representing *Teaching English in the Two-Year College*; John Schilb, then representing *College English*; Lynn Worsham, then representing *JAC*; Cindy Selfe and Gail Hawisher, then representing *Computers and Composition*; Cheryl Ball, then (and still) representing *Kairos*; Alice Horning, then representing *WPA: Writing Program Administration*; and Amy Koerber, then representing *Technical Communication Quarterly*. Collectively, we suggest:

- "Editors and readers appreciate manuscripts that think about the field, or some aspect of it, in fresh, new ways." In this case, the interest in a fresh approach or finding isn't for the sake of newness, but rather is a kind of invention for a fuller, more accurate understanding or representation. What have we missed? What needs to be adjusted?
- "I (and our referees) prefer essays that make a fresh, clear, well-organized, and significant argument that's explicitly situated in relation to existing scholarship." The fresh approach or claim needs to be contextualized: every finding, every new approach, has a history. What is it, and how does it situate the fresh?
- "All publications occur in the context of on-going discussions: situating the manuscript relative to those and representing them fairly, even generously, is helpful to all." To be fair, enacting this point is something of a balancing act. Given the constraints of a print journal's page count—and always, regardless of a journal's medium of publication, an audience's attention space, interest, and patience—an author can't include too much (think trees) without losing space for the fresh; what is included should be the most relevant conversations (think forest),[3] even when that includes scholarship opposing the claim. The question the author is answering, then, is, What are the prior and current conversations on this topic, what are their contours, and why are they important?

- "There's a temptation to simplify and/or to overclaim: instead, 'allow for complexity.'" In their enthusiasm for their scholarship, it's more natural than deliberate for authors to reduce arguments and contexts, often to binaries in which the fresh scholarship is the correct view. A key question here is twofold: (1) Does the claim call for some nuance or qualification, and if so, what might it be? (2) How might scholars ten or twenty or even thirty years from now view the claim?
- "The research design for the project should be elegant and appropriate; the author(s) should explain the methods and results clearly without making discussions of them more complex than they need to be." Sometimes, authors confuse complexity and sophistication. Superfluous complexity, which is confusing, tends to undermine an author's ethos; material, pertinent complexity is helpful.
- "The text needs to be coherent, not 'tenuously held together by the Velcro of metadiscourse.'" Metadiscourse—including signposting, referring to theories, and invoking (sometimes multiple) frameworks—can be helpful when employed judiciously; the key word here isn't *metadiscourse* but *judiciously*.
- "Editors and reviewers are your friends"; they are members of our community. They have their own passions, their own lives, their own commitments. They agree to contribute to a journal—editorial work of all kinds exists in a gift economy—because they too believe in that community and understand that for it to thrive, such participation is required.

That last point leads to my final point.

In providing this account of my editorial practice, I've vacillated between the use of *I* and the use of *we*. On the one hand, as this account details, I was the editor, and certainly I take responsibility for errors and omissions, for aspirations unmet, for issues neglected and concerns unexpressed. On the other hand, in accounting for actions the journal took, I also consistently refer to *we*—as in "we published a large number of articles"—which raises a good question: Who is we? Simply, the we is, in part, a professional reference. This journal is an institution of a kind: editing *CCC* can be understood less as a personal exercise, more as a professional activity representing CCCC itself. The we is also, in larger part, an expression of all the people who have participated in bringing it to life and sustaining it—writers and readers, reviewers and editorial-board members, *CCC* editorial assistants and writers, the people who are, one way or another, members of a community the journal represents, in our case a disciplinary or field-based community, depending on one's perspective. This is the community editors, I believe, want others to join, to share, to participate in, and ultimately, even to change.

Editing a journal, in other words, is an act of supporting community.

NOTES

1. It's worth noting that several of our journals—among them *Composition Studies* and *Computers and Composition*—began as newsletters.
2. A list of roles remarkably similar to the list outlined by Stephen North's (1987) *The Making of Knowledge in Composition*.
3. I am indebted to Amanda May for pointing out the trees/forest metaphor relative to the amount of information included in a text and the shape it takes.

REFERENCES

Bazerman, Charles. 2000. "Letters as the Social Ground for Differentiated Genres." In *Letter Writing as Social Practice*, edited by David Barton and Nigel Hall, 15–30. Amsterdam: John Benjamins.

Holmes, Ashley, Alexis Hart, Anna Knutson, Ide O'Sullivan, Yogesh Sinha, and Kathleen Blake Yancey. 2019. "The Recursivities Project." Research project sponsored by Elon University's Writing Beyond the University Research Seminar.

North, Stephen. 1987. *The Making of Knowledge in Composition: Portrait of an Emerging Field*. Upper Montclair, NJ: Boynton-Cook.

Yancey, Kathleen Blake, ed. 1992. *Portfolios in the Writing Classroom: An Introduction*. Urbana, IL: NCTE.

Yancey, Kathleen Blake, ed. 1994. *Voices on Voice: Perspectives, Definitions, Inquiry*. Urbana, IL: NCTE.

Yancey, Kathleen Blake, ed. 2019. *ePortfolio as Curriculum: Models and Practices for Developing Students' ePortfolio Literacy*. Sterling, VA: Stylus.

Yancey, Kathleen Blake, and Stephen J. McElroy, eds. 2017. *Assembling Composition*. Urbana, IL: NCTE.

PART TWO

Editing Books and Book Series in Writing Studies

8
THE UNIVERSITY OF PITTSBURGH PRESS SERIES
Composition, Literacy, Culture

David Bartholomae
University of Pittsburgh

Jean Ferguson Carr
University of Pittsburgh

1. FROM THE CATALOG

In 1992, we published the first four books in our series with the University of Pittsburgh Press, *Composition, Literacy, Culture*. These books were Patricia Bizzell, *Academic Discourse and Critical Consciousness*; Lester Faigley, *Fragments of Rationality: Postmodernity and the Subject of Composition*; Myron Tuman, *Word Perfect: Literacy in the Computer Age*; and Myron Tuman (ed.), *Literacy Online: The Promise (and Peril) of Reading and Writing with Computers*. Since then (and at the time of this writing), we have published another ninety-seven books, with thirteen in the production pipeline.

Each year we receive twenty to twenty-five prospectuses. We have published, on average, about four books per year, although in some years there have been zero and in others, ten. Once contracts are out, we don't publish a book until it is ready. You can find our catalog here: https://upittpress.org/series/composition-literacy-and-culture-2/. The best way to get a sense of the range and ambition of our books is to scan the catalog. We hope you will.

In university-press publishing (in the humanities), a book that sells five hundred copies is considered to be a market success; three hundred is said to be average. There are fifty-seven books on our list that have sold over five hundred copies, a little more than half the total we have published. We have twenty-four books on our list that have sold between five hundred and one thousand copies, thirty-three that have sold well over one thousand copies, and five that have sold between three thousand and six thousand copies. Our average sales per volume, in other words, is well over five hundred copies.

Below is an alphabetical list (by author) of our top twenty in terms of sales. It is heavily weighted toward the period 1992–2005, when university-press sales in general were higher than they are today (largely but not solely due to cuts to university library budgets, where a series like ours had a standing order). This list is useful, we think, as a way of representing the history of the series. The titles provide a sense of the interplay among the ongoing work of individual scholars, our particular mission as editors, and the evolving interests and concerns of our readers (at least as measured by those who buy books).

- *Academic Discourse and Critical Consciousness*, Patricia Bizzell (1992)
- *The Origins of Composition Studies in the American College, 1875–1925: A Documentary History*, John Brereton (1996)
- *Toward a Feminist Rhetoric: The Writing of Gertrude Buck*, Joann Campbell (1996)
- *Composition-Rhetoric: Backgrounds, Theory and Pedagogy*, Robert Connors (1997)
- *The Powers of Literacy: A Genre Approach to Teaching Writing*, Bill Cope and Mary Kalantzis, eds. (1993)
- *Composition in the University: Historical and Polemical Essays*, Sharon Crowley (1998)
- *Toward a Civil Discourse: Rhetoric and Fundamentalism*, Sharon Crowley (2006)
- *Between Languages and Cultures: Translation and Cross-Cultural Texts*, Anuradha Dingwaney and Carol Maier, eds. (1996)
- *Fragments of Rationality: Postmodernity and the Subject of Composition*, Lester Faigley (1992)
- *Writing Science: Literacy and Discursive Power*, M.A.K. Halliday and J. R. Martin (1993)
- *Illness as Narrative*, Ann Jurecic (2012)
- *Reclaiming Rhetorica: Women in the Rhetorical Tradition*, Andrea Lunsford, ed. (1995)
- *Writing at the End of the World*, Richard E. Miller (2005)
- *Local Knowledges, Local Practices: Writing in the Disciplines at Cornell*, Jonathan Monroe, ed. (2003)
- *Ambient Rhetoric: The Attunements of Rhetorical Being*, Thomas Rickert (2013)
- *Available Means: An Anthology of Women's Rhetoric(s)*, Joy Ritchie and Kate Ronald, eds. (2001)
- *Traces of a Stream: Literacy and Social Change Among African American Women*, Jacquelyn Jones Royster (2000)

- *Eating on the Street: Teaching Literacy in a Multicultural Society*, David Schaafsma (1993)
- *Toward Composition Made Whole*, Jody Shipka (2011)
- *Literacy Online: The Promise (and Peril) of Reading and Writing with Computers*, Myron Tuman, ed. (1992)

Sales figures are never a simple indication of the value of individual titles, to be sure. Some volumes speak to larger audiences than others, but sales figures **are** a good indication of circulation, of how books travel. And books that travel are crucial to the staying power of a series like ours. As editors, we choose books we believe in. We don't make a decision based on projected sales. There is always a point, however, at which the director of our university press asks the marketing people to weigh in. We can speak back during this process, and we have a good track record to fall back on—having made the case for the importance of a number of successful books whose appeal was not immediately evident to the marketing department. It is important to know, however, that university-press publishing is market driven and that the value of a book, in part at least, is measured by its circulation.

Fortunately, our books have sold well, and we continue to have enthusiastic support from the University of Pittsburgh. (But please keep buying our books! And buy the print editions. There is no guarantee we can continue without continued sales.)

It is also the case, we are pleased to note, that in our twenty-six years as publishers, our books have won thirty-five major prizes and awards. Below is a list of prize-winning books. (These are organized by date of the award. You'll note this list differs from the list of best sellers above.) We believe this list of prize-winning books is a way of representing the series' impact both on the field and to scholarship in general.

- Lester Faigley, *Fragments of Rationality: Postmodernity and the Subject of Composition*. Winner of the 1992 MLA Mina Shaughnessy Award; Winner 1992 CCCC Outstanding Book Award.
- John Brereton, *The Origins of Composition Studies in the American College, 1875–1925*. Winner of the 1997 CCCC Outstanding Book Award.
- Thomas Miller, *The Formation of College English*. Winner of the 1997 MLA Mina Shaughnessy Award.
- Sharon Crowley, *Composition in the University: Historical and Polemical Essays*. Winner of the 1998 MLA Shaughnessy Award.
- Jacqueline Jones Royster, *Traces of a Stream: Literacy and Social Change Among African American Women*. Winner of the 2000 MLA Shaughnessy Award.

- Susan Miller, *Assuming the Positions: Cultural Pedagogy and the Politics of Commonplace Writing*. Winner of the 2000 CCCC Outstanding Book Award; *Choice*, 1999 list of Outstanding Academic Titles.
- Paul Kameen, *Writing/Teaching: Toward a Rhetoric of Pedagogy*. Winner of the 2002 CCCC Outstanding Book Award.
- Suresh A. Canagarajah, *A Geopolitics of Academic Writing*. Winner of the 2002 *JAC* Gary A. Olson Award for the Best Book in Rhetoric and Theory.
- Mary Soliday, *The Politics of Remediation*. Winner of the 2004 CCCC Outstanding Book Award.
- Richard Miller, *Writing at the End of the World*. Winner of the 2006 NCTE/CEA James Britton Award.
- Sharon Crowley, *Toward a Civil Discourse: Rhetoric and Fundamentalism*. Winner of the 2007 NCTE David H. Russell Award; Winner of the 2006 *JAC* Gary Olson Award; Winner of the 2008 CCCC Outstanding Book Award; Winner of the 2008 RSA Outstanding Book Award.
- Byron Hawk, *A Counter-History of Composition: Toward Methodologies of Complexity*. Winner of the 2007 W. Ross Winterowd Award (*JAC*); Honorable Mention, 2007 MLA Mina Shaughnessy Award.
- Thomas Rickert, *Acts of Enjoyment: Rhetoric, Zizek and the Return of the Subject*. Winner of the 2007 Gary Olson Award (*Journal of Advanced Composition*).
- Walter H. Beale, *Learning from Language: Symmetry, Asymmetry and Literary Humanism*. Honorable Mention, 2009 MLA Mina Shaughnessy Award.
- Jane Stanley, *The Rhetoric of Remediation: Negotiating Entitlement and Access to Higher Education*. Winner of the 2010 MLA Mina Shaughnessy Award.
- Diane Davis, *Inessential Solidarity*. Winner of the 2010 *JAC* Ross Winterowd Award.
- David Fleming, *From Form to Meaning: Freshman Composition and the Long Sixties, 1957–1974*. Winner of the 2012 CCCC Outstanding Book Award; Winner of the 2013 MLA Mina Shaughnessy Award.
- Ann Jurecic, *Illness as Narrative*. 2012. *Choice*, 2012 list of Outstanding Academic Titles.
- Steve Lamos, *Interests and Opportunities: Race, Racism, and University Writing Instruction in the Post-Civil Rights Era*. 2013 CCCC Special Commendation.
- Rebecca Dingo, *Networking Arguments: Rhetoric, Transnational Feminism, and Public Policy Writing*. Winner of the 2012 W. Ross Winterowd Award for Outstanding Book on Composition Theory.
- Thomas Rickert, *Ambient Rhetoric*. Winner of the 2014 CCCC Outstanding Book Award.
- Risa Applegarth, *Rhetoric in American Anthropology: Gender, Genre, and Science*. Winner of the 2016 CCCC Outstanding Book Award.
- Iswari Pandey, *South Asian in the Middle South*. Winner of the 2017 CCCC Advancement of Knowledge Award.

- Rasha Diab, *Shades of Sulh: The Rhetorics of Arab-Islamic Reconciliation.* Winner of the 2018 CCCC Outstanding Book Award.
- Rebecca Lorimer Leonard, *Writing on the Move: Migrant Women and the Value of Literacy.* Winner of the 2019 CCCC Outstanding Book Award; Honorable Mention, 2017 Winifred Bryan Horner Award.
- Candace Epps-Robertson, *Resisting Brown: Race, Literacy, and Citizenship in the Heart of Virginia.* Winner of the 2019 Outstanding Book Award from the Coalition for Community Writing.

When we first started the series, we expected primarily to receive dissertations that we would help develop into books (and we have done that). Our field had been characterized by articles, book chapters, and empirical reports—not, by and large, by books. So we were (pleasantly) surprised by how many people in the field had a book in their desk or on their computer.

An early interest was to push composition back in time, back from its situatedness in the contemporary academy, or even in its founding as a named discipline, to its forehistory—in textbooks, institutional structures, and traditions of writing instruction. We looked for books on important figures from the past who crossed disciplinary lines (like Gertrude Buck), and we were in search of manuscripts that examined the competing rhetorical and compositional traditions shaped by issues of race, gender, and cultural difference. *Traces of a Stream* (2000) played a major role, we feel, in shaping the conversation in the field on issues of race, gender, and rhetorical history, and it expanded the range of a term like *literacy*. One of our first books, *Eating on the Streets*, focused on how a project that brought together college researchers and high school teachers also navigated divides of race, privilege, and geography. We published two ambitious collections of women's rhetorics, *Available Means* in 2001 and *Persuasive Acts* in 2020. In between, we published books on various genres of women's writing, on particular scenes of rhetoric and race, and on culturally diverse modes of writing.

We also published literacy books that focused on writing happening elsewhere in the academy or in service of particular kinds of social concerns, by writers "at the end of the world" or "on the move." We were interested in expanding the nationalist focus of much of composition studies with books on cross-cultural texts and the "geopolitics" of academic writing.

Many of our books questioned the relationship of writing and politics, the uses of writing in a time and culture like ours; others explore rhetorical theory or tease out the relationship of composition to adjacent fields of study. Books have tracked the growing interest in digital composing and media and have theorized material history, texts, and practices. Some of our books tell stories, some take on critical debates—we hope all of them question ways of reading the past, present, and future. We ask that our books enrich our understanding of the materials of writing, literacy, and culture but also of our ways of engaging with them and reflecting on them.

2. HISTORY

In March 1989, Peter Oresick asked Bartholomae to propose a publication series for the University of Pittsburgh Press. Pitt Press had several successful series in areas that included, for example, poetry, Latin American studies, labor history, urban studies, and dance. Because a series is headed by faculty scholars, it allows the press to focus on a particular field, to develop long-term relationships with potential authors, and to anticipate new directions in scholarship and research—all in ways that would be impossible for an acquisitions editor, who is not a practicing scholar and whose assignments cross fields of study.

As series editors, we work with an acquiring editor (currently Joshua Shanholtzer, a member of the University of Pittsburgh Press's permanent staff and a talented and generous colleague) with whom we are in regular conversation and to whom we present the projects we would like to publish. The acquiring editor, in turn, makes the case to the director of the university press, and the director is responsible to the university provost and to a faculty editorial board.

In the late 1980s, the then director of the University of Pittsburgh Press, Fred Hetzel, was looking to expand the number of series he sponsored. Peter Oresick was a successful Pittsburgh poet, a passionate bibliographer of Pittsburgh writers, a teacher in our composition program, and a good friend. With our colleague Nick Coles, he edited *Working Classics: Poems on Industrial Life* (1990) and *For a Living: Poetry of Work* (1995), both with the University of Illinois Press.

Peter had recently taken a position as the promotion and marketing manager for the University Pittsburgh Press. (He would later serve as associate director and acting director.) He pitched several ideas for new publication series to Hetzel, including a series serving the newly emerging scholarly field of composition. Bartholomae wisely recruited his colleague Jean Ferguson Carr as a coeditor. Carr brought with her serious commitments to feminist theory and practice, to the history of American literacies, and to the history of the book, including early American textbooks. Together, we prepared a proposal, Hetzel discussed the proposal with the university senate's press committee, and the series was approved on March 22, 1989.

In proposing the series, our goal was to promote opportunities for research and publication that recognized the remarkable range of work in the field but also the remarkable range that the emerging field made possible, a range not fully represented by the current terms of use: *rhetoric, linguistics, psychology, ethnography, education*. Hence the series title: *Composition, Literacy, and Culture*.

We wanted to signal that we were interested in a broad history of reading and writing, locally situated; that we were interested in studies of student writing and the materials of the classroom, including textbooks, but also in writing outside the academy—in workplaces, in domestic situations, in private and in public spaces; and that we were hoping this work would be informed by the critical concerns of what, at the time, was known as *cultural studies*. If we have one regret from our opening years, it is that in order to focus attention on the goals of the series, we failed to respond as quickly as we might have to some very significant book proposals that featured work in the history of rhetoric and in rhetorical theory. We never made that mistake again.

When we first met with Oresick, we said that we were interested in the process of book making from beginning to end and that we hoped we could participate in decisions about design, including the design of covers. We wanted something other than the plain gray covers with a title stamped in gold. There was a young production team at the press, and they quickly began to produce mock-up covers with a new look—bright colors, striking images, what at the time we would have called a *postmodern* look. We still have some of the more memorable ones on our office walls. We think our books have always had a distinctive appeal as books, and we think we set a standard for cover design that was quickly followed by other university presses. If you look back to the early 90s, to our catalogs and to those of other presses, you'll see a difference. We continue to have distinctive covers, although the differences are not now so striking across the field.

With the commitment from the University of Pittsburgh Press, we announced the series in the major journals, we had a table at CCCC, and we contacted a number of potential authors and encouraged them to send proposals. Myron Tuman, Pat Bizzell, and Lester Faigley were among the first to respond. Faigley wrote with a proposal for what would become *Fragments of Rationality*, but he worried he book might depend too heavily on literary theory. We responded quickly, saying that a book like his, one that crossed disciplinary boundaries, was *exactly* what we were looking for. Tuman had been working on literacy and the digital and proposed both a collection to bring attention to the field and his own monograph.

We encouraged Pat Bizzell to compile a collection of her published essays, prompting her editorial reframings and anticipating the energy that would come from reading the pieces in juxtaposition. Recalling those days, Pat said, "I remember Dave and Jean being very active editors with this project. They had convinced me that collecting my essays was worth doing, and then they had to push me to introduce the volume with a frank and detailed intellectual autobiography. I wouldn't have done it without their help." Our first books, as noted above, hit the shelves in 1992.

3. ON EDITING

When we are asked, "What are you looking for?," we have a standard answer. We're looking for serious work that is well written and engaging that brings something significantly new to the table. Now, *new* doesn't necessarily mean (or even usually mean) previously unthought, unuttered, earth shaking, paradigm shifting. If you look down our list, you will see many examples of a new critical lens (the work of Bruno Latour, for example, or concerns about multimodality) being brought to the traditional materials and concerns of composition, literacy, and rhetoric. Or, conversely, you will see new materials—often archival, sometimes represented by survey, interview, or ethnographic report—brought to well-rehearsed arguments, usually (but not always) about resistance, assertion, and survival in relation to race, class, and gender. You will see books that turn their attention to the writing of other times, other contexts, that step aside from the US context, that challenge the priority of the academic. You will see books that foreground the framing power of race or gender, of migration or economic condition. You will see others that ask us to rethink the academic as a location, a history, a set of relationships.

Every now and again, though, we pick up a manuscript and begin to read a book that is completely unpredictable and absolutely necessary. And we write notes to each other to say, "Wow. Wait until you read this one." We have been attentive to books that break with academic forms, that intertwine the personal with the critical or that alternate modes of discourse. We are both suckers for beautiful sentences—for well-crafted writing that makes the book move and surprise us as readers.

The book that is both completely unpredictable and absolutely necessary—this book we see maybe once a year. We talked this over and decided it is just not appropriate for us, as editors, to single out titles or authors in this chapter. Some are on our list of prize winners, but not all by any means. We don't have space to talk about every book on our list, and we don't want to just single out a few since so many have made such important contributions to how we think and write and teach. We'd rather you scan the list to make your own selections for the Wow list, or the Books of Greatest Consequence, whatever you might choose to call it. It's worth noting how many of the titles on our lists refer to actions (and not just the expected ones of reading, writing, and teaching) and how many of those actions suggest a going back to look again (reforming, resisting, sounding and resounding, reframing, rereading, reclaiming) or a critical intervention (buying into, assuming the position, weaponizing digital rhetorics). Titles refer to work but also to play, to rhetoric as conversation and distance, as design and network, as inessential solidarity, enjoyment, and wit's end, as experience and as fragments of rationality, as unruly and queer.

We still probably read (or begin to read), twenty to twenty-five manuscripts per year. We continue to do this work year after year because we believe, in general, that it is important to provide publication opportunities for books that matter. Much of the work is routine—making choices, offering advice to writers, convincing the press that a book is significant and that it will find its readership, sending out letters to nominate our books for awards. But it is never fully routine. It would be an easier job if it were. We are buoyed, always, by the "wow" moments and always feel the weight when we have to say no. We are sustained by the expansiveness and passion of our authors, by our pleasure in watching a book take shape.

As editors, then, our first responsibility is to be receptive and attentive readers. We want to spot innovative work that doesn't immediately follow from (or that can't be quickly compared to) the work we have already published or the other published work that best represents our field. In the case of work that *is* more immediately recognizable, that *does* follow from and contribute to more established lines of thought and research, and these are the majority of the manuscripts we read, our goal is to publish the very best—books that are well-written and that define a significant step forward in thought and argument. Having said that, let us add: we wish we received more manuscripts that take as their subject the materials of the composition classroom, particularly student writing.

As readers, we are intrigued by the many shapes possible, and so, as editors, we would argue that monographs need not be so . . . well . . . so monolithic. It is often politically or intellectually important that authors collaborate, that they reflect on the conditions and undercurrents of their work, that they articulate their relationship to (and difference with) disciplinary ethos. Like many publication series, we look for creative responses to the complexities of digital production, large-scale archives, visual and sonic projects. We have used the series to promote work on the complexities of our past—into pedagogy, institutions, discourses and discursive traditions, but we have also sought books that engage the future—focusing on experimental writing, multimodal composition, writing outside the expected locations and contexts.

We continue to love the materiality of the book—the cover, the font and paper, the figures and chapter divisions. We value the moment of rest—of saying this is the book, this is what we have come to, for this moment, here, now; and we value its undoing, when a writer looks again, from a new perspective on what has just been made solid. We value the rhythm of books—the way they place parts in relation, in sequence, in counterpoise. We value the length of books, the space that allows writers to tell of false starts, to show new teachers or scholars how the project took shape, to take the argument to multiple venues. We encourage authors not to feel falsely beholden to the concept of the "mono" graph—of the single voice or position. And we encourage them to take the time to work out their own rhythms, to play with the notion of book structure, the articulation of parts, the sense of sequence, to challenge rather than satisfy expectations. Even in our current speeded-up climate of publish or be exiled, our authors have responded thoughtfully to extensive reviews of their manuscript, have restructured and reworked their text, have felt a kind of permission to let go of the obligatory features of the obligatory dissertation/monograph. We value the moments when they stake out a new space and time for work that initially seemed finished.

4. TO (FIRST-TIME) AUTHORS

The editors of *Behind the Curtain of Scholarly Publishing* asked each contributor to discuss their editorial philosophy and to prepare a section of advice to authors. We don't believe we have anything so grand as a philosophy of editing. You can track the kinds of choices we made in the lists above.

With thirty-plus years of experience soliciting, reviewing, and publishing book manuscripts, we've had many long conversations with authors and potential authors, both at conferences and by email. We do, then, have advice for first-time authors.

The formal process begins with a letter of inquiry to the press or, even better, a prospectus. University presses once had a standard form for a prospectus. The process is now less one size fits all. (You should check individual websites.) In general, for a prospectus, you submit a brief account of the book, a list of chapters, a sample chapter (if available), a schedule for completion, a sense of the expected audience and of other books that engage your subject, suggestions for external reviewers, and a copy of your CV. It is now conventional to submit a proposal to more than one press at a time as a way of soliciting signs of interest.

Take time with the brief summary of your book. It is the crucial piece at this stage and in all that follows. The prospectus must engage the editors with the project, allow them to see its possibilities, its potential significance and interest. It should propose a compelling topic but also suggest how the arrangement of materials and chapters will carry out the project. With it, you are giving the series editors and the acquiring editor language to use as your project is passed down the line. These sentences will travel widely and will be the introduction to your work for all who are engaged at each stage of the process—as the prospectus travels from the acquiring editor to the two us, and then from the press office to the external reviewers, and then, should we issue a contract, to the production staff at the press, including those charged with its promotion and design. It is greatly to your advantage to have a clear and engaging brief summary of your project, one that can be read by nonspecialists as well as specialists.

With a first book, we usually wait to have a complete manuscript before soliciting external reviews (usually two). At this point—that is, once we commit our time and the considerable time it takes for serious external reviews—we expect that the manuscript is committed to our series. We would have, as we say, the first right of refusal. Once we receive the reviews, we read them and make a decision as to whether or not we want to take the next step—to ask for revision and/or to offer a contract. If we remain interested in the project, we send the reviews to the author and ask for a response. The response to readers' reports is an important stage: we do not expect authors simply to bow to the readers' critiques but to work with them, whether they offer concrete advice or symptomatic readings.

We offer editorial advice along the way, usually through the acquiring editor, although sometimes directly. Once the book is ready for production, the press provides copyediting. The most significant intervention, in our experience, comes from the external reviewers.

Our reviewers have been brilliant and generous. They have written long reviews that engage a project from its founding assumptions, to the details of its elaboration, to the sentences and paragraphs that make a sympathetic reader pause. Our readers see themselves as helping move a project forward and, in doing so, keep the field alive. The success of the series has depended heavily and constantly on their care and close attention. We don't think our authors, at least the first-time book authors, are aware of how privileged they have been to receive such attention.

We publish second and third books, to be sure, but the majority of the proposals that come our way are drawn from PhD dissertations. Our advice to authors is to never forward the dissertation itself as a book proposal. The dissertation process is generally fraught and frantic in its final stages. Dissertations are shaped by the need to fulfill the educational contract at a specific institution and by their close address to the dissertation committee, a local audience of three or four. It was once the case that the dissertation was its own genre—the first chapter was a review of the literature, and so on. But more and more, it seems, dissertation committees are taking successful academic books as a model for the work of PhD students in their final years. This is a good thing. Still, it makes no sense to engage professional editors to tell you your dissertation is not yet a book. You want friends and teachers to do that work for you.

We also insist that a book be well written, that the writing is good—engaging, stylish, voiced, and nuanced. In our experience, dissertations are not always well written: they are necessarily defensive documents focused on their demonstrations of field knowledge and the arguments they forward. A concern for the quality of the writing may come to the fore late in the game. So again, step back. Go back to the writers whose writing you have most admired. Look to three or four of the prize-winning books in the field. Take time with them to think about the writing as writing. And, as you reread your dissertation, think about what it would take to engage a broader audience, academics and intellectuals who are not necessarily located in your corner of the field. Again—for several years you may have been writing to no more than three or four readers. Step back and think about the larger range and impact of your work.

So—our advice is to take time, enlist some good local readers, and understand that the first job is to begin the work of turning a dissertation into a book. Start right away. Set a schedule. We are constantly aware that as editors we play a crucial role in local decisions about tenure and promotion. The most difficult cases for us have come when we receive good projects that still require work, but there just isn't enough time.

While it is hard to predict a future for university-press publishing, challenged by declining sales, different modalities of production, and competing notions of authorship, writing, and evidence, we were much heartened to have the opportunity to sit back and to review our list of authors and titles. We can confidently report that there has been no decline in the number, ambition, skill, or eloquence in the manuscripts that come our way. And we know the books we have published have made a difference to our field and to scholarship in general. We are delighted to have had the opportunity to tell our story. And we invite you to keep an eye on our catalog. There are more books to come.

9
OPENING A NEW CHAPTER
Open-Access Publishing in Writing Studies

Mike Palmquist
Colorado State University

Prior to starting graduate school in 1986, I'd lived a rich life as a writer and editor. In high school, I published an underground newspaper with my friend Bob Crim. In college, I contributed to and eventually edited the college's newspaper and literary magazine and worked as a writer in its news office. Following graduation, I moved to Minneapolis and worked in a series of jobs that involved, variously, grant writing, advertising, the creation of mail-order catalogs, and writing and production work on a regional sports magazine. Eventually, following the failure of the magazine, I started a writing business that drew several corporate clients, among them 3M, Control Data, Honeywell, Pillsbury, and the University of Minnesota. A year later, I was billing forty hours per week, working far more hours than that, and thinking about establishing an agency.

My dreams of a career as head of a publishing agency were dashed, however, when my wife decided to pursue a master's degree at Carnegie Mellon University. I followed her to CMU and enrolled in its doctoral program in rhetoric, not realizing that a master's degree would have been an appropriate intermediate step but secure in the knowledge that, as a graduate teaching *assistant*, I would be learning the ropes by observing the teaching of an experienced faculty member. Imagine my surprise, three days before classes began, when I learned otherwise.

A RETURN TO PUBLISHING

I found myself once again in an editing and publishing role a few years after earning tenure and promotion at Colorado State University. It was not a particularly well-considered decision. Instead, as is often the case with academic careers, it was the culmination of a series of choices that began shortly after I completed my doctoral work.

In January 1991, I joined Kate Kiefer, Dawn Rodrigues, and Don Zimmerman on a writing-across-the-curriculum project in our college of engineering. The three of them had worked in various ways on WAC during the 1980s, but they had enjoyed little success with the general approach to WAC used widely at that time. The project they asked me to join would eventually change the way we thought about WAC, resulting in the creation of a network-supported WAC program based in our writing center. The funding we received allowed us to conduct a year-long series of local and national studies of writing in engineering at CSU during the 1992–93 academic year (Thomas 1995; Vest et al. 1995).[1]

What we learned through our studies changed the way we thought about WAC, leading us to create a model we called an "integrated approach to WAC," one that combined the train-the-trainer model that had, by that time, become a kind of WAC orthodoxy with the bottom-up, writing-center-based approach pioneered by scholars such as Tori Haring-Smith (1987). Most important, it was an approach well-suited to the reward structure shaping the work of the faculty at a research-intensive university. Our goal, briefly stated, was to reduce the barriers to adopting WAC in disciplinary courses. We planned to pursue this goal in three ways: (1) providing direct support for student writers through the campus network and writing center, (2) consulting with faculty members, and (3) providing network-based information about WAC for faculty (Palmquist et al. 1995). Beginning that summer, we began to create a series of digital materials—writing guides, interactive tutorials, videos, example documents, and example assignments—and a set of tools for obtaining feedback on drafts from tutors in our writing center. Until we recoded the materials for distribution on the web in 1996, the materials and tools—our "online writing center"—were made available through our university's wide-area network.

Moving our online writing center to the web had a number of consequences. Our videos and interactive tutorials weren't well suited to the limitations of the browsers and servers in use at the time. But because we no longer needed to manually update four hundred computers whenever we made changes to our materials, we found we had more time to develop professional resources for faculty. Not long after moving to the web, we had created a number of guides for faculty who were willing to consider using writing in their courses, and I had begun working on the website that would eventually become the WAC Clearinghouse.

That work involved collaboration with several colleagues at and beyond CSU. At the 1997 national convention for the Conference on College Composition and Communication (CCCC), we started our discussions with a great deal of enthusiasm. Over the next few months, we created a website that provided many of the professional resources we had developed at CSU, a few new resources developed by members of the project team, and a set of links to related sites. By early 1998, however, I noticed that fewer and fewer members of the original group were responding to email messages about what we were by then calling the WAC Clearinghouse. In the brief history of the Clearinghouse published at wac.colostate.edu/about/brief-history/, I credit Bill Condon with pointing out what should have been obvious to me: few departments were giving credit in annual merit reviews (let alone tenure and promotion reviews) for work on a website. It didn't take long to figure out that we could be more successful if we better aligned the WAC Clearinghouse with the reward structures that shaped the lives of potential contributors to the project. With that in mind, I shifted the project from a resource-focused website to an online journal, writing in a May 1998 email message to members of the project team:

> I am imagining a journal that is essentially an evolving, growing document (or, more accurately, a collection of documents) on the Web. Many, but not all materials published in the journal would be peer reviewed. For instance, in addition to peer-reviewed articles (both linear and hypertext), we could post WAC program proposals, successful grant proposals, program evaluations, material collected during research on WAC, and so on. (These would need to be reviewed, of course, but not in the same way as scholarly pubs, and permissions would need to be obtained before posting.)

On March 6, 2000, the WAC Clearinghouse became *Academic.Writing*, a scholarly journal that can now be viewed at wac.colostate.edu/aw/.[2] Members of the project team became editors, editorial staff, peer reviewers, editorial-board members, and contributors to the journal—recognizable roles that allowed them to gain credit for their work under the academic rewards structures then and, for the most part, still in place at their home institutions. The resources found on the original WAC Clearinghouse site were made available on the journal's website, essentially becoming a section of the journal.

The vision of providing a rich set of resources for WAC persisted, however, and almost immediately the new journal found itself home to an expanding set of resources and related publications. Shortly after launching its first volume, *Academic.Writing* began republishing a series of out-of-print books, all of which were released in digital open-access formats.³ The first book, Susan McLeod and Margot Soven's (2000) *Writing Across the Curriculum: A Guide to Developing Programs*, was released in August 2000. Eventually, four scholarly books would be made available through the *Academic.Writing* website. By 2001, *Academic.Writing* was also hosting the digital archives of three other journals—*Language and Learning Across the Disciplines*, *The WAC Journal*, and *RhetNet*.

While it was somewhat difficult, conceptually, to see how several books, three journals, and a growing set of professional resources fit "inside" a single journal, *Academic.Writing* served as the home for the WAC Clearinghouse until early 2002, when we turned things inside out once again. "The WAC Clearinghouse" returned as the name of the website, *Academic.Writing* became one of four journals available through the Clearinghouse, our republished books were made available through the Landmark Publications in Writing Studies series (now available at wac.colostate.edu/books/landmarks), and our resources were made available as a top-level section of the site (wac.colostate.edu/resources).

The immediate motivation for making this move, beyond the growing complexity of the site, was the pending publication of our first original scholarly book, Chuck Bazerman and David Russell's edited collection, *Writing Selves/Writing Societies* (2003). This book would become the first in the Perspectives on Writing series, which I edited until 2011. At that point, Sue McLeod began editing the series and, over the next few years, turned it into one of the leading book series in the field of writing studies. Under Sue's leadership, and later with that of coeditor Rich Rice, and most recently under the leadership of Rice and his coeditors Heather Falconer and J. Michael Rifenburg, the series has published more than forty books, with two earning book-of-the-year awards from CCCC and CWPA.

A more important motivation, however, was the recognition, rooted in part in my work as a professional writer and editor, that any publication—a journal, an academic press, a website, and so on—needs a good story. While the Clearinghouse would likely have failed had we not found a way to situate our work within institutional and disciplinary reward structures, it was even more important to establish a clear purpose and mission. I had struggled with the disconnect between rebranding the Clearinghouse as an academic journal and the initial vision of a set of resources for WAC scholars and faculty outside writing studies who used writing to support learning in their courses. Rebranding our project as an academic publisher allowed us to tell a better story about what we were trying to accomplish with the Clearinghouse. It also provided a more flexible framework for deciding how best to conduct peer reviews, license and distribute our publications, fund our operations, enter into partnerships with other groups, and organize our efforts. We were able, as a result, to establish both a clear identity and a durable framework for carrying out our work.

The Clearinghouse has grown in significant ways since it was relaunched in 2002. It now supports six journals, houses the archives for several others, and has published or republished more than 150 books, with more books in various stages of production. It supports ten book series that publish original books and offers additional books from NCTE and Utah State University Press. It has become home to CompPile and has established partnerships with several WAC organizations, including the Association for Writing Across the Curriculum, CCCC's WAC Standing Group, and the WAC Graduate Organization. Annual traffic on the site has grown to more than three million annual visits (from more than one million distinct IP addresses) and an equal number of annual downloads of journal articles, books, and book chapters in PDF and ePub formats. We have established copublishing agreements with NCTE, Parlor Press, Utah State University Press, and the University Press of Colorado, as well as with a handful of international conferences. Most important, the number of people involved in the Clearinghouse has grown from 14 to more than 180, each of whom serves in an editorial or reviewing role in a journal or book series or serves on the Clearinghouse editorial staff or editorial board.

DEVELOPING AN EDITORIAL PHILOSOPHY: THE PUBLISHING COLLABORATIVE MODEL

In the more than two decades since we launched the Clearinghouse, it has grown into one of the more successful and certainly one of the longest running open-access publishing projects in the humanities. That has less to do with careful planning than with a particular ethos—a philosophical approach, if you will—that has guided our development and shaped my understanding of how publishing can (and perhaps ought to) work. This philosophy is informed by four foundational principles:

- a commitment to the value of sharing scholarly work through open-access publishing,
- a belief that we are strongest when we work together to accomplish shared—or perhaps more accurately, overlapping and compatible—goals,
- a commitment to inclusiveness, and
- a recognition of the importance of aligning our professional efforts with the reward structures that shape our professional lives,

A COMMITMENT TO OPEN-ACCESS PUBLISHING

From the day I first realized my students were being charged fees to read my own articles, I've had a strong commitment to sharing our work through open-access publishing. I believe we should consider carefully the tradeoffs involved in bartering our intellectual property rights for the privilege of publishing in proprietary journals. I've written elsewhere about the role open-access publishing, which I tend to think of as inherently digital, can play in ensuring the broadest possible audience for our scholarly work. In 2001, in a column in *Academic.Writing*, I pointed to the futility of the resistance then being expressed to digital publications by an old(er) guard, suggesting we would soon see most work published in digital formats, largely for economic reasons but also because of the greater reach our work can have if it is distributed online. I also pointed to both the cost of subscriptions to print journals and to the much higher costs borne by students (collectively) in permission fees for work we had assigned to the publishers who owned those journals. My request to readers of *Academic.Writing* was pointed: when one of your colleagues asks what you think of publishing in an online journal, take the time to check out the editorial board and review policies of that journal. Check out, as well, the journal's policies regarding assignment of copyright. Blanket generalizations about the quality of a journal based solely on publication medium reflect poorly not only on the individual making the generalization but also on our field as a whole.

With David Blakesley, Doug Eyman, Byron Hawk, and Todd Taylor (2002), I took up these issues again in a special multi-journal issue of *Academic.Writing, CCC Online, enculturation, Kairos*, and *The Writing Instructor* on electronic publishing. In addition to arguments about the quality of the text and the review process, we pointed out that digital texts had higher citation rates, that open-access publishing in digital formats freed scholars from the market-driven economies that shape most traditional academic presses, and that the involvement of authors in the production of digital texts brought about fruitful collaborations among publishers and the larger scholarly community. I addressed this issue yet again in an editor's column written for the first issue of *Across the Disciplines*:

> Clearly, if our goal as academics is to distribute our ideas as widely as possible, digital publication beats print publication hands down. It's time to dispense with our infatuation with wood pulp and turn our attention to issues of real concern. When tenure and promotion committees evaluate a "tenure book," let's hope that book is available to a wider range of scholars than is typically the case with most codex books, whose small

press runs result in purchase by as few as twenty libraries world wide. (Palmquist 2004)

Open-access publishing has become the norm in our field, as evidenced by the extensive list of journals in the "Resources" section of the WAC Clearinghouse (wac.colostate.edu/resources) and by the number of contributors to this volume who edit open-access journals and book series (Bazerman, chapter 16; Eyman and Ball, chapter 12; Harris, chapter 3; Hawk, chapter 13; Micciche, chapter 2; Pemberton, chapter 10; Powell, chapter 15; Weisser, chapter 6). While my early thoughts on the value of open-access publishing have become more nuanced over the years, the central assumptions informing them have remained stable: as scholars seeking to advance knowledge in our field, we would be wise to embrace publishing technologies that make our work available as quickly as possible to the widest possible audience. Currently, peer-reviewed open-access publishing offers the best means of doing so.

THE VALUE OF COOPERATIVE WORK

I've long embraced the principle that we are strongest when we work together in the pursuit of shared goals. These goals need not be identical. Differences in perspectives and motivations—and the useful tensions that accompany them—have led to some of the most valuable work that has emerged from the Clearinghouse, including the projects housed in our resources section, many of our journals, and several of our book series. I've tried, over the years, to understand how the tensions associated with the efforts to reach shared goals have contributed to the success of the Clearinghouse.[4] Those attempts led me to activity theory (Engeström 1987, 1999, 2014; Leontiev 1978, 2005; Roth and Lee 2007; Vygotsky 1978, 1986, 1989).

A year after the publication of the multi-journal special issue, I introduced the idea of a publishing collaborative in a plenary talk at the CCCC Research Network Forum (Palmquist 2003). I'm not sure whether I came up with the term on my own or heard it elsewhere, but the general notion of collaboratives was in the air, and it seemed well suited to the ethos of the Clearinghouse. We had grown to more than fifty editors and reviewers by that point, and I had been struggling to understand how an organization as distributed as the Clearinghouse had survived. Drawing on activity theory, which I had been exposed to as a result of its central role in Bazerman and Russell's edited collection *Writing Selves/Writing Societies* (2003), I began thinking of the

Clearinghouse as a useful example of the kinds of distributed, collaborative work activity theory had been developed, in part, to interrogate and explain. In an essay I coauthored with Joan Mullin and Glenn Blalock (Palmquist, Mullin, and Blalock 2012), we considered how activity theory could be applied to the kind of work we were doing, respectively, with the Clearinghouse, the Research Exchange (now REx), and CompPile (which has since become an important part of the Clearinghouse). Our conclusion included the observation that activity theory allowed us to understand the development of these three projects "as an expression of the will of existing communities, communities whose members are seeking tools to support and share traditional scholarly work, and as a vehicle for emerging communities, whose members are seeking tools to support and share that work in new ways" (241). As the number of scholars involved in the Clearinghouse has grown, many members of the collaborative not only have not met face to face but in some cases have never communicated with each other online. Activity theory has proven to be a useful framework for understanding the differential contributions and productive collaborations that, even in isolation from each other, have advanced the larger project of sharing resources and open-access publications with the WAC and writing studies communities.

A COMMITMENT TO INCLUSIVENESS

My early work on the Clearinghouse was motivated by a naïve and largely unexamined commitment to inclusiveness. I welcomed anyone who wanted to join the project. All they had to do was ask. Or be asked. In most cases, an invitation to join the publishing collaborative was based on scholarly reputation and shared values. In other words, I invited people who were like me.

Over the past fifteen years, that has changed. My work as a university administrator, which included serving as the hiring authority for more than fifty searches, led me to rethink my approach to inclusiveness, initially helping me to problematize notions such as "fit" and to adopt much more aggressive efforts to recruit candidates who could bring different perspectives to our efforts. My work as an administrator also led me to participate in professional-development activities that deepened my understanding of the challenges facing many of my colleagues and to bring what I learned back to the groups I directed.

Those experiences, in turn, influenced my thinking about the Clearinghouse, in particular how best to build its editorial staff, constitute its editorial board, establish partnerships, encourage submissions, and review those submissions. Most recently, those efforts have been informed by a growing awareness of the challenges highlighted by the Me Too movement and the Black Lives Matters movement. They were also informed by my work on public-relations projects for my corporate clients prior to going to graduate school. That earlier work taught me that projecting an image—in the case of the Clearinghouse, an image of welcoming inclusiveness—is far from sufficient. If it isn't backed up with action, it amounts to little more than virtue signaling—the kind of signaling we see, for example, by corporations who want us to believe they care about climate change even as their products worsen the crisis.

With that in mind, we have both announced our commitment to inclusiveness and established practices to promote it. We developed and published a diversity statement and an invitation to contribute scholarly work. We reconstituted our editorial board and created new editorial-staff positions, including associate-editor positions for our book series and associate-publisher positions for the Clearinghouse as a whole. We recruited new scholars to our Publications Review Board. Most recently, with a goal of increasing awareness of publishing, reviewing, and editorial leadership roles available at the Clearinghouse, we have worked to establish partnerships with groups that focus on diversity and inclusiveness, such the Association for Writing Across the Curriculum and the CCCC Scholars for the Dream Travel Award Committee. We plan to expand these efforts on an ongoing basis, refining our approach based on what we learn from each.

These efforts are not being carried out in a vacuum. They reflect efforts by other publishers, notably journals such as *Kairos* (Eyman and Ball, chapter 12, this volume) and *constellations* (Powell, chapter 15, this volume), to include a wider range of voices than have historically been heard in our field. In their chapter in this collection, Doug Eyman and Cheryl Ball point to the development of editorial practices that encourage submissions from a wider range of scholars. They also outline efforts to promote inclusive writing and citation practices and describe efforts to recruit an editorial staff that reflects the growing diversity of the field of writing studies. Malea Powell points in another direction, describing the establishment of *constellations* as a response to the need to create "a space for the conversations that weren't being heard in mainstream journals." Their efforts, along with those of countless other journals and publishers, are providing a strong foundation for enacting inclusive editorial practices.

Yet it seems clear those practices will be complicated by the very nature of scholarly publishing. As Michael Pemberton (chapter 10, this volume) observes, academic publishing is implicitly tied to the "hierarchical power structure of academic and intellectual politics." Pemberton notes that the criteria publishers and journal editors establish to determine acceptance or rejection are fundamental to decisions "about whose voices get heard and whose don't . . . who's let in and who's kept out." He concludes, "Rather than treating academic publication as merely a *rite* of passage, journals are generally placed in a position of privilege where they get to decide who has the *right* of passage." Dealing with these tensions, he suggests, requires an ongoing effort to maintain an awareness of his ethical responsibilities to both the field of writing studies and the authors with whom he works.

The efforts Pemberton, Eyman, Ball, and Powell describe point to useful directions for enacting inclusive editorial practices. Moving in this direction, with all the contradictions and complications it involves, has been central to the development of my editorial philosophy.

ALIGNMENT WITH INSTITUTIONAL AND DISCIPLINARY REWARD STRUCTURES

My editorial philosophy has also been shaped by the principle that we should either align our professional efforts with existing institutional and disciplinary rewards structures—or work to change them. I've embraced this principle since joining the faculty at Colorado State University. We recognized early in our efforts to design and launch a new WAC program that few members of our faculty would act on the then two-decades-old ethos that WAC should be used because of its clear benefits for students. Our interviews with faculty members in the programs we were working with revealed that, while almost every one of them agreed it would be ideal to use writing to support learning and professional preparation in their courses, they had higher priorities that worked against doing so. Those priorities typically involved publishing and grant seeking, activities repeatedly reinforced in discussions with their senior colleagues and department heads. Our approach, as a result, focused on reducing the time required to use writing in courses by providing direct support for student writing and engaging our faculty in professional-development activities that might help them work as efficiently as possible (Palmquist 2000; Palmquist, Mullin, and Blalock 2012; Palmquist et al. 1995; Siller, Palmquist, and Zimmerman 1998). This approach proved successful, especially in comparison to earlier efforts to enact WAC on our campus. It also led to sustained efforts, in concert with others on our campus who share our commitment to improving teaching and learning, to change the rewards structures at our research-intensive university. This has resulted in substantial changes over the past three decades in how we define, document, and assess teaching effectiveness and in the role those assessments play in our review processes (Colorado State University 2020).

The lessons learned through our WAC efforts have informed my understanding of how to structure the work we carry out in the Clearinghouse (notwithstanding my failure to recognize in 1997 and early 1998 that "work on a website" didn't fit current institutional reward structures). We made a fairly simple set of moves, initially adopting the roles associated with a scholarly journal and, later, expanding those roles to reflect those associated with an academic publisher. This approach has proven effective. The members of the Clearinghouse publishing collaborative can list roles that are easily understood—and, more important, valued—in an annual, promotion, or tenure review. Every member of the Clearinghouse has a clear title, such as publisher, editorial-board member, journal editor, series editor, associate editor, managing editor, associate publisher, or reviewer, among others. These titles serve as a form of intellectual capital that allows the work carried out on Clearinghouse activities to be valued in ways that materially affect the members of the collaborative.

It is not without a sense of irony that I recognize the role both capitalism and Soviet-era activity theory play in my editorial philosophy. It reflects, perhaps, a belief that any good tool is worth considering. But it also reflects the disproportionate role economics has played in academic publishing, where decisions about acceptance or rejection of a book manuscript are routinely informed by an assessment of potential sales, where the number of articles published in a journal is strongly influenced by the cost of adding pages, and where, as a result, promising books and journal articles are rejected because, while they're good, they're not quite good enough. I've asked, for example, what the difference is between the 3 to 5 percent of articles accepted by journals such as *College English* and *CCC* and the next 5, 10, or 20 percent rejected largely for space reasons. Certainly, I recognize that few readers have the time and attention to read twenty or thirty articles in a single issue of a journal. But if our goal is to share good work, we should look beyond the constraints imposed by the economics of traditional publishing technologies and the industries that grew up around them.

FROM THE PHILOSOPHY TO ADVOCACY: CONSIDERING OPEN-ACCESS PUBLISHING

Scholars who are considering publishing with an open-access press or journal will find relatively few differences from submitting work to a traditional academic publisher. The best publishers have strong peer-review processes, work with authors largely via email and other electronic communication tools, and expect authors to play some role in the production process. Because they rely on sales revenue to support their operations, traditional publishers likely do a far better job of marketing a book or journal and of placing it with leading database providers. They are also more likely to provide support for indexing, traditionally a key part of the best books. That said, traditional publishers often take far longer to produce a book than an open-access press, and those books often stay in circulation for a shorter period of time than those produced by open-access publishers. Important, open-access publishers approach issues such as copyright differently than most open-access publishers.

As you consider publishing with an open-access journal or press, keep the following concerns in mind.

Editorial-Review Boards and Peer-Review Processes

Critics of open-access publishers sometimes suggest that the peer-review process can be slipshod. That criticism could also, of course, be leveled against publishers who charge for subscriptions. As you consider publishing with a particular journal or academic press, review their posted peer-review process, take a look at their editorial board, reach out to authors who have published with them, and seek advice from your colleagues. My sense is that the peer-review process is quite similar across reputable publishers. Regardless of whether you are working with an open-access or proprietary publisher, you'll find that scholars are playing key roles in editing and reviewing. Gaining a sense of the reputation of the scholars associated with the journal and assessing the quality of its peer-review process are important steps in deciding where to send your work.

Database and Library of Congress Listings

With a growing number of databases providing access to full-text journal articles and books, it has become more important to understand which databases index the publications in a particular journal or academic press. Equally important is looking for indicators of quality such as Library of Congress publication data in books published by a press, the International Standard Serial Number assigned to a journal, and listings of books in WorldCat, the Online Computer Library Center's union catalog that lists the holdings of more than seventeen thousand libraries worldwide. All other things being equal, it is advantageous to publish your work in an indexed journal or a press that submits its work to the Library of Congress and WorldCat.

Copyright and Licensing

Control over the copyright for your work has become a critical issue, not only for individual scholars but also for college and university libraries. Prior to the rise of open-access publishing, it was rare to see scholars exercising control over copyright to their work. We engaged largely in a barter system, trading our copyrights for the labor and capital required to produce journals and books. As open-access publishers such as *Kairos* and *enculturation* and publishing collaboratives such as the WAC Clearinghouse have allowed scholars to control the production of scholarly work, this barter system has begun to fall out of use. Moreover, many federal agencies are requiring, as part of their grant guidelines, and many colleges and universities have strongly recommended, that scholarly work be published under open-access licenses.

Prior to the launch of the Creative Commons Corporation (creativecommons.org), which provides the legal frameworks under which most open-access materials are released today, the Clearinghouse contracted with authors using a "right-to-present" model, which left the copyright for published material with the author but granted the Clearinghouse rights to present the material on its site. The Clearinghouse now uses Creative Commons licenses. As you consider a home for your work, learn about the options you have for retaining copyright over it and ensuring its wide distribution. While the default licensing option used by most proprietary publishers involves the transfer of copyright to the publisher, you can often negotiate retention of copyright and release of the work in open-access form.

Finally, it can be useful to understand the differences among the many Creative Commons licenses. Key issues to consider include whether you will allow distribution of your work in venues other than your publisher, whether you will allow subsequent works to be derived from yours, and whether you will allow derivatives to be made by commercial entities.

The journal articles and books produced by the Clearinghouse typically use a Creative Commons Attribution-Noncommercial-No Derivative Works license, but this can vary according to the wishes of the author. We use this license largely to offer some protection to scholars who seek to include their work in annual, promotion, or tenure reviews, reasoning that if derivative works exist, it will be difficult for the author to track the impact of their scholarly contributions.

Subvention Fees

Subvention fees are used to support production costs such as copyediting, design, and distribution of work. They are often used to ensure that work published by journals and scholarly presses is available in open-access formats, as is required by a number of federal agencies. Within writing studies, few journals charge subvention fees, but many accept them. Over the past several years, the Clearinghouse has received subventions on a handful of books, most often for those associated with international conferences.

If you are asked to pay a subvention fee and are confident in the quality of the journal or press seeking the fee, look to your institution for support. Most often, you'll find support through your library. Even if a journal or press does not seek a subvention fee, you can support open-access publishers by seeking this kind of funding from your institution. Be cautious, however, about publishing in journals or book series whose editors aggressively seek subvention fees while failing to provide a solid peer-review process and editorial-development support. This is typical of publishers that have been characterized as "predatory." For a recent cautionary tale, see Alan Chambers (2019).

Medium

As Marshall McLuhan (1964) famously argued, the medium in which a publication is delivered can have profound effects on how work is circulated and received. Open-access publishers vary in the formats they offer, with some providing documents in HTML/CSS formats and others providing PDF and ePub. Some offer a mix of formats. Long ago, for example, the Clearinghouse adopted a mixed digital and print approach for our books, in part because some readers want to read a book in print, some want to purchase books to support our continued operation, and some of our authors have found print copies useful during annual, promotion, or tenure reviews.

Manuscript Preparation and Production

Increasingly, both open-access and propriety publishers expect significant involvement from authors and collection editors in manuscript preparation and publication processes. Not long ago, this expectation was expressed as a request to provide "camera-ready copy" (a phrase dating back to the days of offset printing). If you work with an open-access publisher, be prepared to do more of this kind of work than would be the case with a propriety publisher. You will likely be asked to provide high-quality images, to develop tables and charts that will display well on a page (web, print, or both), and even, in the case of books, to create your own index. You are also likely to be asked to secure permissions for use of copyrighted materials. Most open-access publishers provide guidance on their websites, often in the form of a guide for authors and editors.

Similarly, expect open-access publishers to require that you address accessibility concerns in books, book chapters, and articles that incorporate media. Addressing these concerns involves attention to additional aspects of preparation and production, such as providing descriptions of photographs and other illustrations, creating audio transcripts, and providing closed captioning for video. Attending to accessibility might also involve conforming to production practices that ensure long-term viability of work produced in HTML code, such as the practices Bradley Dilger and Kevin Brock put in place for *Composition Forum* (Weisser, chapter 6, this volume). These practices can shape a manuscript in important ways. For example, editors might require that older technologies (various types of video players come to mind) be replaced with modern tools, even when those older technologies are still supported by modern web browsers.

Sustainability

If you take a look at the journal archives on the Clearinghouse—particularly those archived through CompPile (wac.colostate.edu/com pile/archives)—you'll see abundant evidence of journals that have ceased operation. In more than three decades in the field, I've seen the marvelous experiment that was *RhetNet* end its run after only a few years, and I've seen several important journals, such as *Basic Writing E-Journal, English Matters, Inventio,* and *Lore,* among others, come to an end (see Hesse 2019). It's worth noting that—unlike the journals published by academic presses, major database companies (such as SAGE and Elsevier), and professional organizations (such as NCTE and CCCC)—few open-access journals and publishing collaboratives (such as the WAC Clearinghouse and the Computers and Composition Digital Press) have strong financial foundations. This is not necessarily a bad thing, as I'll argue in greater length in an article I'm writing about publishing collaboratives. Those of us who work on these projects know progress is dependent on volunteer labor. To some extent, and from what might seem like a sort of *Alice in Wonderland* perspective, it's less worrisome that a journal has no support than that existing support might go away.

Circulation

One of the most important differences between open-access and proprietary publishers is who can access them. I've written about this elsewhere, arguing that scholars should consider not only the prestige of a journal but also its reach.

> Placing work in a highly regarded journal brings visibility within the field (and confers a degree of prestige to those who are published in such journals). Yet non-subscribers are less likely to have access to new scholarship. In addition, even when the work is released to a database company such as JSTOR, access is still restricted. (Palmquist 2019, 200)

Some of NCTE's journals, for example, are both prestigious and embargoed. This means nonsubscribers will not have access to the articles in the journal until the embargo (typically two years) has passed and then only through a database.

Open-access journals, by definition, make their work available to all readers from the start. The question of sustainability, however, is critical. Fortunately, for open-access journals and books, the end of publication does not necessarily mean an end to access. The cost of storage for a journal's archive, for example, is low enough that it can continue to be available for years (even decades) after the end of circulation. For an example, see the books made available through Utah State University Press's Digital Commons (digitalcommons.usu.edu/usupress_pubs/), which was created when the press merged with University Press of Colorado. In addition, if articles or books have also been added to a database, they will likely continue to be available to those with access through a library or individual subscription.

Perhaps the most important question for books and journals from proprietary publishers is whether access will end if making them available is no longer commercially viable. It is normal practice, for example, for books to go out of print. Fortunately, many traditional presses are making older books available in digital formats even when print is no longer available. And while these books are typically available for a price, a growing number are being released in open-access formats. For an example, see books released through the Knowledge Unlatched initiative (knowledgeunlatched.org).

In contrast, open-access publishers keep journal articles and books available on an ongoing basis. *Kairos* and *enculturation*, for example, provide access to work dating back to the 1990s, while all of the books and journals published by the Clearinghouse continue to be available. Most important, access appears to be strong for both journal archives and books. In the past year alone, for example, the twelve original books published by the Clearinghouse before 2010 saw more than 475,000 visits and more than 460,000 downloads of complete books and individual chapters. This is significantly higher than the typical print sales and paid downloads of books on academic-press backlists.

Citation Rates

For nearly two decades, researchers have reported that open-access publications have higher citation rates than those from traditional publishers (Eysenbach 2006; Gargouri et al. 2010). Recently, it has become clear that this advantage is not as large as it once was (Dorta-Gonzalez, Gonzalez-Betancor, and Dorta-Gonzalez 2017; Dorta-Gonzalez and Santana-Jimenez 2018; Ottaviani 2016; Wang et al. 2015). Jim Ottaviani (2016), for example, has pointed out, "All things being equal, that an article made freely available ought to get downloaded more than a comparable article that costs money to access seems obvious." But, he continues, he mistrusts this observation "largely because all things are rarely equal and confounding factors are not always easy to intuit." The advantage of open-access publications, it seems, has largely been related to the ability to locate articles online. The confounding factors Ottaviani refers to include the growing ease of access to full-text articles through databases. While these articles might be published in proprietary journals, those who have access to the databases can find these articles more easily than was once the case. And since some proprietary journals have high impact factors, they can attract submissions from leading authors in a given field. In addition, as Serio Copiello (2019) suggests in a recent study, some of the citation-rate advantage might be accounted for by a higher likelihood of open-indexing databases (such as Google Scholar) locating open-access publications.

In writing studies, where access to leading journals such as *College English* and *College Composition and Communication* is limited to subscribers and embargoed for two years from databases, it seems likely that open-access publications will continue to have advantages in citation rates for some time.

SOME GENERAL OBSERVATIONS AND ADVICE

If I could offer only one piece of advice, it would be that we continue to work together to reinvent publishing in our field. I have long felt troubled when I become aware of good work that hasn't found a home or when I learn of ambitious and adventurous projects pushed back toward conventionality. I know of a colleague, for example, who might have published one of the first truly multimodal books in our field but who failed to do so in part because of well-meaning but incompetent advice from a department chair. I have for many years questioned the glorification of high rejection rates in journals and book series, and I feel embarrassed to have learned recently that the WAC Clearinghouse Perspective on Writing series is rejecting as many as 95 percent of the proposals it receives. My embarrassment has nothing to do with the decisions made by our series editors, who are wonderful. Instead, I'm embarrassed that our publishing model is not efficient enough to handle more good work.

As a field, we strive to share good scholarship. Our publications are intended to advance our knowledge of theory and practice. They are intended to share excellent research. They are intended to improve our teaching and learning, our scholarly endeavors, and our administrative processes. If we fail to find room for good publications, then we do ourselves, our students, our institutions, and our stakeholders a disservice.

Open-access publishing has helped transform publishing in our field. The majority of our journals now follow this approach, and a growing number of book series are taking it up as well. But open-access publishing is not sufficient. We need a next act. And that next act will require, as some of us have argued, changes in how we reward work in our field and in our institutions (Day et al. 2013). Simply put, we must take greater control of scholarly publishing. That means changing the funding models used by our professional organizations, who rely heavily on subscription-based journals to attract and retain members. It means moving away from using publication in prestigious presses as a placeholder for judgments of quality during annual, promotion, and tenure reviews (and it would be ideal to avoid embracing "impact factors" as well). It means changing, in a fundamental way, our understanding of what "service" means so it can include the work that will allow us, as a field, to regain control over the publication of our scholarly work. And it means taking a hard look at the genres we use to share our work with others. I noted earlier that our field now recognizes, at least to some extent, the value of work on a website. We would be wise to ask ourselves whether we can find value in the publication of other newer genres as well.

Our field is a natural home for experimentation and leadership in scholarly publishing. We have a strong record of accomplishment that includes early work in the development of digital journals and open-access book publishing as well as impressive work in developing citation databases freely available to all. We can build on this strong foundation by continuing to pursue innovative approaches to sharing scholarly work. We can, and should, serve as a model for work not only in writing studies but also in disciplines across the academy. We can, and should, reinvent and improve our practices. We can, and should, retake control of scholarly publishing.

NOTES

1. We received funding from a State of Colorado Commission on Higher Education Program of Excellence grant from 1992 to 1997, as well as internal funding from Colorado State University during and after the grant period.
2. *Academic.Writing* would run through 2003, when it merged with *Language and Learning Across the Disciplines* (*LLAD*, a print journal that housed its digital archives on the *Academic.Writing* site) to form the online journal *Across the Disciplines*.
3. We developed a contract that gave the WAC Clearinghouse (at that time, *Academic. Writing*) the "right to present" the work we digitized while leaving the copyright with the authors. When Creative Commons licenses were launched, we began using those licenses.
4. I'm thinking here of the differences of opinion, often borne out of different perspectives and positionalities, that lead to productive discussions about goals, strategies, and tactics. I do not recall any instances over the past two decades in which differing opinions resulted in the kind of destructive conflict that can derail a project. But I can remember many situations in which we refined and improved our ideas through discussion.

REFERENCES

Bazerman, Charles, and David Russell, eds. 2003. *Writing Selves/Writing Societies: Research from Activity Perspectives.* Fort Collins, CO: WAC Clearinghouse. https://doi.org/10.37514/PER-B.2003.2317.

Blakesley, David, Doug Eyman, Byron Hawk, Mike Palmquist, and Todd Taylor, eds. 2002. "Special Multi-journal Issue of *Enculturation, Academic.Writing, CCC Online, Kairos,* and *The Writing Instructor* on Electronic Publication." http://enculturation.net/4_1/toc.html.

Chambers, Alan H. 2019. "How I Became Easy Prey to a Predatory Publisher." *Science* 364 (6440): 602. https://doi.org/10.1126/science.caredit.aax9725.

Colorado State University. 2020. *Academic Faculty and Administrative Professional Manual.* Fort Collins, CO: Colorado State University Faculty Council. https://facultycouncil.colostate.edu/faculty-manual/.

Copiello, Sergio. 2019. "The Open Access Citation Premium May Depend on the Openness and Inclusiveness of the Indexing Database, but the Relationship Is Controversial because It Is Ambiguous Where the Open Access Boundary Lies." *Scientometrics* 121 (2): 995–1018. https://doi.org/10.1007/s11192-019-03221-w.

Day, Michael, Susan H. Delagrange, Mike Palmquist, Michael A. Pemberton, and Janice R. Walker. 2013. "What We Really Value: Redefining Scholarly Engagement in Tenure and Promotion Protocols." *College Composition and Communication* 65 (1): 185–208. http://www.ncte.org/library/NCTEFiles/Resources/Journals/CCC/0651-sep2013/CCC0651What.pdf.

Dorta-Gonzalez, Pablo, Sara M. Gonzalez-Betancor, and Maria Isabel Dorta-Gonzalez. 2017. "Reconsidering the Gold Open Access Citation Advantage Postulate in a Multidisciplinary Context: An Analysis of the Subject Categories in the Web of Science Database 2009–2014." *Scientometrics* 112: 877–901. https://doi.org/10.1007/s11192-017-2422-y.

Dorta-Gonzalez, Pablo, and Yolanda Santana-Jimenez. 2018. "Prevalence and Citation Advantage of Gold Open Access in the Subject Areas of the Scopus Database." *Research Evaluation* 27 (1): 1–15. https://doi.org/10.1093/reseval/rvx035.

Engeström, Yrjo. 1987. *Learning by Expanding*. Helsinki: Orienta-Konsultit.

Engeström, Yrjo. 1999. "Activity Theory and Individual and Social Transformation." In *Perspectives on Activity Theory*, edited by Yrjo Engeström, Reijo Miettinen, and Raija-Leena Punamäki, 19–38. Cambridge, UK: Cambridge University Press.

Engeström, Yrjo. 2014. *Learning by Expanding*. 2nd ed. Cambridge: Cambridge University Press.

Eysenbach, Gunther. 2006. "Citation Advantage of Open Access Articles." *PLoS Biology* 4 (5): e157. https://doi.org/10.1371/journal.pbio.0040157.

Gargouri Yassine, Chawki Hajjem, Vincent Larivière, Yves Gingras, Les Carr, Tim Brody, and Stevan Harna. 2010. "Self-Selected or Mandated, Open Access Increases Citation Impact for Higher Quality Research." *PLoS ONE* 5 (10): e13636. https://doi.org/10.1371/journal.pone.0013636.

Haring-Smith, Tori. 1987. *A Guide to Writing Programs: Writing Centers, Peer Tutoring Programs, and Writing Across the Curriculum*. Glenview, IL: Scott-Foresman.

Hesse, Doug. 2019. "Journals in Composition Studies, Thirty-Five Years After." *College English* 81 (4): 367–396. https://library.ncte.org/journals/C 5.

Leontiev, Alexei N. 1978. *Activity, Consciousness, and Personality*. Translated by Marie J. Hall. Hillsdale, NJ: Prentice-Hall.

Leontiev, Alexei N. 2005. "The Genesis of Activity." *Journal of Russian and East European Psychology* 43 (4): 58–71.

McLeod, Susan H., and Margot Soven, eds. 2000. *Writing Across the Curriculum: A Guide to Developing Programs*. Fort Collins, CO: WAC Clearinghouse. First published in 1992 by SAGE. https://wac.colostate.edu/books/landmarks/mcleod-soven/.

McLuhan, Marshall. 1964. *Understanding Media: The Extensions of Man*. New York: Mentor.

Ottaviani, Jim. 2016. "The Post-Embargo Open Access Citation Advantage: It Exists (Probably), It's Modest (Usually), and the Rich Get Richer (of Course)." *PLoS ONE* 11 (8): e0159614. https://doi.org/10.1371/journal.pone.0159614.

Palmquist, Mike. 2000. "Notes on the Evolution of Network Support for WAC." In *Inventing a Discipline: Essays in Honor of Richard E. Young*, edited by Maureen Daly Goggin, 373–402. Champaign-Urbana, IL: NCTE.

Palmquist, Mike. 2001. "The State of Publishing in Online Journals." *Academic.Writing* 2. https://doi.org/10.37514/AWR-J.2001.2.1.01.

Palmquist, Mike. 2003. "New Venues for Academic Publishing: From Cooperative Publishing Ventures to Collaborative Web Sites." Plenary Presentation, Research Network Forum. Presented at the Conference on College Composition and Communication, New York, March 19–22.

Palmquist, Mike. 2004. "On Merging LLAD and AW." *Across the Disciplines* 1. https://doi.org/10.37514/ATD-J.2004.1.1.01.

Palmquist, Mike. 2019. "Open or Closed: Observations on Open-Access Publishers." In *Explanation Points: Publishing in Rhetoric and Composition*, edited by John R. Gallagher and Dànielle Nicole Devoss, 199–205. Logan: Utah State University Press.

Palmquist, Mike, Joan Mullin, and Glenn Blalock. 2012. "The Role of Activity Analysis in Writing Research: Case Studies of Emerging Scholarly Communities." In *Writing Studies Research in Practice: Methods and Methodologies*, edited by Lee Nicholson and Mary P. Sheridan, 231–244. Carbondale: Southern Illinois University Press.

Palmquist, Mike, Dawn Rodrigues, Kathleen E. Kiefer, and Donald E. Zimmerman. 1995. "Network Support for Writing across the Curriculum: Developing an Online Writing Center." *Computers & Composition* 12 (3): 335–353. https://doi.org/10.1016/S8755-4615(05)80073-8.

Roth, Wolff-Michael, and Yew-Jin Lee. 2007. "'Vygotsky's Neglected Legacy': Cultural-Historical Activity Theory." *Review of Educational Research* 77 (2): 186–232. https://doi.org/10.3102/0034654306298273.

Siller, Thomas J., Mike Palmquist, and Donald E. Zimmerman. 1998. "Technology as a Vehicle for Integrating Communication and Team-Working Skills in Engineering Curricula." *Computer Applications in Engineering Education* 6 (4): 245–254.

Thomas, Laura Hebenstreit. 1995. "Educating Electrical Engineers for Workplace Communication: A Qualitative Study." Unpublished master's thesis, Colorado State University.

Vest, David, Marilee Long, Laura Thomas, and Mike Palmquist. 1995. "Relating Communication Training to Workplace Requirements: The Perspective of New Engineers." *IEEE Transactions on Professional Communication* 38 (1): 11–17. https://doi.org/10.1109/47.372387.

Vygotsky, Lev S. 1978. *Mind in Society: The Development of Higher Psychological Processes*, edited by Michael Cole, Vera John-Steiner, Sylvia Scribner, and Ellen Souberman. Cambridge, MA: Harvard University Press.

Vygotsky, Lev S. 1986. *Thought and Language*, edited and translated by Alex Kozulin. Cambridge: MIT Press.

Vygotsky, Lev S. 1989. "Concrete Human Psychology." *Soviet Psychology* 27 (2): 53–77.

Wang, Xianwen, Chen Liu, Wenli Mao, and Zhichao Fang. 2015. "The Open Access Advantage Considering Citation, Article Usage and Social Media Attention." *Scientometrics* 103: 555–564. https://doi.org/10.1007/s11192-015-1547-0.

10
GATEKEEPER, GUARDIAN, OR GUIDE?
Negotiating the Dynamics of Power as an Editor

Michael A. Pemberton
Georgia Southern University

In one capacity or another, I've been a rhet/comp editor for more than twenty-five years. That's not a record (I think Muriel Harris has me beat by a mile), but it's a long enough time that I think I've developed a fairly good sense of what the job entails. To briefly summarize the "Editing" portion of my CV, I spent a few years in the late 1990s editing the *IATE Journal* for the Illinois Association of Teachers of English, was a guest editor for a special issue of the *Clearing House* around the same time, and have coedited several books, including *The Center Will Hold* (2003) and *Labored: The State(ment) and Future of Work in Composition* (2017). My longest-running position as editor, though, has been with the academic journal *Across the Disciplines (ATD)*, which I cofounded with Sharon Quiroz in 1994 and for which I have been sole editor in chief since 2004. In 2014, I established a new book series linked to the journal, *Across the Disciplines Books*, and as series editor have had the pleasure of working with dozens of editors and scholars who have contributed to that series.

Enough about credentials. What I'd really like to share in this chapter are my reflections about what it has meant for me to be a journal editor in an academic discipline—not just in terms of the work that's involved (which is extensive) or the behind-the-scenes details of peer reviewing (which can be hair raising) but also about being in a position of power and control I was neither directly trained for nor entirely prepared to assume. As I have occasionally remarked to colleagues, the most challenging part of being an editor is not the *editing*. It's the *decision-making*. It's the act of sitting on a very small throne in a secluded ivory tower, surrounded by a cadre of disciplinary advisors who rarely agree, and making decisions about which of the many publication-seeking supplicants get published and which don't.

All editors of academic journals face similar decisions and similar challenges, but the ethics and philosophies of gatekeeping, of exercising editorial power and control, are rarely discussed among scholarly editors outside a relatively narrow range of publications (such as the journals *Learned Publishing* and the *Journal of Scholarly Publishing*). In writing studies, aside from a few conference panels where editors have talked, for example, about "how to get your article published" or "how to increase diversity in composition journals" (both of which I have participated in), discussions of gatekeeping as a practice are few and far between.

So I'd like to begin that discussion here, filtered through the lens of my own experience as the editor of *Across the Disciplines*, a journal that publishes research in WAC/WID, interdisciplinary communication, and areas "relevant to writing and writing pedagogy in all their intellectual, political, social, and technological complexity" ("Across the Disciplines"). What I argue in this chapter, among other things, is that *ATD*'s positionality as a cross-disciplinary journal has frequently thrown my own gatekeeping practices into high relief and compelled me to reflect on what it means to be an editor, how to be an ethical gatekeeper when standing at the nexus of intersecting disciplinary domains, and what factors are most important to me when deciding which pieces and which authors to let through the gate.

INTERDISCIPLINARY STUDY, WAC, AND BORDER CROSSING

First, a little bit of context. At the time I was applying to grad school, the early to mid-1980s, graduate programs in rhetoric and composition were few in number and several—such as mine at UCSD—offered a concentration in rhetoric and composition housed in a department of literature. This means that although my dissertation was clearly focused on writing theory, my PhD states I have a degree in "English and American Literature," which was the disciplinary domain under which my particular concentration was housed. (Having this degree has caused me a little trouble over the years because accreditation agencies sometimes question whether I have the necessary credentials to teach writing courses.) But because my graduate program was a bit of an odd duck in the department, and because my mentor—Dr. Charles Cooper—encouraged interdisciplinary study, I took courses well outside the traditional domain of literary scholarship. For example, I took courses in cognitive psychology, conversational analysis, and the philosophy of language, all of which informed my dissertation on composing-process models. This disciplinary "border crossing" was not only important to my growth as a scholar but also resonated with rhet/comp's developing positionality as a hybrid discipline. Even at this early stage in composition studies' development as a field, researchers were drawing from fields such as communication studies, philosophy, psychology, linguistics, anthropology, and feminist theory, just to name a few. This expansive approach to scholarly research prepared me for my future career path as a writing center director, program evaluator, writing consultant, and editor of an interdisciplinary journal. In those capacities, I have had to be a regular and frequent border crosser, moving from one discourse community into another. That crossing has often been welcomed, such as when I have helped tutors understand and work with different disciplinary genres, and it has sometimes been resisted, such as when faculty in WAC/WID programs have seen me as an annoying gadfly. I certainly understand this resistance, and I try to overcome it by showing my respect for the expertise of others and demonstrating my willingness to listen when interacting with disciplinary faculty.

GATEKEEPER OR BORDER CROSSING GUARD?

So this is the odd self-contradictory position I find myself in as the editor of an interdisciplinary academic journal. Being the editor of *ATD* places me in a liminal space, right at the boundary between two distinctly different and extraordinarily powerful cultures. On the one hand, the philosophical and theoretical foundation of the journal is aligned with what William Condon and Carol Rutz (2012) refer to as "Integrated" and "Institutional Change Agent" programs, with WAC/WID leaders gradually moving their subject positions away from a missionary or colonial perspective and towards a set of principles similar to Gloria Anzaldúa's (1987) mestiza consciousness—an awareness of duality, a commitment to flexibility and inclusion rather than rigidity and exclusion, and an activist program of coalition building. The goal is not conversion but communication and colearning, not to construct borders and expand them but to deconstruct borders and focus on commonalities rather than differences. The key questions move away from What can I teach you? to What can we learn from each other? In this regard, *ATD* is firmly grounded in the principle that the construction of WAC/WID knowledge is enriched by disciplinary diversity and the contributions that can be made to a complex, nuanced conversation about writing by participants who inhabit different disciplinary worlds. As it says explicitly in our mission statement, "The mission of *Across the Disciplines* is to provide information for—and an opportunity for interaction among—scholars interested in writing, speaking, reading, and communication across the curriculum (CAC)" ("Publish in *Across the Disciplines*" n.d.).

On the other hand, the existence of an academic journal—by virtue of having identified itself as an academic journal—is to implicitly declare its allegiance to the hierarchical power structure of academic and intellectual politics. By establishing criteria for acceptance and rejection, it makes decisions about whose voices get heard and whose don't. It gets to decide who's let in and who's kept out. It constructs borders that disciplinary immigrants can only cross if they display the proper credentials. Rather than treating academic publication as merely a *rite* of passage, journals are generally placed in a position of privilege where they get to decide who has the *right* of passage. And in the case of *Across the Disciplines*, when I refer to the journal as an "it," what I really mean is "me and my editorial board." The journal itself does not make any decisions; a very small, select group of crossing guards does, and I, in my position as *comandante*, am the final arbiter.

Certainly, as an academic editor, I try to remain aware of my ethical responsibilities to the field and the authors I work with. The mandates for ethical scholarly publishing, as described by Darcy Cullen (2012) in "The Social Dynamics of Scholarly Editing," are few but compelling. Among them are "to publish and disseminate original contributions to knowledge in specific disciplines, to promote dialogue across disciplines, and to publish works of scholarship that 'stimulate public debate,' 'extend and challenge prevailing views in the academy and society' . . . and participate in the 'transformation of the intellectual and cultural landscape'" (18). As academics, we're all about challenging the status quo; in rhetoric and composition in particular, we revel in challenging accepted wisdom, we break conventions, we experiment with new textual forms, we introduce and incorporate research from diverse domains of scholarly work. But how far can those challenges and experiments go and still be considered scholarship? And for an interdisciplinary journal, what sorts of texts and scholarship should and should not be considered acceptable for publication? Whose disciplinary standards and conventions, if any, should be privileged, and why? Even Cullen (2012) acknowledges, "challenges to scholarly conventions that at the same time remain within the boundaries of scholarship can be difficult to devise and negotiate" (18).

DISCIPLINARITY, INTERDISCIPLINARITY, AND *ATD*

ATD describes itself as an interdisciplinary journal, but it is probably more correct to say it is a journal that publishes cross-disciplinary scholarship. It is not, in the strictest sense of the word, interdisciplinary in that it does not intentionally seek to synthesize the work of more than one discipline, although that may be a partial outcome of some of the pieces we publish. Neither is it a multidisciplinary journal because it does not merely accept, tacitly or explicitly, that different disciplines approach things differently and therefore refrain from making attempts to understand or bridge those differences. Most of our published articles are about writing research, writing pedagogy, and writing programs that coordinate the efforts of two or more academic disciplines.

Though we publish cross-disciplinary work, our primary audience is housed firmly in the domain of rhetoric and composition and in the subdomain of WAC and WID. Our audience is primarily though not exclusively rhetoric, composition, and WAC scholars, and we expect authors to be familiar with and place their work in the context of research in those fields. We publish pieces that are well grounded in theory and that use methodologies—either quantitative or qualitative—appropriate to the research. We want the articles to appeal to a diverse audience and be, to a certain extent, generalizable. For that reason, we do not publish simple program descriptions or narrative accounts of "this is what we did on my campus." We also do not publish articles that are descriptions of teaching practices or classroom strategies.

According to Richard Rose, the editor of the *Journal of Public Policy*, "The real test of a journal's interdisciplinary character is whether or not it normally engages in interdisciplinary refereeing" (1986, 118), and in *ATD*'s case, the journal falls far short of that criterion. The editorial board of *ATD* is constituted of rhet/comp scholars and writing specialists, not economists and physicists. At times, I believe that may be a bit of a weakness, particularly because I am solely responsible for selecting the members of the board. I have a large number of consulting readers, but again, they are almost exclusively drawn from a pool of people I know in the rhet/comp field (though I have, on occasion, sought out scholars I don't know personally who are qualified to respond to articles in a specific area of expertise, such as reading theory and corpus analysis, just to name a couple of recent examples). In that sense, *ATD* is a tightly focused disciplinary journal but one that respects and invites the insights and perspectives of scholars and researchers from other disciplines. So what implications does this approach have for me as someone who wants to be a responsible disciplinary gatekeeper and also an ethical editor who tries to be open to extradisciplinary perspectives?

GATEKEEPING

A number of professional organizations have produced documents that establish core principles for ethical scholarly publishing, but they focus almost exclusively on guidelines for the efficient and ethical treatment of authors and manuscripts, not the larger questions attendant to disciplinary gatekeeping. The Committee on Publication Ethics (COPE), in its "A Short Guide to Ethical Editing for New Editors" (2016), discusses relations with an outgoing editor, authors, editorial boards, and reviewers and stresses the importance of transparency in the editorial review process. The Council of Science Editors, in its "White Paper on Publication Ethics" (n.d.), replicates, in large measure, the issues addressed in the COPE document. Neither document concerns itself overmuch with larger questions about the editors' positions within their disciplines, such as the extent to which their decisions determine the contours of the field or the degree to which they might have an impact on the directions of current research and scholarly work. (Though Kelly Ritter [chapter 1 in this collection] feels the power editors wield is "often overstated," others such as Christian Weisser [chapter 6] and Kathleen Blake Yancey [chapter 7] believe editors play an important role in guiding and shaping the direction of the field.) These are fundamental ethical issues editors like myself must grapple with, but they don't often lend themselves to simple sets of rules and guidelines.

Gatekeeper, the term most frequently used to characterize the decision-making aspect of scholarly editors' duties, was first introduced by Kurt Lewin in a 1943 article on "Psychological Ecology." Lewin (1951) used the term to characterize the process of food distribution, but the distinction he makes between the "cognitive structure" of gatekeeping and the "motivational structure" of the gatekeeper (177–178) is useful for understanding how disciplinary editors make decisions about which manuscripts to admit and which to turn away.

> **Cognitive Structure**: The terms in which the gatekeeper/editor thinks about the submission in relation to the disciplinary context, including the author's familiarity with the genres, conventions, and structures of knowledge and knowledge making in that particular field.
>
> **The Motivation of the Gatekeeper/Editor**: The system of social and cultural values that lies behind the editors' choices. More specifically, editors must ask themselves questions such as these: Does this manuscript

conform to the readership's social, intellectual, and investigative norms, and will it be accessible to them? Does this manuscript meet readers' needs? How does one describe or present it to reviewers? To what extent are readers flexible enough to tolerate divergent paradigms? Is this manuscript linked with at least some of the audience's values? Are readers getting sufficient exposure to relevant material, methodologies, and paradigms inside and outside the field?

This structure is a fairly accurate description of the process I go through when I'm first considering what to do with a manuscript submission. Do I reject the piece immediately or send it out for review? When I think about cognitive structure, for example, I'm thinking largely in terms of how well the manuscript demonstrates it belongs in the journal. Is this a piece about WAC/WID and/or issues related to interdisciplinary communication? (Strange as it may seem, I've received submissions about biology experiments, public-health policy, and engineering design.) Is this author familiar enough with the disciplinary tropes, language, and genres common to WAC/WID research that readers will accept them—at least provisionally—as an "insider"? Does this author establish a credible ethos by grounding their work in the literature of current WAC/WID research? In terms of motivation, I ask questions that consider matters of disciplinary diversity. Even though this writer and this manuscript may be a little different from "us," am I willing to accept them and their ideas if I think the field can profit by them? In other words, how far am I willing to stretch the disciplinary boundaries that define and distinguish the journal in the name of actually being interdisciplinary?

While I think these are all important questions for scholarly editors to consider and reflect on as they decide whether or not to send a manuscript out for review, it is hard not to see them as disturbingly analogous to the questions asked by border guards or immigration agents. And the decisions made by those agents every day affect the lives and livelihoods of every applicant who tries to cross a border from one country to another. Journal editors, too, make decisions that impact people's material lives. As Stephen McGinty (1999) says, "The journal editor acts as a gatekeeper by funneling manuscripts in one direction or another or rejecting material entirely. In this way, the journal editor has an impact on the professional life of every scholar, because the establishment of scholarly credentials is crucial in higher education" (1). If a scholar wants advancement, a better salary, professional respect, and—most of all—the golden halo of tenure or continuing employment at a great many postsecondary institutions, the stairway to heaven is built on publications in well-known, rigorous, peer-reviewed journals and presses. You must demonstrate you're a full-fledged member of an academic community and scholarly network. The problem is, as Lewis Coser, Charles Kadushin, and Walter Powell (1982) argue in *Books: The Culture and Commerce of Publishing*, that "scholarly networks are close-knit communities, whose core can be quite exclusive" (quoted in McGinty 1999, 2). What this means in practical terms, then, is that the pressure to conform to the norms of that close-knit community—or, more specifically, the editorial judgment of its representatives, an editor and a review board—can be overwhelming, imposing a kind of social and cultural hegemony that encourages submissiveness and assimilation, not independence and originality.

McGinty (1999) draws some interesting parallels between the scholar's quest for publication and Joseph Campbell's characterization of "hero narratives" in this regard, saying that

> the scholar/hero has a long journey that ends with accommodation and submission to the ruling hierarchy.... The scholar/hero expends tremendous effort in order to appear worthy to the elders, who represent the upper echelons of the hierarchy. This involves submission and the display of allegiance. How does one show allegiance? By mastering the accepted way of doing things and showing that one has traveled the path.... The scholar/hero has adopted the language, learned the lessons, and practiced with the tools in order to wield them effectively. (3)

The elders then judge whether the supplicant is indeed worthy, and "reward systems are based on the new generation duplicating what the previous generations did" (3).

This mythic construction of the editor as an "elder" who demands allegiance is certainly unflattering and presents editorial work as a strongly conservative force dedicated to the preservation of the status quo. Though I wouldn't deny these conservative forces are present when it comes to making editorial judgments, I don't find McGinty's comparison to be an entirely accurate representation of an editor's role, particularly in a field as wide ranging and extensive as rhetoric and composition, and most particularly not with a journal like *Across the Disciplines*. If I were to draw a different trope from Campbell's analytical framework to characterize what I—and I think most editors—do, I think it would be the figure of the "Threshold Guardian." The threshold guardian is one of possibly many characters in a hero's quest whose purpose is primarily to test the hero's resolve. The guardian can sometimes be a menacing or threatening figure, but just as often, they can simply be a neutral force, just doing the job destiny has given them, and once the hero has met their challenge and crossed the threshold, the guardian can become an ally, supporting the hero as they continue their quest.

Even so, I would make an important distinction between editors and threshold guardians. When it comes right down to it, editors really WANT to publish scholars and writers in their journals, especially new scholars doing exciting, interesting work (see Horning, chapter 6 in this collection). While we have all likely had run-ins with editors whose perspectives on scholarship can be myopic and exclusionary or whose interactions with authors are brusque and inhospitable, in my experience, most editors in writing studies are encouraging and welcoming to those who want to cross the semipermeable border into the realm of publication, and they are often willing to be flexible and accommodating about disciplinary norms when there are good reasons for doing so. That's certainly true for interdisciplinary and cross-disciplinary journals like *Across the Disciplines*.

Why? Because editors need readers. Without readers and without the interest of a professional community, their publications will not attract submissions. If they do not attract submissions, the journals will disappear. The quantity of submissions a journal receives depends, in part, upon its status in the profession—a "flagship" journal like *CCC* will probably never suffer from a lack of submissions no matter how high a bar it sets—but it depends even more on how useful, current, and relevant the publication is deemed to be by members of the field. So even though *ATD* is pretty clearly a rhet/comp journal, it is definitely not in the journal's best interest to be too doctrinaire and nationalistic about its publication policies. Building a giant wall is not the answer, and neither is a completely open border, but a porous, fuzzy border—a spongey border, if you will—can maintain disciplinary boundaries while still enriching an interdisciplinary journal's perspectives and population.

THE TROUBLESOME "MIDDLE GROUND"

But creating flexible borders and opting to send manuscripts out for review that might not fit fully or comfortably in the disciplinary domain of WAC/WID scholarship further complicates another innate challenge of journal editing: having to make decisions about what to do with manuscripts that have been reviewed and then fall somewhere in the vast "middle ground" of peer-reviewed work. While some pieces are solidly researched and written and receive strong, positive comments in their first round of reviews (garnering an easy "accept with specified revisions"), and while some others miss the mark completely (being either so poorly written or so inappropriate for the journal's editorial focus they are summarily rejected and not sent out for review), the majority of submissions tend to fall somewhere in the cavernous grey area in between. Sometimes reviewers disagree about a manuscript's scholarly contribution. Sometimes they recommend the author(s) completely restructure their paper. Often, they point out structural weaknesses, studies that were overlooked, conclusions that seem unwarranted, and methodologies that appear to be inherently flawed or at least poorly explained. At this point, I (or any journal editor for that matter) must ask myself several critical questions: How much of an investment in time and intellectual energy will the manuscript likely require? Is that investment likely to pay off? How significant are the problems reviewers have identified? Can they be addressed fully in a subsequent draft, or does the research design itself make the chances of an acceptable revision unlikely? Editors (like me) frequently find themselves in this fraught liminal space, torn between the desire to be disciplinary mentors and the need to be responsible academic gatekeepers (and time managers) who sometimes just have to say no.

Since I believe it is important to publish WAC/WID work by non-rhet/comp faculty and to not unfairly privilege a single set of discourse practices, I sometimes have to push myself to be more accepting and forgiving of pieces that are missing expected references in a literature review or revealing a certain naiveté about what constitutes new knowledge in the field. But the fundamental question still remains: Where should I draw the line between being a mentor, either personally or through an extended review process, and being an editor with limited time, energy, and resources?

Every case is different, and every manuscript has its own set of strengths and weaknesses, so it's hard to generalize, but I can offer a few general principles I rely on, illustrated with examples synthesized from the hundreds of article submissions I've considered over the years, that help me make decisions about what to do with challenging submissions.

1. If the design of a study is fundamentally flawed, no amount of revision will produce a publishable manuscript. On occasion an author submits a manuscript that reports the results of a study that claims to measure the improvement of student writing in a course where peer review or multiple drafts or some other aspect of the process approach has been applied, but reviewers point out flaws in the research design that render the article's conclusions either suspect (best case) or completely unwarranted (worst case). For example, authors may not describe their methodology for data collection; they may make broad generalizations based upon a small sample size or "cherry-picked" responses; they may make claims about instructor "perceptions" that student writing has improved but have not collected any empirical evidence to support that claim; they may include excerpts from student work without any indication that these samples were gathered with IRB approval or that students had consented to have their work used in the article. While some of these flaws (like IRB approval and consent forms) might be simple omissions that can be corrected by adding a sentence or two in the next revision, in general, when reviewers express significant reservations about the research design, I am far more likely to reject a manuscript than ask that it be revised and resubmitted.

2. Submissions must demonstrate an awareness of relevant current scholarship in the field and show how their research fills a gap in the existing literature. Here's where research articles written by non-rhet/comp specialists often go awry, and it's easy to see why. Though authors may have read a few articles about WAC principles in writing-across-the-curriculum workshops or on their own, they are usually not conversant with the field and its research literature, so they have trouble placing their work in a larger context or distinguishing what constitutes new knowledge. Papers submitted by graduate students—some obviously written for seminar courses and relying on a very limited range of background readings—can have the same problem. (On a couple of occasions, I've received papers whose entire reference page was a list of articles from a textbook anthology.) Manuscripts with weaknesses in this area might get sent out for review, but reviewers almost always pounce on omissions in the literature review, provide a list of references/links/resources the author should consult, and suggest major revisions. In these cases, I usually send the author a rejection letter because the piece, in my judgment, will likely take too much effort and (probably) too many rounds of review before it gets close to being publishable. On the other hand, if a piece looks promising, I sometimes advise authors to collaborate with a rhet/comp colleague who can help them embed their work in current scholarship and frame their research for an audience of WAC/WID scholars. As one example of how this can work, a recent article published in *ATD*, "Writing in the Disciplines and Student Pre-professional Identity: An Exploratory Study" (Croft et al. 2019), was jointly composed by five authors in disciplinary areas that included history, chemistry, legal studies, and speech pathology. As they worked on this article, they also collaborated frequently with the WAC/WID specialist at St. John's University, Anne Ellen Geller, who offered guidance and feedback as they wrote and revised.

3. I trust my reviewers, but only most of the time. I do my best to find reviewers who will give submissions a fair and thorough reading, but I can't say I'm always 100 percent successful. Most manuscripts are pretty easy to place, especially when they're writing about WAC/WID research that fits neatly within familiar theoretical and empirical paradigms. I can send ethnographic studies to scholars who have done ethnographic research and transfer studies to people who have published articles about transfer. Manuscripts that fall outside those comfortable domains are much harder to place with appropriate reviewers, particularly when they require, for example, specialized knowledge about research protocols in chemistry labs or complex quantitative measures of statistical significance. Sometimes I can find a reader who's got a background in STEM work or is adept with statistical measures of writing assessment, but just as often I must rely on reviewers who can only take their best stab at a meaningful response. The pressure is then on me not only to judge the merits of the submission but also the merits of the review(s) it has received. This is not a position any editor (especially me) wants to be in, and it highlights the importance of finding and recruiting external reviewers who have expertise in all the domains necessary to evaluate articles fully, comprehensively, and fairly, regardless of how difficult that might be.

And even when reviewers are perfectly suited to read and respond to a submission, that's no guarantee they will agree. Probably 90 percent of all manuscripts I send out for the first time receive a revise-and-resubmit rating from their reviewers, but the reviewers usually have very different perspectives on what revisions are necessary. Reviewer 1, for example, might recommend the author expand the literature review to incorporate some recently published research and revise the conclusion to show how the study results are applicable in other institutional contexts; reviewer 2, on the other hand, might state that the exigency for the study is unclear, the methodology is insufficiently explained, and the procedure for selecting assessment criteria is notably absent. In these cases, I step in as reviewer 3 and try to mediate the dispute. Most of the time, I accept the revise-and-resubmit evaluation and write to the author with some guidance about how to navigate the two reviews and some reassurances that I look forward to the next revision. However, if both reviews call for substantial and significant revisions that combined make the entire article look problematic, I send the reviews to the author and politely decline the opportunity to consider it further for publication.

BEING AN ALLY

And with that in mind, I'll close by sharing something that happened to me when I was a young scholar trying to get a piece of my dissertation published in *College Composition and Communication*. I was strongly influenced by Linda Flower and John Hayes and their work on cognitive-process models while I was in graduate school, and my dissertation tried to resolve the seeming differences among competing cognitive models (Bereiter and Scardemalia 2013; de Beaugrande 1984; Flower and Hayes 1981) by looking at them through the lens of modeling theory. A couple of months after mailing three printed copies of my manuscript to Richard (Rick) Gebhardt, then the editor of *CCC*, I received an envelope containing two reviews and a letter from Rick. The first review, which I later found out was written by Linda Flower, was detailed and supportive, making a number of suggestions for revision I found both thoughtful and helpful. The second review was one paragraph long and said, in essence, "This is just more of that cognitive crap; there's nothing here worth reading." As devastating as that second review was, it was Rick's letter to me that had the real impact. The gist of that letter was this: "I'm enclosing the reviews of your article that I received. As you'll see, one of them asks you to revise your piece in some specific ways, and I'd ask that you consider that advice carefully. Just make what you will of the other review. If you decide to revise and resubmit your manuscript, I'll be happy to reconsider it for publication."

Rick Gebhardt showed me that journal editors do not have to be merely gatekeepers or threshold guardians. They can also be an author's ally, someone who softens or deflects unwarranted criticism and tries to mediate between conflicting points of view. That's a lesson I took to heart at the time, and I've tried to emulate that approach in my own work as an editor.

And my article was eventually published in *CCC*.

REFERENCES

"Across the Disciplines." n.d. *WAC Clearinghouse*. Accessed October 31, 2019. https://wac.colostate.edu/atd/.

Anzaldúa, Gloria. 1987. *Borderlands/La Frontera: The New Mestiza*. San Francisco: Spinsters/Aunt Lute.

Bereiter, Carl, and Marlene Scardamalia. 2013. *The Psychology of Written Composition*. London: Routledge.

Committee on Publication Ethics (COPE). 2016. "A Short Guide to Ethical Editing for New Editors." https://publicationethics.org/files/A_Short_Guide_to_Ethical_Editing.pdf. First published in 2011.

Condon, William, and Carol Rutz. 2012. "A Taxonomy of Writing Across the Curriculum Programs: Evolving to Serve Broader Agendas." *College Composition and Communication* 64 (2): 357–382.

Coser, Lewis A., Charles Kadushin, and Walter W. Powell. 1982. *Books: The Culture and Commerce of Publishing*. New York: Basic Books.

Council of Science Editors. n.d. "White Paper on Publication Ethics." Last modified 2018. https://www.councilscienceeditors.org/resource-library/editorial-policies/white-paper-on-publication-ethics/.

Croft, James, Michael Benjamin, Phyllis Conn, Joseph M. Serafin, and Rebecca Wiseheart. 2019. "Writing in the Disciplines and Student Pre-professional Identity: An Exploratory Study." *Across the Disciplines* 16 (2): 34–52. https://wac.colostate.edu/docs/atd/articles/croftetal2019.pdf.

Cullen, Darcy. 2012. "Introduction: The Social Dynamics of Scholarly Editing." In *Editors, Scholars, and the Social Text*, edited by Darcy Cullen, 1–32. Toronto: University of Toronto Press.

de Beaugrande, Robert. 1984. *Text Production: Toward a Science of Composition*. Vol. 11, Advances in Discourse Processes. Norwood, NJ: Ablex.

Flower, Linda, and John R. Hayes. 1981. "A Cognitive Process Theory of Writing." *College Composition and Communication* 32 (4): 365–387. https://doi:10.2307/356600.

Lewin, Kurt. 1951. "Psychological Ecology." *Field Theory in Social Science: Selected Theoretical Papers*, edited by Dorwin Cartwright, 170–187. New York: Harper & Row. First published in1943.

McGinty, Stephen. 1999. *Gatekeepers of Knowledge: Journal Editors in the Sciences and the Social Sciences*. Westport, CT: Bergin & Garvey.

"Publish in Across the Disciplines." n.d. *WAC Clearinghouse*. Accessed October 31, 2019. https://wac.colostate.edu/atd/submissions/.

Rose, Richard. 1986. "Editing an International Interdisciplinary Journal." *Journal of Public Policy* 6 (1): 117–119. https://www.jstor.org/stable/3998368.

PART THREE

Pulling Back the Curtain

Reflections on Editing in Writing Studies

11
REFLECTIONS
Edit to Learn

Victor Villanueva
Washington State University

I'm no longer sure of the date. Maybe it was 1973. I had been assigned to the NCO Academy. Part of the training included grammar. For a number of reasons, though, I left the army after seven years. It was December 1975. Spring quarter, 1976, I walked into a local community college, clutching my *Elements of Style* (1972). This time, though, I did more than follow Strunk's commands. That's when I realized White didn't quite agree with Strunk. I preferred White. Just did. I didn't quite know Strunk was White's professor (even as the book said so). And I didn't know it was White who was the famous writer. Wouldn't read *Charlotte's Web* till some years later, when I read it to my kids.

In graduate school, I was taken aback by the theorists who somehow seemed neither grammarians nor rhetors. I loved Kenneth Burke (1969) somehow, but I loved him more as rhetorician than a rhetor; loved Burke even though so much of what he wrote went without exposition—a willing suspension of incomprehension. It was the same with Mikhail Bakhtin (1981) or even the explanations of Bakhtin by Susan Miller (1983). To Jacques Lacan I said "la can't" (Brooke 1987). And no less for the other somehow engaging yet always foreign continental philosophers and critical theorists. But I saw my inability as *my* inability. By the time I got to Judith Butler (1990), I could read and believed I could understand. Then came the surprise: many who were more savvy than me were critical of her prose. Even Butler's defenders and Butler herself acknowledged the criticism, as Cathy Birkenstein notes (2010). The defenders argued that obscure prose was necessary. I would rethink that by the time I became a professional editor.

But before that, there was the reading—philosophy, critical theory, rhetorical theory, composition studies—and reading what others were doing with the theorists and philosophers. And the more I read, the more I believed I understood, and the more fascinated I became with the sets of theories. Eventually, an academic position. My first attempt at theory, postdissertation: Paolo Freire, Antonio Gramsci, others, like Ernesto Laclau and Chantal Mouffe (see Villanueva 1992, for example). A colleague reads my first "serious" attempt at a paper I wanted to submit for publication. He's an applied linguist whose work concerns contrastive rhetoric. He just turns beet red. I hope the blush isn't about the quality of my writing, hope he's embarrassed because he doesn't know this stuff. I ask another colleague. She's one who is immersed in classical rhetoric and in deconstruction. She would know. She says something like, "Of all the writers to imitate, you choose Marxists?" Thing is, I hadn't intended to imitate anyone or any style. But that's when I started to think that if there can be an *écriture feminine,* why not an *écriture de couleur?*

But I get ahead of myself, except to say the rhetorician and the editor began to take real shape then, with trying to get a point across, though the story goes much further back.

BIRTH OF AN EDITOR-AS-GRAMMARIAN

It's Brooklyn, New York, 1954. Sister Rhea Marie, a Dominican nun, young, inherently peaceful in her traditional white and black habit: the full-length tunic, starched, stiff coif, and black veil. Sister Rhea Marie is petite, not at all intimidating—except for the authority undeniable to those like my parents: Catholics new to this English-speaking world. She is welcomed into our household, seated at the metal and Formica kitchen table, as is the custom, an offering of coffee, as is the custom. I am allowed to listen in on the conversation as long as I stay quiet, as is the custom. The subject is my English. I speak English with an accent, my parents are told. She softly but firmly "suggests" my parents speak with me in English. Mami says, "He speaks with an accent because we *do* speak to him in English," spoken with a smile (the local poultryman used to call Mami "Smiley"). Mom's was a smile that carried authority no less than charm.

Funny how a memory from so long ago still comes to mind so clearly, even the gentle laughter between Mom and Sister Rhea Marie (though Dad stayed poker faced). It was that that prompted my mother to assign me the task of teaching English to her and Dad, even as all Puerto Ricans on the Island had to learn English taught by Puerto Rican teachers with their own accents. Dad never finished elementary school; Mom made it to the junior year of high school; she attended the parish parochial school in Puerto Rico, her entry gained by the priest who employed my grandmother as his housekeeper. In 1954, I was tasked with being the Family Grammarian. I took the task very seriously.

I have been an English teacher since I was six, enjoying reading aloud, enjoying sentence diagramming, dangling not the preposition, never splitting the infinitive (and finding contemporary disregard for that old rule distasteful, even as I knew it was a silly rule), using the double negative only when appropriate (in the neighborhood, away from school and parents), never failing to correct my parents' English.

It's "save face, Dad."

"That makes no sense. It's 'save faith.'"

Hmmm. Right.

I knew it was *save face*, even if I didn't see the sense of it. For some reason, I thought it was a Japanese expression. Don't ask me why. Idiomatic expressions remain somehow foreign to me even after seven decades of English. I didn't argue with Dad; I was just eight or so, after all. I stayed quiet, trying to save face.

I was the Grammarian. The reader in the neighborhood. The reader on the fire-support base in Vietnam, assigned as company clerk when the prior clerk contracted malaria. The reader who became a personnel sergeant, and then a community college student pursuing a high school diploma, and then an English major chasing after an AA and then an MA and then a PhD. The reader turned English professor, still reading, still parsing. Always an editor, as in copyeditor, drawn to "The Study of Error" (Bartholomae 1980), having conversations with two sages of the time, Ken and Yetta Goodman, to figure out if miscue analysis could apply to writing no less than to reading, though for all that, working hard not to correct every error in every paper students submit when I was teaching 101, working against everything in me since I was six, trying to stick to minimal marking (Haswell 1983), especially when working with basic writers, those who came from worlds much like the one I came from but not as taken by the word as I had been. Mina Shaughnessy (1979) had written that we, the New York students of color she met, were lost in the world of oral discourse. Then came others, following Walter Ong (1982; Farrell 1983), who would say the same. For me, it was a fascination with the overlaps and the similarities in the oral and the written, how dialogue in fiction was never really a depiction of the oral and never purely literate. This became—and remains—my obsession.

A personal definition: an editor has an ear for the oral and the written, for the secondary orality and the secondary literacy, the places where orality and literacy "talk" to each other, how to exploit the intimacy of the oral while maintaining the necessary concision of the written. Writers of color tend to know this, thinking of essays about American Indian rhetorics in the collection edited by Ernest Stromberg (2006), for example, and the writings of many African American rhetorics, influenced by the West African storyteller, the *griot*—even when the writer making the case for the rise of the digital paradigm (see Banks 2011, for example). And even as this definition is by an editor of color, it should apply generally no less.

A TRANSITION

About 1987. A mentor (who had been CCCC chair, NCTE president, an editor of *CCC*, the late William Irmscher) recommends me for the Resolutions Committee within NCTE. I had already started attending CCCC some years earlier, thanks to another mentor (a young assistant professor, Anne Ruggles Gere), but it wasn't until the Resolutions Committee that I become active in Cs' organizational matters and those of NCTE (a commitment that remains to this day). Sitting, just chatting, someone mentions that all the past leaders of the organization, NCTE, had been journal editors. Don't know if that was true then, but it took hold. This is my introduction to the word *editor* as concerning a professional role, though I still did not fully understand the differences among the editor of a journal, editor of a collection, or copyeditor. Not in 1987.

It's Flagstaff, Arizona, maybe 1993. An invitation to go to Iowa City to take part in the vetting of potential exams for the ACT. I say no. I felt victim to the biases of high-stakes standardized tests. I would not take part. One of my daughters (ten years old at the time) says that maybe I can learn how to do better in standardized tests by taking part. And maybe I could pass what I learn on to her and her sisters. So maybe being a rhetorician is passed on genetically? This daughter grew up to be one of us, even a Cs award-winner. I consult for and with ACT for the next twenty years or so. The "writing" test is really an editing test. So I learn more of copyediting, more of responding to writing. And for my part, I take issue with testing for idiomatic expressions since whatever the logic or history behind them, idiomatic expressions remain out of reach for the nonnative speaker. When, I would argue, am I not head over heels? Folks around the table would explain. I'd understand once explained. I understand by picturing Charlie Brown making a flip in a Sunday comic panel. Would others understand? How many nonnative speakers can tell you what a *petard* is (or what being *hoisted* means, for that matter)? And I take issue with joining independent clauses with *and* (even as I enjoy opening sentences with *and*) when there is no semantic conjunction to the clauses, when *and* is more of a phatic utterance, an oral device to keep the conversation going. This time, I argue against the orality of the *and* that doesn't mean *and* in the literate.

Flagstaff still, about the same time. Composition studies is in one of Thomas Kuhn's "crises" (see Hairston 1982). The beginning of *Cross-Talk in Comp Theory* (Villanueva 1997 for the first edition). I become the editor of an anthology.

THE PROFESSIONAL EDITOR

Over the decades, I have edited or coedited three editions of *Cross-Talk*, two special editions of *College English*, and six book-length collections and have been the series editor for Studies in Writing and Rhetoric. And in the process, I have learned, and I continue to learn. Beyond that, there's the learning that takes place when working with students: the learning with well over a 150 graduate students on whose committees I have chaired or served; the inevitable editing that is writing instruction for over maybe fifteen hundred undergraduates over the years. So much learning (and never enough).

So why my own reason for being an editor? The most selfish reason is to learn. Ours is a profession of constant learning: the learning we undertake in order to teach, the learning we undertake in order to answer the questions that drive us to scholarship or to research. But in every one of these cases, we become limited by our own interests. If we do read outside our own interests, it might be to keep up with the current conversations taking place in our journals and conferences. But it seems to me that all those reasons can result in clogged terministic screens (Burke 1966) so that we seldom seem to sift through those screens. But as an editor I can't limit myself to those concepts I know I'm interested in. As an editor, I must consider the texts that cross my desk (or my monitor), submissions from throughout the profession—and beyond. And sometimes submissions have me going even beyond my dominant language: I've had to check sources by venturing into Latin or Classical Greek, French, Spanish. I even had to take a crash course in Brazilian Portuguese, a venture into a particular sociologist, José Maurício Domingues, that I then incorporated into one of my own publications (Villanueva 2017). When one agrees to be an editor, it's almost like one agrees to paint oneself into a corner. And it's great!

But there's another dimension to my ventures into editing, one having to do with being a person of color (a tricky identification having to do with the realities of "ethnicity" since I am not "of color" in a physiognomic sense yet subject to racialization). I'll explain. I just mentioned "my dominant language." That's been English since I became an English teacher at the age of six, though mixed with Spanish, as part of my whole life. But language alone doesn't determine one's culture(s). In terms of being an editor, I have had to situate myself within an odd binary. This is how I phrased it a few years ago (2017), for which you can substitute the word *leader* or *leadership* with *editor*.

> In terms of the rhetoric of leadership, when it comes to the leader of color, the binary of self and other always has one faithful to the One and at odds with the Other: Do I stand up, bravely, for the Other? Or do I defend the power of the institution? Must I always find compromise? Or get relegated to leader of the Other but not of the institution, the token leader of the tokenized, not just leader? Do I insist on academic discourse as it's currently defined (or given shape)? Or do I insist on the rhetorics (more than the dialects) of the Other? The code? The code as meshed? Leader? Leader of Color? Leader who happens to be of Color? Always an internal struggle. (487)

I have had the wonderful distinction of having been the first Latino (and since this is a self-reference, the gender is known, so not Latine or Latinx) to head the national organization for rhetoric and composition, CCCC. And I had the same distinction as editor for the organization's principal monograph series, SWR. I don't assume cheap tokenism, but I am nevertheless left with wanting to increase the presence of my fellow scholars and researchers of color. And that means more than being published. It means being published about the matters that mean the most to us *and* being read by the majority in a profession that appears to remain predominately white, whiter than the current national demographic, which the 2017 United States Census Bureau has at 60.4 percent, not including white Latines (2019).

Being an editor for the publications of the profession also means abiding by the rate of submissions. And that means the majority of submissions for CCCC publications would of course be from white authors. I could not—must not—then slight the rate of submissions in order to force publications by people of color (not that I'm opposed to affirmative action, but I was selected as editor for the whole of the profession).

How then to manage the disproportionate levels of the playing field?

For me, my strategy has been to remain conscious of the orality-literacy binary in our writing. But I must remain conscious in a different sense from that which occurred during the discussions concerning the supposed "Great Cognitive Divide" (see Scribner and Cole 1981 for the debate, started, essentially, by Havelock 1963). Havelock's telling is of Plato not necessarily attacking orality but attacking poetry as the source of knowledge, that as such, emotion took precedent over the rational. This is a particular take on orality and is surely (forgive me) prepostmodern, locked into the glorification of rationality (a matter I won't get into here). But here's the thing about the genius of the alphabet. It made for a phoneme-grapheme correspondence, as we know. The alphabet made it possible for a very small number of graphic symbols to represent the sound system of our dominant symbol system—language. Now, I won't get into the discussion of the differences here, only to a way of thinking about editing that allows white authors and authors of color not to seem rhetorically all that different. Maybe I can call it *rhetorical meshing*, worrying less about dialect than rhetorical choices, relying more on some oral rhetorical choices. My attempts have been to have writers demonstrate "that rigor does not have to be displayed as rhetorical rigor mortis" (Villanueva 2010, 582).

So it is that when I find myself with writers who have become immersed within a genre given to density and obscurity, I encourage authors to consider the rhetorics of the literate *and* the oral. I ask them to worry less about "proving" and worry more about teaching. I mean, what if we spoke in our classrooms like Judith Butler or Kenneth Burke write? Most of us, I assume, don't, even if we believe the pro-obscurity arguments. Somehow, we manage to explain (or at least try to) complex theories and philosophies in those classrooms. When we teach, our orality and our literacy intermesh. Our considerations in the disciplines of rhetoric and composition or writing studies often have reason to turn to the philosophical, but we enjoy such broad audiences that we must address as many as we can. We believe our work matters to students and to the world at large. We should write so the work is comprehensible beyond a select few.

That said, I try not to intrude on writers' concepts. I try not to impose my worldview or theory or pedagogy. I just ask that the writers tell me theirs, not sacrifice, not "dummy down," but demonstrate rhetorical acumen. Explain. Teach. And to the extent that writing is epistemological and epistemologies are tied to cultures and genders and sexuality and racism, I invite writers not to feel confined by the rhetorics of Edited American English, rhetorics, not conventions, since I will copyedit. The affectations of dialect are less important (see Gilyard and Richardson 2001 for an example). What matters is more how one chooses to frame the argument so readers have a chance to learn in the process of reading. That is, I try to encourage a style, a dialect, an *écrits féminine et de coleur* that will serve, not override, the message. The writing is to remain integral to the message, not an affectation but a part of the rhetoric. Step away from the stiffness that comes from the necessary exposure to the great (as in wonderful and wonderous) writing of great theorists but not so far away rhetoric's effect becomes rhetorical affectation.

Another definition: If one is a writer, and a teacher of writing, one is perforce an editor. And an editor is a reader, a learner, and perhaps a mentor, one who can speak to the need for every intellectual (and we are all intellectuals) to be a writer. Not just one who writes. But a writer.

WHY EDITING FOR *YOU*

So why do this work of editing? Well, because it's important. It's important for all of us. No less important for those who are of color and to those of us whose first language was not English. I don't just mean telling our stories or providing our worldviews. That's the work of our research, scholarship, publications, and teaching. I mean it matters to all of us for whom this life is as academics in rhetoric and writing. We have developed sets of skills in metalinguistic or metarhetorical awareness. We have skills that can help in the development of publications from everyone, raising the quality of our work for everyone. For all of us, of color or not, multilingual or not (though I hope all of us are to some extent multirhetorical), there are the abilities we bear, if only we'd exercise them, of making the work of rhetoric and writing studies accessible beyond our field. All academics are accused of engaging in closed conversations, of writing and speaking only among ourselves. But our particular fields—rhetoric and writing—are about communication and communicating. What good is what we do if we don't have an effect on the world we're in? We can be instrumental in assuring our colleagues' good work gets out there. And in the process, we learn.

REFERENCES

Bakhtin, M. M. 1981. *The Dialogic Imagination: Four Essays.* Translated by Michael Holquist and Caryl Emerson. Austin: University of Texas Press.
Banks, Adam. 2011. *Digital Griots: African American Rhetoric in a Multimedia Age.* Carbondale: Southern Illinois University Press.

Bartholomae, David. 1980. "The Study of Error." *College Composition and Communication* 31 (3): 253–269.
Birkenstein, Cathy. 2010. "We Got the Wrong Gal: Rethinking the 'Bad' Academic Writing of Judith Butler." *College English* 72 (3): 269–283.
Brooke, Robert. 1987. "Lacan, Transference, and Writing Instruction." *College English* 49 (6): 679–691.
Burke, Kenneth. 1966. *Language as Symbolic Action: Essays on Life, Literature, and Method*, Berkeley: University of California Press.
Burke, Kenneth. 1969. *A Rhetoric of Motives*. Berkeley: University of California Press.
Butler, Judith. 1990. *Gender Trouble: Feminism and the Subversion of Identity*. New York: Routledge.
Farrell, Thomas J. 1983. "IQ and Standard English." *College Composition and Communication* 34 (4): 470–484.
Gilyard, Keith, and Elaine Richardson. 2001. "Students' Right to Possibility: Basic Writing and African American Rhetoric." In *Insurrections: Approaches to Resistance in Composition Studies*, edited by Andrea Greenbaum, 37–51. Albany: SUNY Press.
Hairston, Maxine. 1982. "The Winds of Change: Thomas Kuhn and the Revolution in the Teaching of Writing." *College Composition and Communication* 33 (1): 76–88.
Haswell, Patrick. 1983. "Minimal Marking." *College English* 45 (6): 600–604.
Havelock, Eric. 1963. *Preface to Plato*. Cambridge, MA: Harvard University Press.
Miller, Susan. 1993. *Textual Carnivals: The Politics of Composition*. Carbondale: Southern Illinois University Press.
Ong, Walter J. 1982. *Orality and Literacy: The Technologizing of the Word*. New York: Routledge.
Scribner, Sylvia, and Michael Cole. 1981. *The Psychology of Literacy*. Cambridge, MA: Harvard University Press.
Shaughnessy, Mina P. 1979. *Errors and Expectations: A Guide for the Teacher of Basic Writing*. New York: Oxford University Press.
Stromberg, Ernest, ed. 2006. *American Indian Rhetorics of Survivance: Word Medicine, Word Magic*. Pittsburgh: Pittsburgh University Press.
Strunk, William Jr., and E. B. White. 1972. *The Elements of Style*. 2nd ed. New York: Macmillan.
United States Census Bureau. 2019. "QuickFacts: United States." https://www.census.gov/quickfacts/fact/table/US/PST045219.
Villanueva, Victor. 1992. "Hegemony: From Organically Grown Intellectual." *PRE/TEXT* 13 (1–2): 17–34.
Villanueva, Victor. 1997. *Cross-Talk in Comp Theory: A Reader*. Urbana, IL: NCTE.
Villanueva, Victor. 2010. "2009 CCCC Exemplar Award Acceptance Speech." *College Composition and Communication* 61 (3): 581–582.
Villanueva, Victor. 2017. " 'I Am Two Parts': Collective Subjectivity and the Leader of Academics and the Othered." *College English* 79 (5): 482–494.

12
EVERYTHING IS RHETORIC
Design, Editing, and Multimodal Scholarship

Douglas Eyman
George Mason University

Cheryl E. Ball
Wayne State University Library System

In this chapter, we provide an overview of the work we've done as editors of *Kairos: A Journal of Rhetoric, Technology and Pedagogy*—the longest continuously publishing online peer-reviewed journal in the field. Because we are very strong proponents of collaboration as a primary means for the production of knowledge (and this belief also informs our editorial philosophies), we'll be writing collaboratively as we address our histories, editorial philosophies, contributions, and advice. One theme that appears throughout the chapter's narrative threads is the idea that good scholarship is the result of sound and explicit rhetorical choice, from the methodology of a study, to the organization of the article or chapter, to the harnessing of network technologies and multimedia (in the case of digital work).

Our interplay will also demonstrate how our differing editorial philosophies complement our editorial roles: Cheryl focuses on editing as a pedagogical process, with a strong element of mentorship for both authors and developing editors in the field, while Doug's philosophy focuses on synthesis and networking (both in the social and technical senses) as key practices. In this chapter, we reflect upon the significant editorial changes we've directed as *Kairos* has evolved since its first issue in 1996. Douglas joined the editorial staff of the journal in its first year, Cheryl joined in 2001, and we have collaborated in a number of different ways over the past nineteen years, as of this writing. In our reflection on accomplishments, rather than an exhaustive list of changes, we'll highlight particular editorial practices and our increased focus on access and accessibility.

Of course, we have plenty of advice for scholars working in more traditional projects and in particular for those who want to build digital, multimedia, or multimodal projects. We have enough advice for a whole book, so in this chapter we focus on three key areas: questions for scholars at the stage of invention, editorial interactions, and designing for accessibility.

HOW WE BECAME EDITORS

Doug's Story

My editorial history really started in high school when I joined the staff of our school's literary journal, *Footprints*. The staff voted on submissions (fiction, poetry, art, photography) and provided a limited kind of peer review and feedback. The real technical skill came in lining up the printed-out and exacto-knife-excised sections and securing them to the master pages with rubber cement, using a light table with a grid to align everything. Even then, editing and design went hand in hand. In college, I learned about setting print parameters on the word-processing program provided on the VAX mainframe and then later I worked with and taught WordPerfect and Aldus Pagemaker in the education department's tiny computer lab (it was a large room, actually but only held two Mac IIE computers and a growing number of containers full of 3.5-inch floppy disks). I worked in the writing center at the same time, and while I wasn't editing per se, guiding students through questions of invention and organization is essentially the foundation of developmental editing, just with a smaller audience in mind. After college, I did some freelance editing (of the copyediting variety) and writing and continued working in a local writing center.

I went to the Conference on College Composition and Communication for the first time as I finished my MA, and I met a rowdy group of graduate students who were starting to plan a new kind of online, hypertext-oriented academic journal; the following year I published my first peer-reviewed article in that journal, then called *Kairos: A Journal for Teachers of Writing in Webbed Environments*. I joined the staff at the tail end of 1996, mentored in the editorial processes of the "CoverWeb" section by Michael Salvo, one of the founding editors. My role as editor was to recruit authors to write thematically aligned webtexts and to organize the works and make connections among and between them. It was also my job to clean up any errant code (which was much easier in the days before CSS and the widespread use of multimedia). We had a staff copyeditor at the time, but we didn't have a style guide, and the amount of work was rather much for one person, so our early issues were, at best, lightly copyedited and proofread. In 2000, I moved from "CoverWeb" and took on the role of main editor for the journal.

Cheryl's Story

Those who've worked with Doug and me for a long time know that it's typical for me to respond to an email or a Slack message Doug has already responded to with the simple abbreviation WDS—What Doug Said. And, here it proves useful yet again! WDS

I didn't actually know Doug's editorial origin story until we started working on this chapter together, so that makes it easy to follow after and say that I, too, got my editorial start at my high school literary magazine during the days of paste-up. I, too, picked up odd jobs as a copyeditor during my graduate program, where I learned how to use a Mac while working half time in the writing center at school and half time in the computer lab teaching classes on Word and Pine. I, too, had a critical run-in with a graduate student working on *Kairos* at my first CCCC in 1999—it happened to be Doug!—which prompted me to submit my very first academic publication to *Kairos* and then, two years later as I changed focus from poetry to digital rhetoric and started my PhD program, to apply for the "CoverWeb" position Doug had just vacated. I've told this story so many times and in so many places and publications I have lost track of them all. But, really, it seems my professional trajectory with *Kairos* has been set from the start!

Doug

Perhaps one of the best editorial decisions I've ever made was to hire Cheryl and Beth Hewett as coeditors of the "CoverWeb" section. From my perspective, Cheryl and Beth made a formidable team: Cheryl had organizational and design skills and was developing the seeds of the staff mentoring program for our assistant editors, and Beth had an eye for detail and a laser-like precision as a copyeditor. Both were equally adept at developmental editing and production. Copyediting is a very particular skill, and having taught technical editing classes and served for a period as copyeditor for H-Net book reviews, I can say it requires both attention to particulars and an ability to identify issues with content, organization, coherence, and continuity.

Cheryl

When Beth and I started collaborating as editors in 2001, virtual collaborations were still fairly new, and we had to be crafty in how we proceeded. We learned a lot from each other in those early years of working together, and we each brought different strengths to the table, as Doug mentioned. While I began work with *Kairos*, I was also being trained by Dànielle DeVoss to do print-based scholarly publishing and editing with *Computers & Composition*. She had formed a team of assistant editors to teach them how to copyedit the articles in production at that journal, which is where I learned APA style. Dànielle's mentoring of us more junior editors provided a framework I could take to our editorial work at *Kairos*, which, as Doug mentioned, didn't have a staffing structure in place that could satisfy the growing demands of *Kairos*'s publication output. I wanted to bring the professional workflows I had learned from Dànielle, as well as those from my time in trade publishing, where I worked more closely with graphic designers and page-layout technicians, to bear on the design-based texts we worked on with authors at *Kairos*. This was the beginning of *Kairos*'s perhaps infamous eight-stage copyediting process we still use, with some tweaks along the way. We adapted a professional editorial workflow to this experimental publication and began introducing it to assistant editors in our section, and eventually—once Doug and his coeditor James Inman became senior editors and promoted Beth and I to coeditors of the whole journal—to the assistant editors in other sections. *Kairos* became a training ground for many of the editors who now lead webtext-based scholarly publications in the discipline.

As *Kairos* has tried to expand its outreach beyond the current staff, we have begun implementing our mentoring practice with authors and other editors as well, running publishing workshops at major conferences for most of the last decade and more recently introducing digital publishing and editing workshops—what we've colloquially dubbed KairosCamps—geared specifically for academic authors, editors, and publishers outside digital writing studies who have just begun to recognize the equal importance design and code play in relation to the rhetoric of authors' words.

EDITORIAL PHILOSOPHIES

Doug

As editor of *Kairos*, I find the scope of editorial work greatly expanded. We look not only at the quality of ideas, argument, and expression but also at design (as a rhetorical component that enacts the argument in digital scholarship) and at code. Just as we use a style guide for consistency in language, we have an in-house style guide that specifies how certain aspects of code should be carried out, mostly based on best practices from the perspective of web development but also with an eye toward sustainability and accessibility. I've been increasingly concerned with issues of access—making sure the work we publish is findable, useful, usable, and accessible. In terms of editorial philosophy, I would say I attend to the technical, disciplinary, and social infrastructures of scholarship. Technical infrastructure includes both physical components (networks, servers, routers) and digital components (metadata, well-formed code, nonobsolete file formats). At this point, all journals are digitally produced, even if the end product is often also print—and that means knowledge of technical infrastructure should be required for all editors (I'm not suggesting the need for technical expertise, but a basic understanding of the issues and challenges is necessary). Disciplinary infrastructure includes citation formats, genre expectations, and the means to circulate the work to its intended audiences (getting indexed in the appropriate databases and library catalogs, and increasingly, a well-managed social media presence). The social infrastructure includes the peer-review and communication processes of editing, interactions between editors and potential authors and between editors and readers. The social and disciplinary infrastructures are both present when journals are represented at and participate in scholarly conferences and workshops. A number of past attempts to develop and promote online journals (not only in our field but also across disciplines) did not succeed because they paid insufficient attention to one or more of these infrastructures—all three are critical for the success of any journal.

My overall approach, and one Cheryl also practices, is to consider editorial work as a form of mentorship—our task is to provide guidance to authors to help them shape their arguments, strengthen their research skills, and reach the most appropriate audiences for their work. Editors also must keep up with the field as a whole in order to best understand how an individual work will connect to the research and theories of the field both historically and in the present moment. I feel strongly that editors must know the history of their discipline so they can point out gaps in the literature review when authors assume their current work is absolutely novel. It's certainly not sufficient for editors to simply be adept at the craft of wordsmithing and rhetorical shaping—they also must have fairly solid knowledge of the fields in which they work. Some of that knowledge is of course developed over the course of an editing career, which is one of the benefits of the work (it's not all labor without reward!). Editors have a responsibility to the authors they work with, to the field as a whole, and to the editorial board or peer reviewers who provide the critical work of evaluating and helping strengthen the work we publish by lending their expertise to the enterprise. This is one of the reasons the initial review of submissions is so important—a work must not be passed on to a reviewer if it is not ready for review (and having been a reviewer who has received incomplete work to evaluate, I make doubly sure this critical act is not overlooked in my own editorial practices). But what constitutes "ready for review" may look radically different for a digital webtext, which might actually not be fully complete and polished, as the peer-review process may demand changes impossible to make once the code and design are fully integrated and complete.

Cheryl

In 2012, as I was revising my teaching-philosophy statement for the umpteenth time in my career, I realized I had hit a point in my career where everything I worked on could be witnessed through the lens of my editorial work, so I reframed my teaching philosophy into a professional philosophy I have called an *editorial pedagogy* (see Ball 2012a, 2012b, 2012c). As I said in a series of *Hybrid Pedagogy* articles in 2012, "An editorial pedagogy builds on the recursive and reciprocal nature of professionalization through editing, writing, mentoring, and teaching."

> *Kairos* mentors authors through multiple revisions of their webtexts (usually through multiple "Revise & Resubmits") because many of the journal's authors are composing these mixed-genre, mixed-media, and multi-technological texts for the first time: They are developmental webtext authors who need to revise multiple times before their submissions can be accepted for publication. Like students. (2012a)

This mentorship applies not only to authors but also to the journal's staff and any other editors embarking on digital publishing, all of whom will need to know and follow the latest web accessibility and design requirements when publishing media-rich scholarship. As well, readers may need to be trained to understand how to read and analyze such webtexts, which can be particularly true for tenure readers. Every user of the journal is a "developmental user who should be mentored into becoming a more professional communicator in that situation" (Ball 2012a). This editorial pedagogy focuses "inwards, towards a 'home' field that I call digital writing studies while simultaneously focusing outwards, towards digital publishing studies as a specialty that embraces the collaborative, open-access, and professional [development] values of the digital humanities" (2012a).

Because of this mentoring, pedagogical approach, *Kairos* does accept webtexts that aren't *quite* finished (yes, running slightly counter to WDS above), because we expect authors to go through multiple rounds of open peer review, where section editors and eventually (if a text passes muster at the initial round of review/revision) the editorial-board members collaborate with each other to craft revision feedback worthy of a journal espousing the best practices in writing research. We are all writing teachers, after all, and we want our authors to succeed, so we mentor them through our three-tier peer-review process and provide them with all the feedback possible to help them craft and recraft their work for publication. Editorial pedagogy requires extensive mentoring and creates an incredibly rigorous and welcoming environment in which experimental scholarly multimedia can be produced.

REFLECTIONS ON CONTRIBUTIONS AND SUCCESSES

Kairos is the longest continuously publishing, online, peer-reviewed journal in the field; while there was a brief moment of transition in the midst of Y2K that featured only one issue, the journal has published a significant archive of digital scholarship since January 1, 1996. Over the years, we've changed our name to indicate a wider audience and an interest in submissions in a wider range of fields, and we've redesigned the journal twice (both times aiming to improve usability and accessibility—our most recent redesign won awards from *Computers and Composition* and from the Council of Editors of Learned Journals). Webtexts published in the journal have been republished in textbooks and included in the annual *Best of Independent Journals* collections. We typically see about ten thousand visitors each month, with readership peaking as issues are released (our record was forty-five thousand visitors in a single month); these readers hail from every top-level domain and country code in the world (including places we didn't know existed until they showed up in our server logs!).

The journal has demonstrated a number of innovations, in terms of both design and editorial practice. We were one of the first journals to insist on scholarship that integrated design as an integral part of the argument and invented the term *webtext* to describe this new genre (and to make a distinction between this new scholarly approach and hypertexts: as founding editor Mick Doherty [1998] argued, "The kind of writing we are hoping to reward is *not necessarily hypertextual*"—it's "not that webtext provides a minor, and unimpressive subset of the larger category 'hypertext,' but that hypertextual authorship is only one of the few important things that the larger category 'webtext' can allow.").

The founding editors and editorial board also developed an open peer-review process that allowed many reviewers to weigh in on a submission with a smaller team working directly with the author in a developmental editing capacity. Although we've made small adjustments to this model over the years, *Kairos* uses a three-tiered mentoring process when working with authors and their submissions. In the first tier of review, section editors collaboratively review an author's webtext by assessing its viability for the journal, the section it's been submitted to, and its readiness for review by the editorial board. These reviews have taken place in a number of media over the years, from email threads to Slack, and most recently we have begun using monthly, synchronous video meetings. More often than not, the section editors (of which there are currently eighteen, including the managing editors and senior editorial team) determine the text needs more revision before the board sees it, so we write up a review letter based on our collaborative discussion of the text and include specific revision strategies for the author to work on before resubmitting. All reviewing editors' names are appended to the letter. Once a text is ready for the second tier of review, we send it to a group of five to seven editorial-board members, via an email chain, for the external-review dialogue to begin. After a period of about a month, we collect that email thread, edit it for clarity and concision, and append it to an overview letter outlining revision suggestions (most webtexts at *Kairos* receive an R&R on the first and second review), with the board members' names appended to their reviews. During this stage of revision, authors can request a staff mentor, who works with them to provide on-going feedback for a twelve-week period (we call this the Tier 3 review), after which the text returns to a second-tier rereview. During every part of the process, the reviewers know who the author is and the authors know who the reviewers are, so it's a partially open review process. (If it were fully open, authors would collaborate with reviewers during the review process. Only a very few journals, such as *Hybrid Pedagogy*, use that fully open process.) This open and community-based review system is the heart of the journal's peer-review process and something we are very proud of having maintained and strengthened over the years.

One of the elements we are most proud of is the editorial mentorship and training system Cheryl developed and refined. Many scholars have been part of the *Kairos* family over the years, serving as editors, peer reviewers, and participants in the journal's experiments (see the *Writing Studies*

Tree for a list of past and current editorial-staff members). We now have robust documentation of our multistage reviewing and editing processes, and our guidelines for developing and designing multimodal scholarship have been consulted and used by other journals and presses such as *Southern Spaces*, *Ground Works*, Stanford University Press Digital Projects, and Computers and Composition Digital Press, as well as featured in the Library Publishing Curriculum. We also secured NEH grant funding to run a series of summer workshops for authors (KairosCamp) and shorter workshops for publishers and editors. With these efforts and with our publications, we continue to share our hard-learned lessons about the challenges of publishing digital work (Ball 2004, 2013, 2016, 2017; Ball and Eyman 2015; Eyman 2008, 2019; Eyman and Ball 2014, 2015, 2016).

We're also proud we've been able to give back to the computers and writing community by presenting annual awards for best webtext and best digital project, as well as awards for graduate students and contingent faculty who deserve recognition for their exemplary teaching, service, and research in the field.

Finally, we have been working to develop better systems and platforms to help scholars who wish to develop their own online journals. As Doug notes in his editorial philosophy, we have identified three types of critical infrastructure: social, scholarly, and technical (see Ball 2017; Eyman and Ball 2015). As part of an NEH grant in 2010, we mapped the general forms of infrastructure, from the social requirements of audience and peer review, to the scholarly norms of citation and disciplinary genre expectations, to the need for accessibility and usability as key features of the technical platforms that support the work of digital publishing, as well as our extensive peer-review and copyediting workflows at *Kairos*; Cheryl then used our framework and documentation to support the development of Vega, an academic publishing platform for scholarly multimedia and other digital scholarship, funded by a major grant from the Andrew W. Mellon Foundation in 2015.

Both the NEH and Mellon grant projects focused on building a platform designed from the outset to facilitate multimedia publishing, from submission through peer-review, editing, and publication. To date, no current systems do this well, as the primary model is based on the workflows and requirements of print-based genres (starting with Open Journal Systems, the most common platform for online-journal publication, but even for newer systems like Fulcrum). We also needed a system that would allow for design to be an integral part of the webtexts we publish (which is why we evaluated and rejected the use of a general CMS such as Drupal, which could conceivably be configured to support digital scholarly publishing but would impose its own design framework on every webtext; there was no way to suppress the "container" of the CMS to allow authorial design in the foreground).

Vega has workflow features similar to other publishing platforms, including submission tracking, notification systems, user-info databases, and front-end reader interfaces. Unlike other platforms, Vega was designed from the start to support the editing, review, and publication of scholarly multimedia. Vega is not a multimedia-authoring platform; rather, it provides a holistic beginning-to-end publishing system that supports the tasks of each stakeholder in the publishing process, from authors to editors to publisher. Vega is licensed under a generous MIT open-source license and is available at https://github.com/VegaPublish/ (in prerelease as of this writing, with more active development coming in 2020; for more on the development of Vega, see Ball 2017).

ADVICE FOR EDITORS AND AUTHORS

We could write an entire book on advice to editors and authors interested in creating or publishing scholarly multimedia (and, indeed, we are in the process of doing so), but following our practice of being guided by the theories and methods of rhetoric, we have distilled three key elements: understanding how the choices made during the invention stage impact the process and production of the work; understanding audience, especially the multiple audiences represented in the editorial process itself; and understanding the importance of accessibility and usability as critical infrastructures of delivery for digital scholarly publications.

Invention: Begin at the Beginning

Our first piece of advice applies to any digital media or digital humanities project, but it can also be read with an eye toward any publication project. We suggest authors and editors use the following heuristic to explicitly detail their understanding of the project, its audiences, its designs, and any infrastructures needed to complete its construction.

The Big Questions
- What are you researching?
- What do you want to make?
- Why do you want to make it?

- Where will it live?
- Who is your audience?
- Who are your stakeholders?
- Who benefits from your DH project?
- Who will sustain your project?

The Difficult Questions
- What role does the digital play?
- What digital media do you have?
- What digital media do you plan to collect?
- What does this media show?
- What does it argue?
- How does it change the way you can argue?
- But what does it *mean*? (with a focus on *ethos* and *pathos*)
- Does the media align with your research scope?
- Is your scope too big?

The Fearless Questions
- How do you strategize your project?
- How do you sustain your project?
- Whom do you collaborate with?
- What are your next steps?

This heuristic has been taken up by publishers, especially those in library publishing, who tend to focus on digital humanities-type projects and who have used this heuristic to create intake proposals to help faculty members plan their publications in advance. Cheryl initially wrote this heuristic for Sarah McKee at the Fox Center for Humanistic Inquiry at Emory University, who asked her to develop a workshop for faculty members just beginning their work on digital humanities projects. We spent three hours reviewing the questions in relation to specific examples and then providing one-on-one feedback to authors who had project ideas so we could pinpoint early pain points and potential successes and collaborations for their DH projects. It's funny how a little rhetorical understanding goes a long way. This kind of editorial pedagogical outreach is one of the ways *Kairos* has extended its success beyond digital writing studies into the broader DH and academic-publishing community.

EDITORIAL INTERACTIONS: UNDERSTANDING THE EDITING AND PUBLISHING PROCESSES

We've written elsewhere (Eyman and Ball 2014) how authors must pay attention to not only the rhetoric of their arguments but also to the design and the code in which they are writing. Over the past few years, Cheryl has worked to make visible on social media platforms several dozen editorial "Professional Tips of the Day" we've learned from design editing *Kairos*, with the aim of helping authors understand the behind-the-scenes work editors and publishers perform. Many authors think editors are gatekeepers meant to prevent their work from reaching its audience, but it's actually the opposite, in our experience: editors serve authors and are at their best when they are shepherding an author's work to its appropriate audience through a publishing venue. Each publishing venue has its own requirements for content, rigor, style, usage, and so on, and it's an editor's job to guide an author towards meeting those requirements. It's the author's job to step up in the attempt to meet that bar. But, once the bar has been met, the editor feels a sense of accomplishment and gratification in moving a text from the development stage of editing to the production stage.

Let's interject briefly to explain these two terms:

> The development process occurs as an author is composing and revising their text (article, chapter, book, website, and so forth). Developmental editing refers specifically to the part of that process in which the editor or group of editors interacts with the author (e.g., through editorial or peer review) to provide revision feedback the author must incorporate as they revise.

> The production process occurs after an editor (or whoever is in charge) decides a piece is suitable for publication. For a piece of scholarly writing (regardless of genre or medium), production begins when the author submits the fully revised version for copyediting, layout/design, or other production-oriented tasks.

In terms of understanding the editorial and publishing processes, it's the *production* portion of the process authors generally have no clue about. And we don't blame them. With the exception of those of us who truly get excited by moving commas into the right place, the production process sounds dull and even more nerdy than most PhDs can stand. But it's the part of the process that actually gets an author's text to its readers.

One of the things Cheryl often says to authors new to production practices is, "Remember the sixteen pairs of hands that will be on your text after you deliver it." Here are some examples of those hands (the titles of which may vary depending on the publishing venue you're working with):

- **developmental, managing, or acquisition editors,** who will have likely worked with you during the revision process and will review your manuscript to make sure your revisions are suitable;
- **production editors,** who are likely to focus on coordinating the copyediting and design process of the copyedited text, as well as seek permissions for quotes, images, and so on, all of which may be outsourced to **multiple freelancers**;
- **copyeditors,** who take the acceptance manuscript, after it's been approved by the acquisitions, developmental, or production editor, to complete multiple tasks including fact-checking and reference checks, as well as edits for grammar, style, usage, and so on. This job may be **outsourced** from the publishing venue itself;
- **designers, art directors, or layout specialists,** who do the graphic-design and page-production work on your manuscript, preparing it for publication (whether it's for print or screen consumption).

Each of these roles serves a different function to prepare a manuscript for publication, and each person in those roles requires the manuscript to be prepared in a different manner, which becomes part of the editorial workflow at a publisher. For instance, all that painstaking hand formatting you do to a print article in Word to submit it? In most publishing venues, every last bit of it will be stripped from the manuscript at the beginning of the production process so the publisher can add their own formatting styles—and, frankly, most authors don't know how to use their word-processing software very well at all, so there are all **sorts** of mistakes in the formatting authors provide to publishers. So, our best tip? Learn to use Styles in whatever program you're writing in, whether it's Word, Pages, InDesign, or HTML.

The sixteen-hands rule is true at *Kairos*, although we have different names and responsibilities than those listed above, in part because of the unusual nature of the scholarly multimedia we publish. The above job titles/types are often found in print-based academic publishing, so in addition to those jobs, *Kairos* editors—and others from journals, presses, libraries, and venues that publish similar kinds of scholarly multimedia, including digital humanities projects—must design edit and code edit the technological platforms those texts are created in. *Kairos's* design style guide for authors is one of the longest in the business because it is thorough (even as it points to even longer documents, like the W3C Accessibility Initiatives guidelines) and is emulated by many other publication venues.

DESIGNING FOR ACCESS AND ACCESSIBILITY

Because we are an online journal, one of our key concerns is accessibility. Accessibility is typically invoked via technical solutions—making sure screen readers can adequately render a website into a spoken text, adding transcripts to videos, podcasts, and other media, and making sure the site works well across all the likely platforms a user might be on, from desktop computers to mobile phones. But accessibility also requires access in a broader sense—making sure the journal's work is findable, impactful, citable, usable, and sustainable as well (see McCormick 2018).

This larger view of accessibility accounts for our insistence on using nonproprietary and open-source programs for the development of webtexts (e.g., Flash was a very popular choice for more interactive digital scholarship in the early 2000s, but it is now no longer supported and is essentially unusable—which means works in that format are no longer usable, much less accessible).

Keeping with our theme of rhetoric, design, and code, we think it is important for authors to consider accessibility from the point of invention—it's not something that can be figured out later, particularly as fundamental choices about infrastructure and approach should be considered through the lens of usability and accessibility. And it's not just the technical issues that must be addressed: aligning style and audience expectations and needs, as well as making sure any argument is presented in a way that doesn't intentionally add unnecessary complexity, also contributes to a scholarly work's overall accessibility. We're not necessarily advocating a pure plain language approach (such as Randall Munroe's [2015] "ten hundred" words model), but we do believe scholarship and research should be as accessible as possible given the constraints of needing to work within the technical discourses of one's field or discipline. Similarly, design choices—including consideration of metaphors and analogies used in a given webtext's design, color, navigation schema, and overall document design—should privilege accessibility and usability over innovation. (But, we also acknowledge some innovative works have a lot of impact and may need to be delivered in forms that might not make them wholly accessible in similar ways to every reader at the point of publication.)

For a fairly comprehensive overview of accessibility issues in digital publishing, we recommend both authors and editors explore "Access/ibility: Access and Usability for Digital Publishing" (Eyman et al. 2016), which was developed in collaboration with twenty-seven scholars from a wide range of humanities and information science disciplines during a summer institute Cheryl hosted in 2015.

What we haven't covered here in terms of accessibility is the ways we practice inclusivity in our editorial decisions, staffing, and publications. This is an area we actively strive to be better at every day we work on the journal so we can proudly answer the question of how we are making the journal a more inclusive place for digital scholars and digital scholarship. Some of this work is as easy as saying we pay attention to and correct towards inclusive language in our copyediting—an easy practice for authors to pick up in their own writing. The CELJ has published a list of inclusive editing style guides (http://celj.org/projects), which authors can use to find more information on writing for inclusivity in terms of race, gender, and sexuality. We also try to ensure authors don't rely exclusively on white, male authors (which, tbh, is not difficult in digital writing studies because of the feminist approach of our field) just as much as we try to ensure authors avoid only citing print-based publications, particularly monographs, when we have a plethora of online venues of multiple genres in our discipline. A large part of changing the shape of citation practices in our field to be more inclusive of not only gender but also of multiple races, ethnicities, and abilities comes with changing the make-up of our editorial board, which we have been working on throughout 2020.

We have also been striving to hire more scholars of color into our editorial ranks, and to create spaces for scholars who don't necessarily have the advanced design-editing chops some of our associate editors need, so that we can mentor folks into more advanced editorial ranks. The staff has been engaging in multiple conversations and action plans during 2020, within our own journal and across other publication venues and publishing organizations, to live up to one of our goals of making publishing more inclusive, particularly for scholars that tend to go unpublished in our field. In line with other publication venues that worked on creating diversity statements in 2020, *Kairos* created an inclusive publishing action plan that would help us espouse antiracist practices. Modeled on the demands-forward statement authored by April Baker-Bell, Bonnie J. Williams-Farrier, Davena Jackson, Lamar Johnson, Carmen Kynard, and Teaira McMurtry of the 2020 CCCC Special Committee on Composing a CCCC Statement on Anti-Black Racism and Black Linguistic Justice, Or, Why We Cain't Breathe! (Conference), *Kairos* published its own Inclusivity Action Items list in the August 2020 issue of the journal (Ball 2020). *Kairos* strives to be radically inclusive and equitable in its publishing practices, to push against the way we have defined access/ibility even further, and we welcome feedback on this action list and any of our practices and mentoring ideas that might better foster a sense of inclusivity for scholars of color in our or other disciplines.

Editing and publishing in any field is constituted through a set of rhetorical practices, and carrying out both authoring and editing activities with an explicitly rhetorical frame leads to a great degree of effectiveness in the whole knowledge-making enterprise. Through our experiences as editors (and as authors), we see the importance of making our processes transparent, of centering the work on our understanding of audiences and users, and of striving for accessible, usable, and sustainable platforms that support the circulation of research in our discipline. As we continue our work as editors, we will continue to support new and established scholars who can see the value of building disciplinary knowledge through both text and design, and we plan to continue to theorize and frame our work from a rhetorical perspective. And of course, *Kairos* always welcomes queries and submissions from authors interested in crafting and publishing webtexts—particularly ones that push the field to see new possibilities in the affordances of digital scholarship.

REFERENCES

Ball, Cheryl E. 2004. "Show, Not Tell: The Value of New Media Scholarship." *Computers and Composition* 21 (3): 403–425.

Ball, Cheryl E. 2012a. "Editorial Pedagogy, part 1: A Professional Philosophy." *Hybrid Pedagogy*. https://hybridpedagogy.org/editorial-pedagogy-pt-1-a-professional-philosophy/.

Ball, Cheryl E. 2012b. "Editorial Pedagogy, part 2: Developing Authors." *Hybrid Pedagogy*. https://hybridpedagogy.org/editorial-pedagogy-pt-2-developing-authors/.

Ball, Cheryl E. 2012c. "Editorial Pedagogy, part 3: Developing Editors and Designers." *Hybrid Pedagogy*. https://hybridpedagogy.org/editorial-pedagogy-pt-3-developing-editors-designers/.

Ball, Cheryl E. 2013. "Pirates of Metadata or, the True Adventures of How One Editor, Fifteen Undergraduate Publishing Majors, and 25,000 Media Elements Survived a Metadata Mining Project." In *Extend and Unify: Outreach and Education for Scholarly Communication and Information Literacy Programs*, edited by Stephanie Davis-Kahl and Merinda Hensley. Chicago: Association of College and Research Libraries.

Ball, Cheryl E. 2016. The Shifting Genres of Scholarly Multimedia: Webtexts as Innovation. *Journal of Media Innovations* 3 (2). http://dx.doi.org/10.5617/jmi.v3i2.2548.

Ball, Cheryl E. 2017. "Building a Scholarly Multimedia Publishing Infrastructure." *Journal of Scholarly Publishing* 48 (2): 99–115.

Ball, Cheryl E. 2020. "Logging On: Inclusivity Action Items." *Kairos: A Journal of Rhetoric, Technology, and Pedagogy* 25 (1). http://kairos.technorhetoric.net/25.1/loggingon/index.html.

Ball, Cheryl E., and Douglas Eyman. 2015. "Editorial Workflows for Multimedia-rich Scholarship." *Journal of Electronic Publishing* 18 (4). http://dx.doi.org/10.3998/3336451.0018.406.

Ball, Cheryl E., and Rich Rice. 2006. "Reading the Text: Remediating the Text." *Kairos: A Journal of Rhetoric, Technology, and Pedagogy* 10 (2). http://kairos.technorhetoric.net/10.2/binder2.html?coverweb/riceball/.

Conference on College Composition and Communication. 2020. "This Ain't Another Statement! This is a DEMAND for Black Linguistic Justice!" By April Baker-Bell, Bonnie J. Williams-Farrier, Davena Jackson, Lamar Johnson, Carmen Kynard, and Teaira McMurtry. https://cccc.ncte.org/cccc/demand-for-black-linguistic-justice.

Doherty, Mick. 1998. "As We May Link . . ." From the Editor's Desk(top). *Kairos: A Journal for Teachers of Writing in Webbed Environments* 3 (1). http://kairos.technorhetoric.net/3.1/binder.html?loggingon/doherty.html.

Eyman, Douglas. 2008. "Learning from Kairos: Value, Visibility, and Virtual Teamwork." In *Handbook of Research on Virtual Workplaces and the New Nature of Business Practices*, edited by Pavel Zemliansky and Kirk St. Amant, 590–598. Hershey, PA: IGI.

Eyman, Douglas. 2019. "Text/Design/Code—Advice on Developing and Producing a Scholarly Webtext." In *Explanation Points: Publishing in Rhetoric and Composition*, edited by John Gallagher and Danielle DeVoss, 206–209. Fort Collins: University Press of Colorado.

Eyman, Douglas, and Cheryl E. Ball. 2014. "Composing for Digital Publication: Rhetoric, Design, Code." *Composition Studies* 42 (1): 114–117.

Eyman, Douglas, and Cheryl E. Ball. 2016. "History of a Broken Thing: The Multi-journal Special Issue on Electronic Publication." In *Microhistories of Composition*, edited by Bruce McComiskey, 117–136. Logan: Utah State University Press.

Eyman, Douglas, Cheryl E. Ball, Jeremy Boggs, Amanda K. Booher, Elkie Burnside, Scott Lloyd DeWitt, Jason Dockter, Jay Dolmage, Traci Gardner, Sara Georgi, Hal Hinderliter, Susan Ivey, Michael Keller, Rachael Kelley, Sarah Kennedy, Rebecca Kennison, Pamela McClanahan, Alex Ries, Kassi Roberts, Melanie Schlosser, Karl Stolley, John Paul Walter, George H. Williams, M. Remi Yergeau, and Sean Zdenek. 2016. "Access/ibility: Access and Usability for Digital Publishing." *Kairos: A Journal of Rhetoric, Technology, and Pedagogy* 20 (2). http://kairos.technorhetoric.net/20.2/topoi/eyman-et-al/index.html.

McCormick, Monica. 2018. "Findable, Citable, Usable, Sustainable: A Checklist for Rigorous Digital Publishing." Scholarly Communication Institute. https://trianglesci.org/2018/07/17/findable-citable-usable-sustainable-a-checklist-for-rigorous-digital-publishing/.

Munroe, Randall. 2015. *Thing Explainer: Complicated Stuff in Simple Words*. New York: Houghton Mifflin Harcourt.

Writing Studies Tree. n.d. http://writingstudiestree.org/live/content/kairos-journal-rhetoric-technology-and-pedagogy.

13
ENCULTURATION AND SCHOLARLY EDITING AS NETWORK COORDINATION

Byron Hawk
University of South Carolina

In 1996 I cofounded *enculturation: a journal of rhetoric, writing, and culture* with David Rieder at the University of Texas at Arlington. We were graduate students at the time, so how we got started was easy: we built a website and opened up shop. The why is perhaps not so hard to grasp either: we were students caught up in our emerging interest in the field and didn't see any reason we shouldn't start a journal. During the early days of the internet, there were few academic journals online, and the freedom to start a journal was very much of the times. We had no long-term aim, only a desire to do a journal. We intuitively knew the nature of knowledge production was changing but also felt strongly that an academic journal should preserve what is important about traditional scholarly practices, as well as move into a new technological era. So we kept the traditional anonymous-review process, as well as feel and usability, of the print journal with issues, tables of contents, and articles while also being open to wider variety of work being done by academics. As a two-person team, David and I produced six issues, and after David stepped down as coeditor in 2003, I continued to produce issues as a boutique journal published at George Mason University.

In 2008 I brought in Jim Brown as managing editor and the journal began to grow. And in 2011 Casey Boyle came on as book-review editor and quickly moved up to comanaging editor along with Jim. Their efforts significantly expanded the journal's scope and solidified its consistent publication, as well as its recognition in the field. Laurie Gries came on as managing editor in 2015, and the journal expanded in both scholarly scope and editorial teams, with Donnie Sackey in charge of special issues and responses, Anthony Stagliano managing production, and Caddie Alford editing book reviews. We also expanded into sonic rhetorics, with Eric Detweiler editing a new special section that features audio works, and expanded into essays longer than journal articles but shorter than monographs with the special section *Intermezzo* edited by Jeff Rice. *Intermezzo* publishes on a variety of topics both academic and non-academic, and authors are encouraged to experiment with form, style, content, and medium in their use of the liminal space between the article and the monograph. Scot Barnett stepped in as managing editor in 2020 with a vision for further expanding the journal's ability to showcase outstanding work from emerging and established scholars in the field and increasing the diversity of its citations, authors, and issues. Today the journal is supported by the University of South Carolina with an RA and sports its largest number of editors and editorial-board members to date.

As a purely open-access, nonprofit journal with no budget, *enculturation* is run through gifted labor, and I've found building networks and distributing the work is the best way to make sure the journal runs effectively. My current understanding of editing in this context is quite a bit different than when I first started. It has moved from an individual effort to review manuscripts to a larger process of network coordination. In *Aircraft Stories* and *The Body Multiple*, both John Law (2002) and Annemarie Mol (2002) respectively emphasize coordination as a key aspect of connecting multiple versions of their objects of study across their networks of coproduction. Law focuses on the brochure and Mol medical files: the former articulating various aspects of the TRS2 aircraft across multiple inter- and intra-institutional groups; the latter articulating various versions of atherosclerosis across the hospital, lab, and clinic. While both emphasize textual practices, their accounts reveal how networks function and how writers participate in networked coordination. Mol argues, for example, that something like a disease is not a fixed, essentialist object but a function of coordinated sets of practices that are always local, enacted in a particular place at a particular time. Consequently, in Mol's parlance, an object like a disease is a multiple object continually coproduced by the specific practices that sustain it. Coordination, in other words, "doesn't depend on the possibility of referring to a pre-existing object. It is a task" (70). The question, then, is always how these tasks perform the object of study—how does the multiple object "hang together" through various forms of coordination across time.

Since producing scholarly knowledge is a function of enculturation into disciplinary practices and networks, the primary role of the editor becomes to engage in ongoing tasks that coordinate and facilitate this process by establishing and sustaining these networks, connecting authors to these networks, and moving texts through these networks and their coproductive relations. Both the networked practices of managing a journal and editing manuscripts, in other words, don't simply replicate but intervene in scholarly conversations to coordinate the coproduction of objects of study and coproduce new disciplinary knowledge by altering the networked conditions of enculturation—enculturation is an emergent, not a deterministic, process.

ENCULTURATION AS PHILOSOPHY OF EDITING

As a concept, enculturation is the process of learning the norms, values, and practices of a culture through unconscious, tacit repetition. The totality of actions within a culture—everything from institutional procedures to everyday behaviors—sets the conditions for what is possible in a society. Learning in this context becomes a life-long process that happens continuously every day across all aspects of life and increasingly includes forms of speech, textual commands, modeled images, and sonic cues along with countless gestures and practices, all of which coproduce the technological, economic, political, social, ideological, and philosophical bases of the culture. This sense of learning is a critical concept for anyone working in the areas of rhetoric, culture, and education. Rhetoricians, for example, cannot ignore the emergence of social media as a new context for enculturation, from the productive circulation of cultural forms and events, such as hip hop and the Arab Spring, to the disruptive circulation processes initiated by both state and nonstate actors, such as Russia and QAnon. Likewise, educators cannot ignore the unconscious, habitual elements of their own classrooms, both the ways they continue to tacitly model disciplinary traditions and the ways they can explicitly create new or alternate conditions for enculturation. In short, enculturation is a continuous process of change that makes it possible to internalize the norms of a culture but also to enact cultures differently, coproducing the system otherwise, even to the point of coproducing a new cultural system that displaces an established one.

Of course, journal editing fits well within such processes and practices. Even though courses on scholarly methods and genre exist, much of what scholars learn about research comes from doing rather than knowing; the journal editors and anonymous reviewers function to coordinate processes of disciplinary enculturation. An editor's role is not simply to function as a gatekeeper but to tacitly cultivate a scholar's acquisition of discursive practices. Layered processes of review consolidate professional issues and conversations, guide new scholars into the discipline via responding to those conversations, and direct future inquiry by revealing alternative connections and possibilities opened up by those conversations. The editor's task is to function as a facilitator of enculturation through the bottom-up movement of scholarly production. If the aim of research is the production of new knowledge rather than simply the repetition of prior knowledge, then editors coordinate the conditions of this coproduction that generates the new through the old. Any editor's philosophy should recognize the ethical coresponsibility that comes along with ensuring disciplinary conversations change and reflect that recognition in their scholarly practices.

One of the initial ethical practices an editor engages in is the selection of manuscripts to send out for review. It is of utmost importance to identify initial submissions that have the potential to embody certain scholarly characteristics. As we all know, when a journal changes editors, the "flavor" of the journal can change because the orientation of the editor toward these characteristics can vary in both form and content. My own orientation toward scholarship, for example, tends toward careful, close writing and detailed interconnectivity of argumentation. Editors must be mindful of such assumptions so they can be attentive to manuscripts that carry the potential for these traits rather than simply select ones that have them already, and be attentive to alternative forms and styles of academic discourse that nevertheless enact a scholarly ethos that opens up disciplinary conversations (Bizzell 2002; Thaiss and Zawacki 2006). Finding manuscripts with real potential and helping them move toward greater clarity, insight, or nuance, whatever their stage of development, position of argument, or style of engagement, is always a major goal. While editors also have their "flavors" in terms of content, these should never become unconscious assumptions, especially when the issues or theories being engaged are emerging ones or are put forward by newer or diverse scholars. Because newer scholars especially aren't accustomed to the process, they at times take extensive feedback as evidence the editor is performing the role of gatekeeper. But if an editor has taken time with a manuscript, they have already recognized its potential and shifted into the role of coordinator with the aim of transitioning the author into the process and helping them develop the manuscript into a contribution to the field. This is a tacit process of enculturation that isn't deterministically normative but that coordinates the author's arguments with conversations in the field in order to move the field forward, simultaneously coproducing the arguments, the conversations, and the field.

Additionally, while anonymous peer reviews are critical to academic integrity and development, another key ethical practice of editors is negotiating diverging reviews. In practically all cases, this warrants a third reviewer and careful attention by the editor. First, it is critical to send manuscripts to the right reviewers, and oftentimes a diverging or disparaging review is the fault of the editor's choice of reviewers, not the manuscript or the reviewer. Choosing the right third reviewer in such cases becomes vital. Second, it is critical for the editor to mitigate the impact of the disparaging review by repackaging it for the author so the critical or negative commentary can become the basis for productive revision.[1] Every review, even the most terse or vehement, tells the editor and author something about potential readers in the field and therefore some aspect of the conversation being engaged. The editor's role is to listen to the reviewer's concerns while rearticulating those concerns so the author can hear their potential without acquiescing to or dismissing them. This process is similar to a teacher's cultivation of alternate conditions for enculturation in a classroom. Negotiating and enacting certain conditions for the production of discourse and learning is what teachers and editors do. The aim, for me, is to support scholarly *ethoi* and practices while making it possible to produce new knowledge that changes conversations.

In terms of managing a journal, I feel a key editorial practice is to develop a collective network of scholars and a collective set of processes that allow the editorial team to work without much of a hierarchical presence. As I've moved out of the role of managing the review process and into the role of senior editor, I see this as my primary task. Open-access journals run through gifted labor, and my role is to continually build and coordinate these networks, create processes that distribute work equitably across the system, and sustain these networks and processes as they shift over time. Part of the aim is to make sure no one person, save the managing editor perhaps, is over extended. Ultimately this is what makes an independent journal sustainable. Independent journals without an affiliation with an organization or press can dissolve once an individual editor decides to step aside or retire. But if I've done my job respectably, gathered a collective to work on the journal, and enacted an antimicromanaging philosophy behind this work, then *enculturation* as a network should sustain itself well beyond my editorship. People have actually told me they didn't know I started the journal or didn't know I was still senior editor. I actually think this bodes well for the future of the journal and is an important aspect of creating tacit conditions for processes of enculturation.

COORDINATING CONVERSATIONS

Scholarly research is about practices of not just discovering but also inventing the conversations authors are responding to as they are engaged in them and making sure that through the process, new exigencies, connections, ideas, and practices are coproduced that set the stage for others to discover and invent the discipline in return. Editors coordinate this process both implicitly and explicitly. In "Discipline and Publish," Collin Brooke (2012) argues that graduate level writing instruction is often more akin to current-traditional rhetoric's tacit transfer than process pedagogy's explicit engagement, and our graduate courses are organized more around topics and canons than disciplinary conversations—canons are primarily norming while conversations are open to change. Brooke's solution is to address the issue more directly and explicitly by teaching conversations rather than canons and foregoing the seminar paper for more direct rhetorical instruction in intervening in these conversations. In my own course on scholarly articles as a genre, I've tried to follow Brooke's advice and move these pedagogical moments from the office to the classroom. Since disciplinary knowledge isn't something that stands outside its productions but is intimately a function of disciplinary conversations and the collective networks that produce them and give them salience, the advice I give my students is in line with the kinds of coordinating practices I engage in with authors. In order to extend the enculturating work of graduate school into the networks of editorial practice, I follow key works in the field to ground my "flavor" and turn it toward more explicit advice to authors.[2]

First, in editorial feedback, I always prompt authors to trace the disciplinary conversations around their objects of study. A scholarly manuscript can't take a position in relation to a field without first being attentive to its larger movements and issues. Gary Olson (1997) argues that scholarship is a series of ongoing conversations that engage issues in the field through conferences, articles, and books that don't always reach consensus. Rather than build toward consensual truth, the conversations are generative: they coproduce discourse, ideas, rhetorical and pedagogical practices, and ultimately the objects of study themselves. Olson's advice for a first move, if the author wants to join these conversations, is to listen to what is being said, both in the field writ large and in the particular journal or journals the author aims to publish in. The conversations have major and minor perspectives, can be hotly debated, and are usually practiced indirectly through writing rather than direct exchange or even citation in some cases. Some issues have already been settled or exhausted and don't need to be rehashed. Others may need to be resurrected or reinvigorated, but only listening to the conversations will provide a sense of which issue is which at any given time. These conversations perform a coordinating function in relation to objects of study authors ultimately intervene in and coproduce.

Second, I prompt authors to explicitly gesture toward knowledge of these conversations in their manuscripts. Authors typically lay out versions of these conversations in writing to establish an exigency for their work. Richard McNabb (2001) studied a corpus of submissions to *Rhetoric Review* and found the majority of rejected manuscripts failed to situate their claims in the field. The key rhetorical gesture, McNabb found, is to shift interpretive authority out of nonepistemic individual, practical activity (classrooms, workplaces, department meetings, conferences) and onto a constructed epistemic disciplinary matrix (subjects, works, ideas, and methods). Nonepistemic gestures typically show no recognition of current disciplinary problems or conversations. Instead they locate the problem in the author's personal experience, defer disciplinary context through more general details, or describe the field's knowledge in an acontextualized literature review. Epistemic gestures, on the other hand, draw immediate attention to the disciplinary conversations that provide an exigence for the author's research. Authors should coordinate their claims through the field's current knowledge, published authors, and recognized methods to show they are producing new knowledge in the discipline rather than replicating it, which ultimately shifts the epistemic gesture into an ontological one that coproduces new versions of the discourses, objects of study, and world.

Finally I ask authors to foreground the cost of the disciplinary problems they identify. Authors should always be clear and direct about what is at stake in the disciplinary problems that ground their contribution. Oftentimes proposals or articles point to a "gap" in the disciplinary conversations to show something hasn't been addressed. But this, in and of itself, isn't enough to constitute a disciplinary problem. Joseph Williams (2011) argues introductions should include a destabilizing condition that generates costs or consequences for the field. A gap in knowledge or flaw in understanding only constitutes a problem if not developing a response incurs a cost to the field or its practices—readers need to see the problem as a significant one that has an impact on them, their students, the field, or the larger public. Williams derives a useful heuristic for article introductions: stasis, problem with condition + cost, and solution or response. Stasis is some established position in the field that is then disrupted by a problem. The problem should include both an articulation of the conditions that create it and the costs that come from ignoring it. The solution can be laid out in detail or suggested as a response to the problem and left to the rest of the article for further elaboration. This rhetorical move holds back from fully giving the argument away and creates some tension or suspense for the reader, who will want to read on if the costs are seen as disciplinarily significant. Most important, this disruption means scholarly production isn't simply normative in a deterministic manner but is always a function of change.

What I am asking authors to do is become reflective about their production of scholarly knowledge, seeing it as a process that disrupts a disciplinary conversation and coproduces its object of study. As Mol (2002) notes, these aren't universal objects that preexist and are unchanged by our scholarly interventions into them. I'm asking authors to recognize their own practices that enact those multiple objects. What this means is that scholars aren't simply fracturing preexisting objects but instead are enacting forms of coordination in order to coproduce versions of those objects of study that "hang together" in a particular way.[3] For Mol, clinical exams, various measurements and tests, multiple symptoms and multiple findings are "brought together in the patient's file," giving the disease a "manyfoldedness" more than disparate fragmentation (84). Law (2002), in *Aircraft Stories*, is very explicit about the textual strategies of coordinated objects like the TSR2 aircraft, and he sees his academic book in the same light: "It is an attempt to perform decentered or allegorical knowing. It is an attempt to edge toward and perform a set of alternative academic sensibilities having to do with association, resemblance, and similitude.... It imagines objects—and the worlds in which they subsist—to be fractionally coherent. Oscillatory between singularity and multiplicity" (193). Our editorial forms of practice help enact these forms of coordination through both implicit and explicit means, and the work we do as editors becomes a part of the multiple objects of scholarly study the field produces through our coparticipation in its networks, which ultimately disrupts disciplinary conversations and ontologically coproduces something new through this engagement.

INTERVENTION AS INVENTION

Overall, I think working on *enculturation* from such an early stage in my career allowed me to develop a real interest in editing that has extended through edited collections, special issues of other journals, and editing a book series through the independent publisher Parlor Press. As I shift into the last third of my academic life, I expect I'll be doing more of this kind of work, especially reviewing manuscripts for journals and presses, as well as working with various research networks at CCCC, CW, and RSA and reviewing submissions for conferences. This kind of work really is a form of teaching writing and seems almost a natural extension of working in the field. And even though *enculturation* continues to publish predominantly textual scholarly articles, I think the continued focus on written discourse is an understandable extension of our field and our institutions. We continue to receive submissions in the genre of the scholarly article, and even when the tone and style of many of them become more essayistic over the review process, as Douglas Hesse (2019) recently noted, they are still steeped in disciplinary theories, methods, and conversations (384). As print publication becomes ever more precarious with the reduction in institutional support, there is still a need for this kind of discursive knowledge production and editors, reviewers, and board members at *enculturation* work hard to fill that niche in the now not-so-new medium.

Looking back on *enculturation*'s development over the past twenty years or so, I can see how its role has emerged to fill such a niche. In a brief response I wrote for *College English* (Hawk 2013), I argued that a journal is a function of disciplinary networks and practices and that as these networks grow, it becomes increasingly difficult for a journal to claim "flagship" status—in other words, while there will clearly be primary journals produced by a discipline's dominant organizations, they can no longer represent the entirety of a field or its diversity of subfields. In such a scenario, independent journals and niche journals connected to subfield conversations or specific methods or approaches within a field will become increasingly important. *enculturation*, for example, has become increasingly focused on publishing works on rhetorical theory and rhetorical criticism in relation to composition and new media. In 2018 I was asked to participate in the CCCC's Rhetoric SIG on "What Is Rhetoric's Role in CCCC?" It was a very interesting and spirited conversation. My takeaway from the conversation was that rhetoric currently operates at the level of warrant in most CCCC's presentations. In other words, what rhetoric *is* is assumed and deployed rather than interrogated and supplied with backing. Most of the work that interrogates rhetorical theory, history, and criticism has shifted over to RSA as it has grown over the past twenty years. I see *enculturation* as having tacitly moved with this shift and focused on publishing work in composition that highlights the rhetorical as that work has moved away from central conversations in composition writ large. If there is a broad contribution made by *enculturation*, it is providing a forum for these conversations, as space in other journals for these works has narrowed. Having such a venue not only keeps the conversations going but also allows them to change and develop over time.

In other words, in addition to changing with conversations, editing participates in changing conversations. In Law's (2002) discussion of coordination, he sees it as a kind of intervention. Describing, tracing, and writing an object of study is "colluding to enact it into being," which "interferes" with it to perform it in particular ways that do not simply reproduce it (7). Jackie Rhodes (2012) describes this as "disrupting the unending conversation." Rather than attempting to reproduce conversations, she advocates looking slant at them, using them to produce failures, generating side conversations, enacting affective responses to them, and "courting your own slippage of signification" while engaging them (162). Rightly, she notes the constructedness of those conversations and thus the potential to make them "fail to perform as expected" (163). By engaging in this kind of intervention, research is changing the nature of objects of study as multiple objects, extending the coordination of networks that do not simply support but that also coproduce the worlds we perform as academics, scholars, and editors. In "Editing as Inclusion Activism," Kelly Blewett, Christina M. LaVecchia, Laura R. Micciche, and Jaline Morris (2019) provide an excellent overview of conversations around scholarly editing in rhetoric and composition and also an excellent example of how establishing a conversation isn't necessarily acquiescing to it but instead can provide a forum for changing it. They argue that editorial work builds and sustains professional networks, which puts editors in a position to more actively consider and enact those coordinating practices. Doing so can and does change the conditions for the coproduction of scholarly knowledge—or said differently, scholarly conversations—and Blewett et al. provide a detailed set of sustaining practices for enacting inclusive networks in relation to those conversations to further ensure they coproduce the new.

In short, academic authors don't simply discover and cite the preexisting, or preassumed, scholars or conversations. Editors help authors play an active role in inventing what those conversations are, who is having them and how, and by doing so disrupt any preexisting sense of what that conversation is, what knowledge and objects of study get produced, and by extension who is provided a forum to produce them. Ultimately editors should orient themselves in this way to Burke's parlor metaphor. Conversations might already be there in a certain sense, but our interventions into them already make them something else. There is always a coproductive dance. As conversations and thus objects of study emerge and change over time, editors must recognize editing's coresponsibility in and to this emergent enculturating process.

NOTES

1. A recent study has noted the consequential effects of unfairly negative reviews, especially on marginalized groups. Christie Wilcox (2019) notes various strategies for responding to this problem. I advocate here one she doesn't note, which is to not send the review but repackage it. If there is simply nothing productive that can be found in it, automatically sending to the third reviewer is the course of action to take.
2. This section is a reworking of my advice in "You *Can* Do That in Rhetoric and Composition" (Hawk 2019), and the chapter on the whole is a response to and extension of what I argue there.
3. One way to read my recent *Resounding the Rhetorical* (Hawk 2018) is to see it as an extensive look at the kinds of practices involved in making recorded musical sounds "hang together" as a single quasi- or multiple object.

REFERENCES

Bizzell, Patricia. 2002. "The Intellectual Work of Mixed Forms of Academic Discourse." In *Alt/Dis: Alternative Discourses and the Academy*, edited by Christopher Schroeder, Helen Fox, and Patricia Bizzell, 1–10. Portsmouth, NH: Boynton/Cook, Heinemann.

Blewett, Kelly, Christina M. LaVecchia, Laura R. Micciche, and Jaline Morris. 2019. "Editing as Inclusion Activism." *College English* 81 (4): 273–296.

Brooke, Collin. 2012. "Discipline and Publish: Reading and Writing the Scholarly Network." In *Ecology, Writing Theory, and New Media*, edited by Sidney Dobrin, 92–105. New York: Routledge.

Hawk, Byron. 2013. "*College English* as Network." *College English* 75 (4): 436–443.

Hawk, Byron. 2018. *Resounding the Rhetorical: Composition as a Quasi-Object*. Pittsburgh: University of Pittsburgh Press.

Hawk, Byron. 2019. "You *Can* Do That in Rhetoric and Composition." In *Explanation Points: Publishing in Rhetoric and Composition*, edited by Dànielle Nicole Devoss and John Gallagher, 32–34. Logan: Utah State University Press.

Hesse, Douglas. 2019. "Journals in Composition Studies, Thirty-Five Years and After." *College English* 81 (4): 367–396.

Law, John. 2002. *Aircraft Stories: Decentering the Object in Technoscience*. Durham, NC: Duke University Press.

McNabb, Richard. 2001. "Making the Gesture: Graduate Student Submissions and the Expectation of Journal Referees." *Composition Studies* 29 (1): 9–26.

Mol, Annemarie. 2002. *The Body Multiple: Ontology in Medical Practice*. Durham NC: Duke University Press.

Olson, Gary. 1997. "Publishing Scholarship in Rhetoric and Composition: Joining the Conversation." In *Publishing in Rhetoric and Composition*, edited by Gary Olson and Todd Taylor, 19–33. Albany: SUNY Press.

Rhodes, Jacqueline. 2019. "Queer/ed Research: Disrupting the Unending Conversation." In *Explanation Points: Publishing in Rhetoric and Composition*, edited by Dànielle Nicole Devoss and John Gallagher, 161–165. Logan: Utah State University Press.

Thaiss, Chris, and Terry Zawacki. 2006. *Engaged Writers and Dynamic Disciplines*. Portsmouth, NH: Boynton/Cook, Heinemann.

Wilcox, Christie. 2019. "Rude Paper Reviews Are Pervasive and Sometimes Harmful, Study Finds." *Science*, December 12. https://www.sciencemag.org/news/2019/12/rude-paper-reviews-are-pervasive-and-sometimes-harmful-study-finds.

Williams, Joseph. 2011. *Problems into PROBLEMS: A Rhetoric of Motivation*. Fort Collins, CO: WAC Clearinghouse.

14

BUILDING A FIELD THROUGH EDITORIAL WORK
The Case of Second Language Writing

Paul Kei Matsuda
Arizona State University

One of the central concerns of my academic career thus far has been to help build the field of second language writing—a transdisciplinary field situated simultaneously in writing studies and language studies. From early on, I recognized the need for establishing an identity for the field, building the disciplinary infrastructure, generating interest among a broader population of scholars and teachers, and mentoring newcomers to the field. This line of work has many facets—engaging in philosophical and historical scholarship, developing courses and programs, contributing to organizations, organizing conferences, editing journals, books, and book series, and building an interdisciplinary network of people.

Among these forms of engagement, editorial work has played a particularly important role in my career. When people look at my CV, many of them comment on the large number of edited works. Over the last two decades, I have produced ten edited volumes and three special journal issues. These edited works have helped shape my professional identity while also allowing me to mentor younger scholars. In this chapter, I focus on the role of editorial work in my professional development and in my efforts to help shape a field and its directions.

THE BEGINNING

My initial experience as an editor of academic publications involved working on two editing projects while I was a doctoral student at Purdue University. My coeditor was Tony Silva, my PhD supervisor and one of the co-founding editors of the *Journal of Second Language Writing* (*JSLW*).

In my third year of PhD studies, I noticed the lack of disciplinary infrastructure—particularly a conference where second language writing specialists could advance knowledge in the field. I went to his office to discuss the possibility of organizing a conference, which became the beginning of what has come to be known as the Symposium on Second Language Writing (SSLW).

The first SSLW was designed to be a small conference involving 12 invited speakers only and about 150 participants in the audience. During the initial planning stage, Tony brought up the idea of asking all the speakers to bring a written version of their presentations suitable for publication. With those manuscripts, we produced our first edited volume, *On Second Language Writing* (Silva and Matsuda 2001b), which was designed as a state-of-the-art collection. Given the caliber of the authors, all of whom were well-known experts in the field, we decided to publish the volume as an edited book rather than conference proceedings because the latter would make the volume less impactful than would an edited collection.

Because of our shared interest in bringing writing studies and second language studies together, Tony and I looked for a publisher that was well represented in both fields. We decided to work with Lawrence Erlbaum Associates (which later became part of Taylor and Francis/Routledge). We contacted Naomi Silverman, who was the acquisitions editor for applied linguistics and teachers of English to speakers of other languages (TESOL) at that time. When we met at a TESOL conference, she was enthusiastic about the idea and gave us a copy of the proposal guidelines.

At about the same time, Jerry Murphy, then the sole editor of the *Landmark Essays* series, asked Tony if he would edit a volume in the Landmark Essays series, and he invited me to work with him as a coeditor of *Landmark Essays on ESL Writing* (Silva and Matsuda 2001a). If the goal of *On Second Language Writing* was to provide a synchronic overview, *Landmark Essays* was designed to provide a diachronic perspective. Although the series was also published by Erlbaum, it had a different acquisitions editor, Linda Bathgate, who worked with the composition market. It seemed that the disciplinary division of labor between writing studies and second language studies (Matsuda 1999) was also being institutionalized at the publisher level. In order to reach the audience of second language writing specialists in both fields, we asked Erlbaum to market our volumes in both fields.

Working on these two volumes gave me opportunities to experience different kinds of editorial work. *On Second Language Writing* was an edited volume consisting of manuscripts written by experienced authors in the field, which made the editorial process relatively painless. Most of the authors completed their manuscripts by the deadline and brought paper copies to the symposium. The manuscripts were invariably well written and well formatted, requiring little revision or editing. Although they were somewhat varied in style, Tony and I saw that variation as a strength, reflecting the disciplinary diversity of the field. One of the authors, a senior scholar, used the European convention for punctuation marks, putting commas and periods outside the quotation marks. We initially converted them to the APA style, but the author expressed her desire to keep the original usage to maintain her own voice, and we decided to honor her request.

In contrast to *On Second Language Writing*, which was a collection of original works, *Landmark Essays on ESL Writing* was a reprint collection consisting of previously published articles and book chapters. The main task was to choose chapters to be included and to write an introduction that provided a historical overview of the field to contextualize the selected pieces. Tony and I agreed on a number of criteria for the selection and organization of the chapters. First, we wanted to start with early publications that gave a sense of how things were back in the old days—to illustrate how far we had come as a field. Second, we wanted to represent some of the key players who contributed to the development of the field. Another important task was to obtain permission to reprint from publishers—sometimes with the help of the authors. Since the pieces had already been published, we did not need to edit the texts extensively, although we did correct some of the obvious errors in the original publications.

BENEFITS OF COEDITING

Working with a collaborator-mentor proved to be a useful learning experience. Tony and I brought unique and somewhat overlapping assets to these projects. Tony was about ten years ahead of me in his career. As a co-founding editor of a journal, he had experience in working closely with publishers and authors. A detail-oriented and well-organized person, he was also highly skilled as a copyeditor. He had also been compiling—and continued to compile until recently—the most comprehensive annotated bibliography of second language writing, which has been shared as a book (Silva, Brice, and Reichelt 1999) and as a regular feature of the *JSLW*.

As a relative newcomer to the field, I did not have the kind of experience or network Tony had. But I brought my experience as a second language writer. I was also developing my own network through my active involvement in several major professional organizations—the American Association for Applied Linguistics (AAAL), the Conference on College Composition and Communication (CCCC), and TESOL. Being a conference organizer and editor while still in graduate school also helped me expand my network. My primary asset was the historical knowledge of the field of second language writing, as well as writing studies and language studies. Inspired by Tony's influential piece on the history of second language writing pedagogy (Silva 1990), and with my formal education in rhetoric and composition since my undergraduate years, I had developed an extensive knowledge of the history of these fields.

Each of us had a fairly comprehensive knowledge of the field; both of us had independently collected and read virtually all publications on second language writing written in English since the 1950s—and in my case, I also had read most of the key publications on second language writing in Japanese. Our shared knowledge base helped us during the proposal-writing process—as we identified which authors and topics to include, what kind of publications would fill the current gap, and which existing publications would compete with the proposed volume.

For our collaborative process, we met regularly in Tony's office. He led the collaboration by providing frameworks and criteria, and we often brainstormed together. We drafted proposals and introductions together, sentence by sentence. Initially, Tony was at his keyboard typing, and I sat next to him offering my real-time comments. At some point, Tony suggested we switch roles, and I composed as he watched and offered comments. This collaborative process worked surprisingly well for us.

Because of our shared knowledge of the field, we seemed to be on the same wavelength most of the time, which made the collaboration easy and fun. I felt Tony treated me with respect as a colleague and equal partner rather than as a student, although I deferred to him on rare occasions when we had differences of opinion. In editing the collection, each of us read and commented on the manuscripts independently and then consolidated the comments during our regular meetings. As I have documented elsewhere, my approach to mentoring through collaborative work has been influenced by this experience (Matsuda 2016; Simpson and Matsuda 2008).

Tony and I went on to coedit two more volumes together, including *Second Language Writing Research* (Matsuda and Silva 2005) and *Practicing Theory in Second Language Writing* (Silva and Matsuda 2010). Using a process similar to *On Second Language Writing* (Silva and Matsuda 2001b), we started by asking invited speakers at the symposium to provide manuscripts. Although I had already completed my PhD and had left West Lafayette, the previous collaborative experience helped us work together over a series of email exchanges and a few meetings at conferences with the publisher. For introductions, one of us developed the initial draft while the other provided feedback.

MENTORING AND LEARNING

A few years after finishing my PhD, I was still looking for ways to integrate a second language perspective into writing studies. Through my scholarship, I had pointed out the importance of paying attention to the presence and needs of second language writers in college writing classrooms, but I felt the need to make insights from the field of second language writing more accessible to the broader composition audience. One day, while attending CCCC, I walked by Bedford/St. Martin's Press booth where they were promoting the latest sourcebook—an edited collection of previously published works on a specific topic. "What better way to promote an important but neglected topic than free books!" I thought to myself. I found Leasa Burton, who was a senior editor at the time, and discussed my ideas. I was given a go-ahead to submit a proposal for a volume entitled *Second-Language Writing in the Composition Classroom: A Critical Sourcebook* (Matsuda et al. 2006).

For this project, I chose to work with two of the PhD students I was working with at the time: Christina Ortmeier-Hooper and Michelle Cox. I also invited Jay Jordan, a PhD student from Penn State who was becoming active in the L2 writing community at CCCC. My original intent was to give them some experience and exposure, but as we discussed the project, I was also excited by different perspectives they brought, and I decided to take more of a coordinator role, letting them lead the efforts to organize sections and draft section introductions. I did have to impose some restrictions. Because the primary audience for this collection was first-year writing teachers at the college level, we had to exclude some of the topics the coeditors were interested in including. My contract with Erlbaum for the *Landmark Essays* also limited my ability to include pieces from the previous collection in order to avoid competition. The resulting product, though somewhat different from what I had originally envisioned, was probably more appealing to a wider variety of readers than if I had edited it by myself. (I have described this mentoring process in more detail in Matsuda 2016.)

A FAILED PROJECT?

After the success of *On Second Language Writing* (Silva and Matsuda 2001b), which was based on the first SSLW in 1998, I tried to edit another collection based on the second SSLW held in 2000. For this project, I invited Kevin Eric De Pew, a new PhD student starting at Purdue, to be my coeditor. The theme of the conference was "Contexts of Second Language Writing," the purpose of which was to encourage research in contexts outside US higher education. Unlike the first iteration of SSLW, SSLW 2000 took the regular conference format with four plenary speakers and many concurrent sessions. Because we wanted to avoid the conference proceedings, we opted to develop a collection by soliciting proposals from presenters. Developing a focused edited volume out of solicited proposals was challenging, as was ensuring the quality of contributions. Although we initially developed a proposal for an edited collection that sought to expand the scope of the field, we were not able to obtain enough quality submissions to develop robust sections.

To ensure the authors' efforts were not completely wasted, we provided additional feedback and suggestions for possible venues for publishing each chapter. But in the process, we noticed there was a cluster of strong papers that dealt with issues involving young second language learners—between the ages of five and eighteen. Instead of abandoning the entire project, we decided to reshape it into a special journal issue with a focus on early second language writing, which was a neglected area within the pages of the *JSLW*. It was not that research on young second language writers was not happening, or that the journal was not interested in those issues. Rather, the journal was caught in a vicious cycle—because research on young second language writers was not being published in the *JSLW*, many people seemed to assume the editors were not interested in the topic. I had often heard Ilona Leki, the founding coeditor, say that "we can't publish what people don't submit" when people asked her if the journal was not interested in certain topics. A special issue on early second language writing seemed like an opportunity to break the mold. Kevin and I proposed the idea to the *JSLW* editors, and the special issue was published toward the end of 2002.

A PHILOSOPHY OF EDITED WORKS

Both as an editor and reader, I am drawn to the edited collection because of its dialogic and generative potential. If a monograph can be compared to a plenary talk and a journal article to a conference paper, an edited collection is akin to a colloquium or symposium. In fact, some of the best edited collections evolved out of colloquia and symposia at conferences. Like a well-conceptualized colloquium, an edited collection can create a space for a focused exploration of an issue by bringing together authors who represent different positionalities or perspectives. It can also benefit from contributions by multiple experts who can address different aspects of the topic.

Monographs and journal articles tend to be driven by centripetal force. They take the perspectives and insights from existing works and move toward a synthesis, critique, or alternative proposal. The new knowledge presented by the author or authors of monographs and journal articles tends to come from a unified perspective, privileging their own contributions over existing perspectives or possible alternatives often systematically refuted or dismissed in the process. In monographs, authors can construct their own rhetorical narrative in which competing perspectives play the villain—the bad, the old, and the ugly—and out of which their own favorite theories or interpretations emerge as the victors. Of course, edited volumes also have their own purposes and can paint the picture of the field in similar ways. Yet, because of their multivocal nature, edited collections can also create spaces for more dialogic and open-ended explorations.

By engaging multiple members of the field in exploring the same topic and putting them in conversation with one another, the edited collection can help create a synergy that moves the field in a new direction—and do so more effectively than a single monograph or journal article can. Because of the possibility of representing diverse perspectives, which can sometimes be contrary or even contradictory, the edited collection can create *dissoi logoi* or expose knowledge gaps, stimulating further discussion and inquiry. In other words, the centrifugal force created by the diversity of positionalities and perspectives makes edited collections potentially more generative than other genres.

The edited collection can also be an instrument of inclusion. On any given topic, editors can choose to include marginalized voices more systematically. It also allows editors to mentor novice or traditionally underrepresented researchers, who often bring fresh perspectives. Editors can provide specific guidelines, outlines, or extensive comments with multiple revision opportunities, which is not always possible for journal articles. The inclusion of alternative perspectives can further stimulate the development of the field by challenging the status quo, by exposing the limits of the conventional wisdom.

THE CHALLENGES OF EDITED WORKS

The biggest challenge in producing edited volumes is the lack of support and recognition. Although edited collections have a unique function that can help move the field forward, they have often been undervalued in comparison with other forms of intellectual work. Editing a journal is often considered significant service to the profession, and institutions sometimes provide support for editors in the forms of course releases and editorial assistants. Editing a book, however, does not usually warrant much institutional support.

Edited collections do not rank high in the academic reward system. At one of my previous institutions, editing work did not count much, if at all, toward annual review, tenure, or promotion. At ASU, edited volumes traditionally ranked lower than book chapters, but after the recent revision of the tenure and promotion guidelines, edited collections came to be evaluated based on the assessment of external reviewers in the respective fields.

The devaluing of edited volumes also affects the ability to assemble strong and relevant contributions. Although book chapters can create a space for the publication of important insights less suitable for journal articles, they tend to count less than journal articles, partly because edited collections do not have impact factors. In the world of scholarly publication driven by institutional ranking, authors from some countries and institutions now prefer to spend their time and energy focusing on publications in indexed journals with high impact factors.

Another challenge is the amount of time it takes to work with authors. Editors of journals—especially highly coveted ones—have the option of rejecting manuscripts for the quality of writing because articles to be included in regular journal issues do not have to work together. Chapters in edited volumes, on the other hand, must cohere. To make it happen, sometimes editors must work extensively with authors who have important insights but are not fully comfortable with the particular genre. Working with less experienced authors (or authors unfamiliar with the genre) can be especially time consuming, requiring multiple cycles of feedback and revision, which can be frustrating for both authors and editors. But if they persevere, the fresh perspectives of young authors can be stimulating and inspiring to readers. For this reason, I consider editorial work to be an important form of mentoring.

Working with experienced authors also has its challenges. Experienced authors who are already tenured full professors are not desperate for another publication. To involve these authors as contributors, the edited collection must be well conceived and relevant to the authors' professional agendas. Working with them can be like herding cats, and it can be particularly challenging for less experienced or less well-established editors. Rejecting proposals—especially complete manuscripts—submitted by senior scholars can also be an issue. One of the ways of dealing with this power dynamic is to have at least one coeditor who is a senior scholar and can work more comfortably with authors at different levels of their career. Another strategy would be to shift the agency—by referring to comments by anonymous reviewers as the ground for revision requests or rejections.

SOME ADVICE FOR ASPIRING BOOK EDITORS

Based on my experience with various types of edited collections—both as an editor and contributor—here are some of my suggestions for aspiring book editors. First and foremost, editing books effectively requires a broad understanding of the field—its history, key issues, existing publications, and people. Reading widely and attending conferences regularly can help identify potential projects that can fill existing gaps. Networking with other scholars and publishers is also important in identifying and assessing potential projects. It is also useful to develop panels, colloquia, or symposia to test ideas, to generate materials, and to garner interest among potential contributors and readers. It is also important to become familiar with various types of publications, their possible functions in advancing knowledge, and their advantages and disadvantages.

Having a coeditor is also helpful—in fact, all my editing projects have been collaborative. As with any form of collaboration, working with a coeditor can sometimes take more time and effort, but the process of articulating goals, assumptions, and procedures can help editors make more deliberate decisions. Having another person to work with can also help ensure the project keeps moving forward. Working with a coeditor can also help take the project beyond the personal comfort zone, resulting in new knowledge and insights. For inexperienced editors, working with a mentor is a great way to learn not only about editing but also about some of the tacit assumptions and practices in the field and in the academic publishing industry. Having a senior collaborator can also be useful in negotiating with authors and publishers and in anticipating some of the issues and challenges that might come up in the editorial process.

Another consideration is the economy of publishing. Due to the lack of institutional recognition, spending time and energy on editing projects can hinder a young scholar's career. The lack of institutional recognition did not bother me personally because I was driven by the need to help build the field rather than the need for publications. I have always had enough publications under my belt and was able to spend my remaining energy working on projects not highly valued by the institution but nevertheless important to the field, such as editing books and organizing conferences. In the end, it is up to us to consider how our editorial work is evaluated by the institution and to maintain a balanced academic profile.

REFERENCES

Matsuda, Paul Kei. 1999. "Composition Studies and ESL Writing: A Disciplinary Division of Labor." *College Composition and Communication* 50 (4): 699–721.

Matsuda, Paul Kei. 2016. "The Will to Build: Mentoring Doctoral Students in Second Language Writing." In *Graduate Studies in Second Language Writing*, edited by Kyle McIntosh, Carolina Pelaez-Morales, and Tony Silva, 93–110. Anderson, SC: Parlor.

Matsuda, Paul Kei, Michelle Cox, Jay Jordan, and Christina Ortmeier-Hooper, eds. 2006. *Second-Language Writing in the Composition Classroom: A Critical Sourcebook*. Boston: Bedford/St. Martin's.

Matsuda, Paul Kei, and Tony Silva. 2005. *Second Language Writing Research: Perspectives on the Process of Knowledge Construction*. Mahwah, NJ: Lawrence Erlbaum.

Silva, Tony. 1990. "Second Language Composition Instruction: Developments, Issues, and Directions in ESL." In *Second Language Writing: Insights for the Classroom*, edited by Barbara Kroll, 11–23. Cambridge: Cambridge University Press.

Silva, Tony, Coleen Brice, and Melinda Reichelt. 1999. *Annotated Bibliography of Scholarship in Second Language Writing: 1993–1997*. Stamford, CT: Ablex.

Silva, Tony, and Paul Kei Matsuda, eds. 2001a. *Landmark Essays on ESL Writing*. Mahwah, NJ: Lawrence Erlbaum.

Silva, Tony, and Paul Kei Matsuda, eds. 2001b. *On Second Language Writing*. Mahwah, NJ: Lawrence Erlbaum.

Silva, Tony, and Paul Kei Matsuda, eds. 2010. *Practicing Theory in Second Language Writing*. West Lafayette, IN: Parlor.

Simpson, Steve, and Paul Kei Matsuda. 2008. "Mentoring as a Long-term Relationship: Situated Learning in a Doctoral Program." In *Learning the Literacy Practices of Graduate School: Insiders' Reflections on Academic Enculturation*, edited by Christine Pearson Casanave and Xiaoming Li, 90–104. Ann Arbor: University of Michigan Press.

15
MAKING SPACE FOR DIVERSE KNOWLEDGES
Building Cultural Rhetorics Editorial Practices

Malea Powell
Michigan State University

This is a story.

This story begins in an outdoor bar at an all-inclusive resort hotel in Puerta Vallarta in 1999. At that bar, on a muggy Mexican seaside evening, I became a journal editor just a year after completing my PhD and taking my first tenure-track job. I'd left graduate school with the goals of changing the way people learned about American Indians, intervening in canonical discourse about rhetoric histories in rhet/comp, and contributing to the growing body of Native scholarship in Native American literary studies. I just didn't know that editing a scholarly journal would be one of the ways I'd begin to accomplish those goals. Since then, a substantial part of my twenty-plus years of work as a scholar has been spent engaged in editorial work, first as editor of *Studies in American Indian Literatures (SAIL)*, then as a founder and editor in chief of *constellations: a cultural rhetorics publishing space*, and now as editor of *College Composition & Communication (CCC)*. As an editor, my baseline understanding has always been that we need more spaces for diverse scholarly voices and for diverse forms of scholarship and knowledge making in the fields, interdisciplines, and disciplines where my editorial work took place. In this chapter, I'll clear a path through my own diverse editorial career to highlight some ways to engage in Indigenous and cultural rhetorics practices as an editor. In walking that path together, we'll stop at some strategic places of advice gathered from the challenges I've faced in making slightly more space for scholars to theorize a diverse disciplinary future instead of just replicating a traditional past.

So, back to that bar. It was the hotel bar at the 1999 American Literature Association's first-ever Native American Lit Symposium. The symposium was a watershed moment for many Native scholars and writers. It was run as a real symposium conversation—one room with a large rectangular table where presentations took place sequentially. Our conversations during the symposium were very exciting, though sometimes contentious, as Native scholars spoke with longtime nonnative allies about the necessity of centering Native voices in scholarship focused on Native intellectual and creative practices. At the end of the second day, I found myself sitting at that bar alongside John Purdy and Bob Nelson—the editor and managing editor of *SAIL: Studies in American Indian Literatures*. *SAIL* was (and is) the only journal in the United States to focus exclusively on American Indian literatures (broadly defined to include all written, spoken, and visual texts created by Native peoples). Up until 1999, it had been edited by a string of non-Native folks. Those editors had always seemed to work hard to get Native scholars published, but the journal's editorial operations were more aligned with an older, less competitive academic culture than with the ways newer scholarly journal practices were supporting the increasing pressure on new scholars to be publications active.[1] John's approach to soliciting submissions was congenial and grassroots—he talked to folks at conferences and through his network, often working with young writers for months to mentor them to publication or relying on established ally scholars to do so. Bob's approach to the production work was hands on—he did it all, from copyediting to loading the finished files onto the journal's website to sending a list of *SAIL*'s content for each volume series to the MLA publications manager[2] so it could be listed in the MLA database (he also ran the website).

Anyway, there I was at that bar with John, Bob, and my very first Native graduate student Daniel Justice.[3] Somehow, the subject of the journal came up and John said something like this. "Malea," he said, "I'm ready to step down as *SAIL* editor but no one seems to want to take it over. Bob can keep doing his part of it, but we need a new editor. What kind of editor would you want for the journal?" I remember I said *SAIL* needed a Native editor, one who could bring the journal to a university press and bring Native scholarship front and center, like the *American Indian Quarterly* was doing. I know I made a long list of dreams about how the journal could mentor young Native scholars, bring back its creative writing features (where some very famous Native writers had been published first), and a lot of other things I only vaguely remember now. John praised my ideas and said, "Well, *you* ought to be the editor!" I laughed outright. Bob joined in with more encouragement, and John started pitching it seriously—the kind of support I'd need from my university, when he could make the transition, why a younger Native scholar was the right choice. Daniel chimed in too—he'd been an editorial assistant for *Great Plains Review* and knew how a journal run by a university press should operate. By the end of that night, I'd agreed to become the new editor of *SAIL* in my second year on the tenure track. The next day, I told my mentors—midcareer Native women scholars—and they freaked out completely. In retrospect, I understand their concern; back then, though, my own naïve, ambitious excitement far outweighed their good sense. I went back to the university, negotiated with my department chair and dean, and spent eight years as *SAIL*'s editor.

During those eight years, we published twenty-seven peer-reviewed issues of the journal (a total of about 135 individual essays plus poetry, short stories, and book reviews), to an audience of four hundred to seven hundred members. This was easily the equivalent of an edited book collection each year.[4] When I began that editorship, *SAIL* was xerographically produced at a local copy shop and listed only in the MLA index. Submissions were not regularly peer reviewed, and there was not a regular publication schedule. Immediately, Daniel and I created an editorial board (including a former book-review editor, Eric Gary Anderson, and a creative editor, Joe Bruchac), a doubly anonymous peer-review process, and a regular production schedule. Then I started pitching the journal to several university presses, eventually signing with the University of Nebraska Press in 2004 as one of the original ProjectMuse publications. During those first years with the press, we gained Thomson ISI coverage in the Arts and Humanities Citation Index and Current Contents: Arts and Humanities databases, as well as inclusion in the ERIC database. In other words, during the eight years of my editorship, *SAIL* went from a grassroots, self-produced insider venue to a peer-reviewed scholarly journal scholars in Native studies could use in their own cases for merit, tenure, and promotion. What that meant was that I had to teach myself a lot about how scholarly journals work, how they're valued in tenure and promotion processes, and how to actually pay for the brick, mortar, paper, ink, and labor of creating them.

All those things are important to universities, of course, but some of the other things we instituted were important for the interdiscipline of Native studies and the field of Native literatures. In creating a reliable, respected space for all scholars in that community (new, experienced, Native, non-Native) to engage in meaningful conversations with one another, we helped guide the field towards its current form. This meant I had to learn to deal with authors in a way my rash, hip, younger self hadn't quite envisioned. One part of that work was to cultivate and mentor Native and Indigenous scholars who'd consistently been trained to believe the academy wouldn't allow them to write or theorize from their own experiences *as* Native/Indigenous people and, instead, expected them to "support" their own knowledge with that of non-Native scholars. The work of encouraging them to center themselves and their community's knowledge in their scholarship was consistently rewarding. But another part of that work was to learn to see the value of those mainstream scholars who had, in fact, argued for the significance of Native writing during those formative "ethnic studies" years and had produced much of the scholarship in the field up to that moment. That work challenged who I thought I was and what I thought I believed. In fact, it was A. LaVonne Ruoff and Kenneth Roehmer who gently and kindly, but firmly, taught me the value of my non-Native elders in Native studies circles. I'm forever grateful to them for their gracious support and for their very real commitment to making space for all of us. And now, looking back, I can see how the way I was trained to aggressively and mindlessly critique any and all traditional work/structures actually damaged my ability to be a thoughtful, generous scholar.

Once I learned—through my relationship with very diverse scholars inside what was then a very small field of study—to see more nuance and complication than sheer positionality, to think rhetorically about the strategies being used to create (or close) space for conversation, I became not only a much better editor but also a better scholar.

Below are some of the more straightforward things I learned as editor of *SAIL*:

- Building editorial trust with diverse/Indigenous scholars is a long, careful process even when you are also Indigenous—it takes consistency and persistence over the long haul plus a willingness to learn new things, new ways to talk with folks about their work so they trust you with those revision suggestions;
- Small things can become really important—one of the first things we needed was to provide a contact list for all the Native nations referred to in each article and author bio—this made the sheer number and cultural multiplicity of Indigenous groups highly visible at a moment when the mainstream academy imagined them as quite the opposite;
- Collaborative editorial practices take more time, and they aren't comfortable for a lot of folks trained in Western scholarly traditions (this was as true for Native scholars as it was for many non-Native allies)—finding ways to norm collaborative practice inside these structures takes a lot of conversation and reflection, mistakes, and apologies;
- Editing is one of the best ways to make change in a field—editing provides an opportunity to shape and represent the breadth of conversations that take place, to practice equity and inclusion in order to maintain productive balance, and to contribute to a growing field

of scholarship by *making community* instead of just accumulating your own publications (which I was also doing).

I took those lessons into my nonediting work—program building, national leadership, graduate student mentoring, teaching, scholarship, and so forth. In the years between leaving *SAIL* (2008) and creating *constellations* (2014), I learned more about how the internal structures of the university worked *and* how the internal structures of large disciplinary organizations worked. My commitment to cultivating and mentoring scholars of color grew, especially those who've been told their work is "marginal" to their field/discipline/interdiscipline. Alongside that long-term commitment, I became increasingly interested in finding ways to make the invisible work of *creating community* in scholarly practice (like journal editing or national-organization service) both visible and rewarded. I also learned that making mistakes is okay, that it's a standard part of trying to create space and create a future for diverse disciplinary work.

My years in the CCCC chair's rotation helped me gain a substantial sense of the breadth, depth, and diversity of work scholars and teachers in rhet/comp were doing. But when I looked to our mainstream journals for meaningful representation of that diversity, I was sorely disappointed. The kind of diverse scholarship I had seen and heard at conferences, in visiting other universities, on social media, and in personal conversations was mostly absent from those mainstream publications. There are some standard (and true) reasons for that—print journals are expensive and simply can't publish all the excellent submissions they receive, for example. But during my time as CCCC chair, I had also accumulated a large and disturbing pool of stories from a range of folks (grad students, pretenure, nontenure, early, mid-, and late-career tenure-system faculty) who were also members of particular kinds of "affinity groups" (of color, queer, disabled, or living other minoritized[5] identities). Their stories had an intertwined set of common experiences. Each person had—implicitly or explicitly—been told by a journal editor (or a reviewer with whom the editor agreed) that their scholarship didn't "belong" in rhet/comp and/or that their approach to that scholarship didn't "fit" in rhet/comp. So, while I was personally seeing the level of scholarship in these minoritized areas increasing in both quantity and quality, that scholarship was less represented in our disciplinary publications than it had been when I was a grad student in the nineties. This was especially disturbing to me given my own belief that these were the very scholars envisioning and creating the future of the discipline.

In fact, inside my own NCTE/CCCC caucus, the joke was that while a nonnative scholar could easily publish *about* Native writing/rhetoric in our flagship journals, actual native scholars were consistently told their work didn't fit inside the discipline. The easy analysis here is, of course, as old as colonialism itself and eerily mirrored the conditions in Native literature studies that marked the early days of my *SAIL* editorship. That is, in order for Native knowledge to be "palatable" to non-Natives, it needed to be written from a non-Native (a.k.a., "unbiased") perspective and authorized by non-Native sources of knowledge. Frequently those non-Native scholars were speaking directly to/from a non-Native perspective that simply used Native writing to illuminate a more general point instead of investigating Native writing, rhetoric, theory, or methodology.[6] The word from Native rhet/comp scholars was that you had to "dumb down" or "white-ify" your Indigenous-centered analysis and representations in order to publish in a flagship journal. And I heard this from other minoritized scholars—Indigenous, Latinx, Chicanx, Black, African, Caribbean, Asian, Asian American, Arab, LGBTQIN, disabled, and so forth. So, I decided to do something about it. After all, what good was the privilege I'd earned during my years as a CCCC leader and as a full professor at research university if I didn't use that privilege to create something more—a space for the conversations that weren't being heard in mainstream journals —and do so by engaging in both collective and collaborative practice with other scholars? Thus: *constellations: a cultural rhetorics publishing space*.

As Phil Bratta and I say in our introduction to the cultural rhetorics special issue of *enculturation* (Powell and Bratta 2016), there are four interrelated events that led up to developing *constellations* as a digital, open-access journal: the collective scholarship that led to the publication of "Our Story Begins Here" (Powell et al. 2014), authored by members of the Cultural Rhetorics Theory Lab at MSU (this laid the groundwork for cultural rhetorics theory and methodology as collective, decolonial practice); the first-ever international Cultural Rhetorics Conference held at Michigan State University in October 2014 (CR-Con14); the "Cultural Rhetorics" special issue of *enculturation*, which garnered submissions from the 2014 conference participants; and, the formation of the Cultural Rhetorics Consortium, a collective of scholars whose research and teaching is substantially engaged with cultural rhetorics as a field of study.

Perhaps the most important of those events was the business meeting held at the end of CR-Con14. During that meeting, participants overwhelmingly asked for a publishing space where we could talk to each other without having to explain every single assumption of our work to a nonexpert audience, that the scholarship published there be doubly anonymously reviewed so it would "count" for institutional scholarship requirements, but that there be some way for cultural rhetorics scholars to be mentored as writers/makers during the editorial process. They also asked that this "dream" journal be multimodal and open access and that we develop some space for pedagogical conversations as well as the peer-reviewed publishing space. So, four of us (Phil Bratta, Cindie Tekobbe, Alexandra Hidalgo, and I) sat in a room one summer and started dreaming about a journal that would do all those things. It took a while to make it happen. Funding was an issue, so we spent several grant cycles attempting to fund the platform we wanted to build. We tried out several open-access-journal systems (like that offered by the Public Knowledge Project) and even some digital humanities installation platforms before we decided the relatively low learning curve of a WordPress site (plus a YouTube channel and a Vimeo account) would be best for us. At the same time, we spent hours figuring out how our editorial practices could match up with the methodological and ethical values of cultural rhetorics scholarship. Then we only had to recruit an entire community of scholars to help us fulfill the editorial vision we had built. The community that runs *constellations* is made up of an editor in chief, seven managing editors, five editorial-board members, thirty-three review-board members, a social media manager, a pedagogy blog editor, copyeditors, a full-time RA, and a technical editor.

As I said before, as a publishing space, *constellations* was explicitly designed to make space for the scholarship that didn't seem to fit into the mission (implicit or explicit) of many mainstream rhetoric and writing journals. It's a space for scholars and makers who've made a commitment to the values of cultural rhetorics scholars to engage in meaningful scholarly exchange and experimentation without always having to pull their efforts back to the so-called mainstream center. For me, *constellations* is a gathering space for scholars who will produce the future of the discipline in a radically different form than might be possible otherwise. At the same time, a piece published in *constellations* is still be recognized as a peer-reviewed publication for merit, promotion, and tenure at mainstream universities.[7] However, the collective work of creating this space presented (and continues to present) some interesting challenges. First, we had to think through what it meant to create a deliberately diverse and inclusive digital publishing space with a mentoring-focused editorial practice in relation to the "regular" mechanisms of publishing, like anonymous peer review. One of our solutions to this challenge was to run the early stages of submission as doubly anonymous, only launching the mentoring part of the process after a piece has been accepted, but this also meant talking frankly among ourselves and with our review team about the qualities we were looking for in a piece evaluated as accepted. Second, we had to pay close and careful attention to the human infrastructure that supported the publishing space. This meant our weekly meetings included both the work of the journal *and* a check-in for how everyone was doing: learning who needed help with tasks, making sure we were sharing equally across the community, and recognizing *all* efforts and engagements with the work of the journal. It meant caring for one another as humans and caring for our contributors as humans too. Third, we had to find ways to deliberately make the unseen, often unrewarded labor of digital builds and editorial practice persistently visible in the attribution practices of a publication. So we created a "Credits" section for each published piece so every person whose hands/minds touched that piece gets credit for their work. Not only does this reflect the collaborative nature of *all* disciplinary publication, it emphasizes the community/collective approach cultural rhetorics scholars center in their own intellectual activity.

Finally, as we worked our way through developing common workplace practices that reflected our theoretical and ideological commitments (remember, there are literally fifty people in the editorial community of the journal), we ran up against some entrenched inequities our efforts alone couldn't change. One big example of this came during one of our collective conference presentations at FemRhet 2017, when an audience member asked how we were going to manage the "gold-standard" metric for scholarly publication—rejection rates. I may or may not have gotten on a soapbox about the cruelty and violence of a profession that holds high rejection rates as a standard of prestige, especially when that profession is focused on writing and rhetorical practice. Nonetheless, the answer we gave came out of dozens of conversations we'd had across the journal's editorial community about just these kinds of inequities. Simply put, we wanted to change that standard. Surely we can imagine ways to see a different kind of prestige in a journal that is proud of its high rate of publishing submissions, of mentoring great ideas into publishable pieces? Our central goal at *constellations* is to *publish excellent scholarship*, not to send it on to another journal or to reject it because that first submission draft wasn't quite there yet. Yes, I know, this is why so many print journals use "revise and resubmit" to catch these kinds of submissions. But an "R&R" feels like a very different thing than an "accept with mentoring and revision." And our decision to choose a digital platform for the publishing space guaranteed we could, indeed, publish all the excellent scholarship that came our way.

So, how to go from working in such a radical, collective editorial community to taking on the editorship of *CCC*, one of the most mainstream of our discipline's journals? I won't lie. It's been a tricky transition. There's an editorial management system[8] already in place that took me nearly a year to learn to use at a basic level. It's a system that makes building relations with authors more difficult since it favors boilerplate responses instead of personal ones. While we've learned to work around that, it does add labor for my editorial assistant (Tania de Sostoa-McCue). There's a set of traditions in place as well that create inaccurate assumptions about what should/shouldn't be published in *CCC*. And there's also some significant lore about the lack of diversity (both demographic and scholarly) in the journal's history. But I took on the *CCC*'s editorship knowing these things already. So, I've made some fairly straightforward changes to bring cultural rhetorics editorial practices into my *CCC* work thus far. First, I revised the journal's mission to match that of the CCCC as an organization—a move that substantially broadens its scope and clarifies the journal's role as a place where scholarly conversations across the breadth of the discipline should be taking place. Second, I took a page from John Purdy's grassroots approach and have tried to initiate new lore via in-person and online conversations. Simply put, I want to see all kinds of scholarship from all kinds of scholars in our submissions pool.[9] Fourth, we also added dozens of new reviewer "tags" so we can more precisely match a manuscript with someone who does the same or very closely related work. Fifth, I've added a new category of acceptance.[10] We have a few more ideas in the works to improve engagement and create conversational spaces online, but work that fundamentally changes the culture of an environment like a mainstream print journal takes time, collaboration, and luck.

I'm not sure what's at the end of this *CCC* gig, but I think it's best if my path in this chapter ends with the core practice that has guided my life as a scholar, a teacher, a mentor, an editor, and a human. In some ways, Toni Morrison (2003) says it clearly in her now famous quote, "If you have power, then your job is to empower somebody else. This is not just a grab-bag candy game." For me, editorial practices in our discipline have often been too much of that "grab-bag candy game," too much hiding behind the supposed equity of our anonymous review practices that pretend each of us has the same access to the kinds of support and mentoring that lead to "publishable" prose, too much sleight of hand in relation to ideas and writing that don't speak directly to the most homogenously whitestream disciplinary audiences—ideas and writing that might challenge and upset those audiences. As I move forward as editor of *CCC*, then, I'll be guided by the visions of generations of BIPOC women/queer scholars and activists whose practices are so clearly summarized in Morrison's exhortation. It's that vision, forged in resistance and love, that has always led me to the key components of my editorial philosophy. That is, professional/scholarly journals (whether print or online) should create space for conversations; they should reflect both the now-established scholarly traditions that have created structure for the discipline/field and the new, edgy, challenging, risky, forward-thinking, future-building scholarship that will *be* the new tradition in twenty-five years. Journals should be lively, accessible spaces where *all* who engage in disciplinary/field conversations are welcomed, encouraged, supported, and represented. Journals should be a touchpoint for the community to create, reflect, and revise its practices. The job of an editor, then, is to foster that community even in the most mundane of editorial practices. What does that mean? It means taking chances, yes, even with the most mainstream of our disciplinary journals. By the time you read this, I imagine you'll have an opinion about how I'm doing with this kind of visionary balance. I hope you'll let me know what you think. Each of you is, after all, part of my intellectual community. Even if we don't agree, even if we don't like each other, we are connected as a large, diverse, lively community of humans dedicated to creating knowledge with, against, alongside one another.

NOTES

1. One of my senior colleagues at the University of Nebraska (my first tenure-system home) told me I had published more as a graduate student than he had when he got tenure at UNL.
2. *SAIL* is the journal for the Association for the Society of American Indian Literatures, an MLA organization.
3. Now professor of First Nations and Indigenous Studies and English at the University of British Columbia and the person who, along with Dr. James Cox (professor of English at the University of Texas at Austin), followed me as *SAIL* editor in 2008.
4. Thankfully, my new institutional home—Michigan State University—actually counted each volume series of the journal as an edited collected for the purposes of merit, promotion, and tenure.
5. I use *minoritized* here to emphasize that this scholarship has been narrativized as "minority," but, in my opinion, isn't marginal to the growth of our field at all.
6. This isn't to say there aren't non-Native scholars doing excellent work in Native/Indigenous rhetorics; in fact, there are quite a few non-Native scholars who've had the same experiences of having scholarship that centers Native theory or methodology rejected as not fitting inside the discipline.

7. I'm grateful Alexandra Hidalgo has continued and expanded on these practices since she's become editor in chief of *constellations*.
8. Literally called Editorial Manager, EM for short. This is the system all NCTE journals use, though Jonathon Alexander and I were the first two *CCC* editors to do our transition via EM, and the process had some significant bumps.
9. The previous editor, Jonathon Alexander, told me this work desperately needed to be done. He'd taken on diversifying the editorial-board during his term and advised I do the same with the reviewer pool. When we began reviewing submissions, there were about 50 active reviewers in the system. Now there are about 230. Given that each of the 182 submissions we received last year needed to be reviewed by at least two people, that's still a pretty small pool.
10. After all, despite being writing scholars, many of us never get good writerly mentoring in grad school or in the early years of our career. It's time we just admitted this instead of pretending we all have all the writing support we need.

REFERENCES

Morrison, Toni. 2003. "The Truest Eye." Interview with Pam Houston. *O Magazine*, November 2003. http://www.oprah.com/omagazine/toni-morrison-talks-love/all#ixzz520t7eq6c.

Powell, Malea, Daisy Levy, Andrea Riley-Mukavetz, Marilee Brooks-Gillies, Maria Novotny, and Jennifer Fisch Ferguson. 2014. "Our Story Begins Here: Constellating Cultural Rhetorics Practices." *enculturation* 18. http://www.enculturation.net/our-story-begins-here.

Powell, Malea, and Phil Bratta. 2016. "Introducing the Conversation: Engaging with Cultural Rhetorics." *enculturation* 21. http://enculturation.net/entering-the-cultural-rhetorics-conversations.

16
WON'T YOU BE MY NEIGHBOR?
How to Build Scholarly Community

Charles Bazerman
University of California Santa Barbara

By disposition I have tended to follow my own path, often at my own peril. Early on, however, I realized I needed companions, support, and communal wisdom in my journeys. I needed friends and neighbors to learn from and connect with. As I learned more about how disciplines communicate and form shared projects of knowledge building, I engaged more intentionally with networks of scholars. Consequently, I have repeatedly participated in and organized study groups, attended and organized conferences and seminars, built organizations, and edited special issues, volumes, and book series. These activities allow me to contribute to an academic world I can happily be part of. I see editing as part of this larger project of discipline building and the advancement of knowledge. While this essay is largely a personal narrative of editorial and related projects, it will, I hope, elaborate themes about the meaning and value of such work and what it can accomplish both for oneself and the profession. It will end with some explicit lessons I have learned about doing such work.

When in the late sixties I found literacy teaching to be a fulfilling way of life, research in writing studies was still in its early stages. As I developed my approach to teaching, some emerging ideas and lines of research helped me think through how I taught—whether Mina Shaughnessy's (1977) conception of basic writers; the use of noncanonical, popular texts (vide Donald McQuade and Robert Atwan's *Popular Writing in America* 1974); attention to students' thought and mental growth (in the styles of Ann Berthoff 1971 and James Moffett 1968); or focus on writing processes (as being explored by Linda Flower and John Hayes 1981). I also was an early member and first secretary of the CUNY Association of Writing Supervisors, where I began learning about conference organizing and building reading groups.

INTO THE SOCIAL WORLDS OF DISCIPLINARY WRITING

But I felt compelled to scratch a more social itch. The work that spoke most directly to me was James Britton, Tony Burgess, Nancy Martin, Alex McLeod, and Harold Rosen's (1975) investigation of how writing was tied to curricular structures, framed by assigned tasks and genres, which evoked different kinds of intellectual, stylistic, and personal practices. When Britton's project for writing across the curriculum in British schooling shook hands across the Atlantic with the emerging WAC movement in higher education, it created space for engagement with teachers of all disciplines and eventually an inquiry into the practices of those disciplines. I finally found a welcoming workspace that fit my intuitions and engaged me with others of similar interests.

As I started looking into the writing in different disciplines, I got drawn into questions of the intellectual and social arrangements of those fields. The sociology of science showed me how the organization, values, practices, and communicative channels of research disciplines formed within social networks and institutions, including publications. The role of journals in sponsoring, formulating, regulating, and creating space for the dynamic evolution of genres became even more clear as I studied the history of genres and their relation to particular journals. My own research revealed how much the emerging social structure of science was tied to editorial, reviewing, and readership roles created around the production and distribution of genres (Bazerman 1988). A bit later when I was studying the emergence of modern citation practices, I confronted Joseph Priestley's millenarian communal vision of scientific inquiry as a social process to be documented through recognition and discussion of each other's texts (Bazerman 1991).

As I went down this road connecting science studies and writing studies, I gathered fellow travelers in a series of symposia on rhetoric at science studies conferences throughout the '8os (see, for example Bazerman 1989). Review essays (Bazerman 1983, 1985) helped me sort through my own ideas and connected with others', especially Carolyn Miller's ground-breaking work on genre first presented at the 1979 CCCC (eventually appearing as Miller 1984). Her theoretical formulation of genre became central for a series of genre conferences (Ottawa 1992; Aarhus 1997; Vancouver 1998; Oslo 2001; Ottawa 2012) and related publications. These events showed me the importance of powerful concepts to bring people together, inspire work, and create venues for contribution and sharing.

EDITING AS ENGAGING OTHERS IN A RESEARCH SPACE

Miller's connecting the rhetorical contexts of situation with the phenomenological theories of sociology helped me articulate my own vision of the social structuring of discursive situations. The volume *Textual Dynamics of the Professions* I coedited with James Paradis (Bazerman and Paradis 1991) created space for others to build those connections through their own investigations of academic and professional writing. In this volume, as in almost all my editorial projects to follow, each of the submissions had to be based on detailed empirical study described with methodological precision and transparency. Every idea had to be earned through showing where and how it resided in the world. This stance was from the beginning skeptical of our received knowledge about writing and insisted we look into how writing was actually done in the world, what it looked like, and most of all, what it accomplished in the situations it was part of.

In working with authors developing their projects from initial proposals to final chapters, I started to experience the value and excitement of engaging in developmental dialogs. I appreciated the integrity of others' research data and the fundamental insights they got from working with their data. As the authors articulated what their data told them, my own vision grew, and my ideas modified to take into account what they were showing me. In trying to make useful comments, I learned to incorporate their perspective and reflect it back to them but as filtered through what I saw as the potential in their work.

Shortly thereafter David Russell and I coedited another kind of editorial project pulling together and interpreting earlier work in relation to current practice and programs: *Landmark Essays on Writing Across the Curriculum* (Bazerman and Russell 1994). David introduced me and the readers of the volume to the documents that lay behind his important historical research (Russell 1991). Making selections posed for us fundamental puzzles about the conceptual basis of WAC as a way of knowing about writing, which we addressed in two introductory essays on how WAC challenged traditional understandings of composition and rhetoric. Editing this volume deepened our understanding of how genres were responsive to systematically organized activity, and in turn structuring for those social organizations and activity—leading us to placing genre within activity and structurational theory frameworks. To foster work elaborating these ideas, David and I coedited a special issue of the journal *Mind Culture Activity* (Bazerman and Russell 1997). Each of the articles grew out of particular inquiries and advanced the views of the authors, yet each contributed to a general approach to understanding writing. To further develop the genre and activity theory perspective, a few years later, David and I coedited a volume *Writing Selves, Writing Societies* (Bazerman and Russell 2003). Many of these projects were already well developed before they were proposed for this volume, but they emerged out of a growing body of work supported by the earlier publications.

Simultaneously, starting in the mid-1990s I had been editing a series on *Rhetoric, Knowledge, and Society* with Erlbaum Publishers. This series, which was ultimately to include eleven volumes,[1] gave authors greater space to investigate how writing, genres, and rhetorical activity supported knowledge-based social systems. As books often took a number of years from initial proposal to final publication, I got to know the authors and their projects well, learning from their distinctive empirically grounded visions based on long study of their cases. Some books came as almost complete manuscripts, challenging me to respect their perspectives in order to provide a sounding board to help the authors present their visions for audiences that might not be so familiar with their points of view. Other projects were born more in dialog over dinner conversations or conference coffees as I learned the richness of what they were seeing in their research and reflected back the coherence I sensed they were reaching towards. Other books were between these poles, but each provided opportunities for discussions that expanded my own view. For each volume I wrote a brief introduction, which helped me articulate how the book looked from my perspective and how it expanded my vision.

Over the years, I have also been fortunate enough to be asked to provide introductions or commentary chapters on volumes edited by others. Although I was not engaged in developmental dialogs, writing these comments put me in a dialogic relation with the chapters, making sense of and commenting on them from my point of view, making connections to my own world and expanding my vision of the neighborhood I was visiting. I readily admit I was the beneficiary of the principle of the accumulation of advantage, or the Matthew Effect (Merton 1968). My editorial connections kept me current with much research and theory while building relationships with some of the more active contributors to the field. I was being nourished by this work even while, I hope, helping others.

MAKE KNOWLEDGE AVAILABLE

Another editorial project then catapulted me into the worlds of reference volumes and of open-access online publication. I was invited in

1999 to coedit a series of reference volumes in composition and rhetoric, but the print publisher soon dropped out, as did the coeditor. I, nonetheless, remained committed to the idea that the field of rhetoric and composition needed reference works to make it grow. Further, given the practical nature of the field, it was important to build connections among research, theory, the history of practices, and current best guidance for practice and programs (in this I was following the model of Joseph Priestley, whom I had studied recently—see Bazerman 1991). The publication dilemma came at an opportune moment, as Mike Palmquist of the WAC Clearinghouse was contemplating republishing out-of-print works as an open-access resource. The clearinghouse struck me as the right vehicle for newly published reference guides to reach teachers and researchers at many kinds of institutions, not all of which would have well-funded libraries. These books have in fact been downloaded widely internationally and have been a vehicle by which US composition research and practice has been connecting with the development of writing programs elsewhere (see Bazerman et al. 2008). I have continued to use the WAC Clearinghouse for other projects, as I discuss below.

One of the challenges of editing a reference series has been to maintain the volumes' focus on reporting the history, state of knowledge, and practice in the field rather than on the authors' particular arguments or research—at the same time as giving the authors the flexibility to present their subjects in the way they see best. An initial controlled outline to guide all books soon morphed into a list of functions that authors needed to fulfill, however the book was to be organized. The series now has ten titles with several more in process.[2] In 2011, I was joined by two younger editors, Anis Bawarshi and Mary Jo Reiff, to ensure titles continuing into the future.

Increasingly aware of the need for integrative reference works in writing studies, in 2003 I began work on a *Handbook of Research on Writing* (which appeared in 2008), with a particular focus on historic and social aspects of writing but also including school, individual, and textual issues. To make the book comprehensive and balanced and to identify strong international authors, I formed an international review board for the volume, who commented on the proposed table of contents and suggested possible contributors. The board members also helped me in reviewing particular chapters in their areas of expertise. The authors were all accomplished scholars with specific expertise and addressed specific expectations for the chapters; consequently, the main editorial challenge was to bring chapters down to length parameters since so much had been produced in some of the fields and so little consolidation had been done previously.

Text analysis also suffered from fragmented approaches, as studies and teaching materials tended to adopt a single perspective, whether rhetoric, linguistics, literary, content, cognitive process, or ethnography. Even when there was discussion of one or two alternatives, the alternative was viewed through the lens of the dominant perspective of the analysis. Students accordingly were likely to be introduced only to a single approach. To introduce students and scholars to a wider range of alternatives and to evaluate which would be most appropriate for each research question, Paul Prior and I organized and edited a collection in which each chapter was written by a scholar experienced in a particular method (Bazerman and Prior 2004). To ensure the chapters would provide a solid practical introduction to each of the methods with detailed instructions, elaborated examples, explanation of the underlying theoretical assumptions, practical guidelines, and bibliography for pursuing each of the methods more deeply, we provided the authors detailed outlines for structuring their chapters. As editors we then helped authors shape their presentations to meet the outline goals.

ADVANCING RESEARCH THROUGH CONFERENCES AND SEMINARS

Working on reference projects increased my appreciation of the different perspectives contributing to the growth of writing studies, though the knowledge remained fragmented. Although we had strong conferences focused on practices and programs, such as the annual CCCC, NCTE, IWAC, IWCA, and WPA meetings, as well as many other smaller independent events, research tended to take a back seat to more immediate practical issues. I initially tried to enrich the CCCC meeting through floating the idea of the Research Network in 1987 and with the help of Cheryl Geisler got it into the 1988 CCCC meeting as a preconference event, where it has remained. In 1991, in collaboration with Janice Lauer, we organized another group that has continued to meet preconference, the Consortium of Graduate Programs in Rhetoric. These organizations, under evolving leadership, have fostered the development of many emerging scholars and have supported the growth of a research culture in the field.

More recently, with the help of very engaged graduate students (including Paul Rogers and Suzie Null) and colleagues in the Santa Barbara Writing Program (including Karen Lunsford, Chris Dean, and Madeleine Surapure), I initiated what started as a small regional research-focused conference at UCSB in 2002 and 2005. This grew by 2008 into a much larger international Writing Research Across Borders Conference in Santa Barbara. This conference has since met in 2011 in Virginia, 2014 in Paris, and 2017 in Bogota; but for the pandemic, it was to meet in 2020 in Xi'an. Plans are now well underway for the 2023 meeting in Trondheim, Norway. WRAB in turn spawned the International Society for the Advancement of Writing Research, which now runs the conference. This conference brings together researchers of different perspectives, disciplinary backgrounds, theoretical orientations, and methods from many regions. Participants study writing at all stages of life, from early childhood through old age, as well as writers with atypical abilities. The studies reach far beyond classroom and formal educational settings to consider writing in workplaces, informal communities, social organizations, and even retirement activities. Starting in 2008, each of the conferences has been the basis of a volume of fifteen to twenty selected chapters. In each of these I have led teams of editors who have helped authors working in particular disciplinary, geographic, or theoretical settings to make their work accessible to readers of other backgrounds—providing contexts, elaborating and justifying assumptions, becoming more explicit about methods and findings, and identifying the value of the findings. Editors on these projects provide important mirroring functions as readers from outside the authors' intellectual worlds. Since these projects have large teams of editors, each editor can work closely on just three or four articles, allowing them to form a close relation with the authors, though in coordinating the editors I must make sure they align standards and goals and keep to similar deadlines. In some cases, I must provide additional assistance to address specific challenges posed by individual manuscripts. Also, in recent years we have been producing multilingual volumes to facilitate exposure to work from the conference-host region alongside work produced in English.[3]

During this period, my facilitator and editor roles stretched out in another direction, which was a totally unanticipated serendipitous gift. Because of my work on genre, I began receiving invitations to conferences and campuses in Brazil, and I soon became the international coordinator for a biannual conference on genre, SIGET (**Simpósio Internacional de Estudos de Gêneros Textuais**). I also helped edit conference volumes and special issues of multilingual journals, arising from the 2007 and 2009 SIGET conferences.[4] It was especially rewarding to mentor scholars with limited experience in international publication to make their work and research visible more widely with clarity and force.

The SIGET and WRAB conferences also began connecting me to scholars in other South American countries and Mexico, and I became aware of the emerging role of writing in higher education of the region. When I then had the good fortune of being advisor to a pair of doctoral students from Colombia and Chile and a number of other visiting scholars from South America, I saw the opportunity to connect separate initiatives being taken on different campuses in different countries. To encourage the building of regional networks, with a team of researchers from various countries I facilitated a project to document what was going on through surveys, interviews, and public website ILEES.org. The team produced a number of publications analyzing the emerging tendencies and their underlying institutional conditions and theoretical orientations.[5] I also coedited with a Brazilian scholar a special issue of the Brazilian journal *Ilha do Desterro* on the growth of writing in the region (Bazerman and Moritz 2016). As the network became self-sustaining with local leadership, including the formation of a regional society ALES.org, I stepped back, consulting only when asked.

This engagement with South American writing worlds has been truly enlightening and gratifying. I had previously been ignorant about the history and social complexity of the region, let alone the educational institutions, policies, and practices or the role literacy and writing was taking in education. I became aware of the great differences in the educational systems, educational cultures, and dominant intellectual traditions among the countries. But I also found very eclectic and open theoretical worlds, with strong dialog among proponents of different approaches. The teachers of writing are highly motivated and committed, seeing the importance of writing for developing their students, their social worlds, their democratic cultures, and prosperity, with implications for the development of their countries.

I also have long sensed the need for a summer seminar focusing on developing research methods and helping emerging researchers form mutually supportive research communities. Working with Christiane Donahue with the support of her institution Dartmouth University, an ideal location for a two-week summer retreat, we were able to realize this project in 2011, where it has continued since then. We (along with other contributing faculty and the support of interested organizations such as the Association of Writing Program Administrators) have provided opportunities annually for around twenty-five scholars of all levels to come together, develop their projects, provide each other feedback, and develop enduring collaborative networks. The alumni of this seminar now total well over two hundred. It has been a privilege to work with new generations of scholars and see many projects eventually come to publication and prominence.

ENGAGING A DISCUSSION ABOUT LIFESPAN DEVELOPMENT OF WRITING

Despite the work of reference books and increasingly broad-scope conferences, studies of writing still remained fragmented across ages of interest, and the developmental picture remained discontinuous. To advance discussion of developmental issues, I arranged a series of meetings of leading scholars working with different ages and from different perspectives: psychological, social, linguistic, multilingual, curricular, and assessment. Supported by the Spencer Foundation, we met face to face and virtually for four years. Even with the accomplishment, knowledgeability, and collaborative spirit of the team, advancing the discussion depended on strategic facilitation and mediation among the various viewpoints—to surface differences in assumptions, approaches, and methods and to help each appreciate the full implications of each other's positions. At the same time, I did not want to give up my own voice as a participant, so I often shifted roles—handing the management of the discussion over to another participant who was less caught up in the issue of the moment. We recorded and transcribed these discussions, and those transcriptions themselves provided the basis for further discussion and commentaries. These meetings were stimulating and deeply informative for all of us, broadening our views, as the participants often commented.

We regularly produced and circulated documents, comments, and drafts, at our face-to-face meetings and between meetings, to articulate our separate positions and to provide materials for group statements. De facto, I became the editor of our various statements, making connections among positions and organizing the group voice. Many of these documents were internal, but eventually we were able to agree on a public statement about principles to guide research on lifespan development of writing. This set of principles became the basis of a commentary article in *Research in the Teaching of English* (Bazerman et al. 2017) and appeared in more extended form in the volume from the project, *The Lifespan Development of Writing Abilities* (Bazerman et al. 2018). In these publications, we all served as reviewers of each other's work and the group statements, with me monitoring the whole project, setting deadlines, stepping in where needed, and assuring coherence—though I have never worked with such an efficient hard-working group, so I barely even had to hint at a nag.

To engage others in exploring developmental perspectives, I then edited a special issue of *Writing and Pedagogy* (2018). Then when a Writing through the Lifespan Collaborative formed, led by Ryan Dippre and Talinn Phillips, I gladly entered into those discussions https://www.lifespanwriting.org/.

MAKING RESEARCH OPEN ACCESS

As I have been pursuing these various editorial and profession-building projects, the publication landscape has been rapidly changing, with corporate consolidation and manipulation on one side and the rise of open-access digital production and distribution on the other. In studying the history of scientific and scholarly writing, I became familiar with the previously beneficial alliance between scholarly networks and commercial publishing industries, which often share common values and goals. Recently, however, this traditional symbiosis has been destabilized. Small publishers have been taken over by large corporations with little cultural affinity with academics and increasingly predatory practices. Digital publication and the internet then decreased many of the services provided by the publishers in a paper and print world. Nonetheless, the corporations attempted to use their hold on prestige and copyrights to increase monopolies and prices. On the other hand, these same new digital tools and communicative media provided means to return publication control to the academics who were doing the core work of writing, evaluating, refereeing, developmental editing, and using the texts. Mike Palmquist has done heroic work to build open access for our field at the WAC Clearinghouse, and I have taken advantage of the opportunities he made possible. Collections from the genre conference and the reference guides were among the first projects I moved to digital open access. I have also used the platform for volumes from the WRAB conferences and other volumes. Further, I have steered others to the clearinghouse. Digital publication has also allowed the opportunity for copublication or republication from other sources, including books published in various languages. While I still work with some of the remaining ethical commercial publishers when the nature of the project would benefit from it, open access has become my default, and I now refuse to review for the most predatory publishers.

LESSONS

The stories of my editorial and discipline-building projects over the preceding pages contain ways to perceive opportunities for productive scholarly discussion and strategies to nurture high-level exchange. Here more explicitly are some of the editorial lessons I learned along the way.

1. *Forming projects: Perceive the situation and frame the moment*
   a. Start with your own curiosities and budding projects but think how they connect with the interests of others and how a project that enlists the energies of others might carry your curiosities and ideas forward. Be open to the opportunities that might emerge and think how you might use them to advance issues you find important. Use editorial and discussion projects to build community, build research programs, and make a home where your own projects fit.
   b. Identify uncrystallized needs and energy that can be mobilized with the right forum or project. Look for pockets of potential energy that can be engaged and given direction. Look for the concept or idea, or concrete situation, that will give participants the clarity and focus they previously have not had.
   c. As good as a project might be, unless it can mobilize participation, it has not found the right place and moment for communal action. Sometimes projects are personal, with only you being able to see the potential and ready to go down the path. If so, it may be best pursued as your own project. But if it needs symbiotic growth with others, hold the project in your files until the right opportunity comes along. Similarly, if opportunities arise that don't match the values and goals that engage you, let them pass if you can afford to. If you don't place high value on your editorial projects, you cannot effectively communicate energy and enthusiasm to those you are enlisting in the discussion.
2. *Shaping and directing projects: Use your knowledge*
   a. Use your rhetorical knowledge to think about what you want to accomplish, what roles and projects you might take on, what needs the project addresses, and what form your participation and project might most effectively take on.
   b. Use your social knowledge of the publication distribution system, how disciplines are organized through texts, how genres are deeply purposeful, and how writing changes over time through strategic creativity to give shape to your proposals and seek venues.
   c. Use your knowledge of writing processes and how writers work to provide timely, tactful, and useful support.
   d. Use your teacher's knowledge of strategic facilitation, group processes, effective editing, and feedback in order to gain maximum engagement from your authors.
   e. Understand that texts are temporal interventions, not for all time, and the subjects will look different later. Help the authors to make the best case they can at this moment, as long as they are indeed showing something new. If they are onto something, then further publications can elaborate and answer technical objections.
3. *Relating with authors: Disciplined generosity*
   a. Once you are committed to a project, be generous with your time and

energy to keep the projects going, even if this sometimes means you must take on more of the work or difficult tasks than others to make the project succeed. Delegate, but supervise where necessary, and quietly pick up the pieces where needed.

b. Be generous in understanding the views and work of others, being willing to assume there is something to learn from them, but urge authors to articulate and refine their ideas when needed and raise concerns as issues to be discussed and addressed. Try to spot emergent messages in early versions of work or even unexpected potentials of the authors' projects they may not have yet focused on. Mirror back to the authors what you find that they might bring out more strongly.

c. Be prepared to be surprised, enlightened, and expanded by what others share. Remember the purpose of the article is to show you and other readers the new things the author has seen or understood.

d. No matter how pointed are your comments to authors, be encouraging and pose your concerns as solvable problems. Remind the authors that a publishable article can require a long process.

e. Be demanding but in harmony with the visions of the participants. They are following their own lights, and as an editor, it is your job to make that light as bright and penetrating as possible.

f. Keep in mind, and make sure the authors keep in mind, that the readers need to have an intensely rewarding experience, to engage with a clear, powerful, persuasive meaning in the final version.

g. If you are using reviewers, their comments can provide strong and demanding guidance, particularly if reinforced by your transmittal comments that show suggestions are not just the quirky demands of one individual. But also don't hide behind the reviewers to avoid your own editorial judgment. Think through what the reviewers say and how their comments can be synthesized, but it is also your role to identify what is most useful and to downplay that which is distracting or contradictory.

h. While you should not hold back on your views, in the end the piece of writing is the statement of the author, as long as they meet the criteria of the publication.

4. *Sharpening manuscripts: Power of facts and data, power of ideas, power of language*

a. Everything is potentially data of something, but of what? Believe in and demand evidence but be open to seeing what others see. Data can be of many sorts. As long as methods are defensible, take seriously what they show, even if they don't conform with what you think they might show. On the other hand, the data may be open to multiple interpretations or may show something beyond what the authors recognize. Help the authors see the true value of their data.

b. The power of facts and well-designed empirical work relies on detailed transparent presentations of methods for readers to understand and be persuaded by the evidence. Don't let the writer skip past the detailed presentation of the methods and initial findings or even reasoning to get to interpretations and conclusions. The reader needs to see

what is found and how it is found before being ready to consider the authors' characterization of what the data mean.
  c. Transparency of reasoning, organization, and coherence not only helps ease reading, it enables the readers to comprehend and accept the evidence and argument.
  d. Keep the reasoning and presentation moving forward, with the reader learning something new every sentence. Each sentence should reward attention and help readers cumulatively build a picture of what is being said. If potential objections are answered as they arrive or even before, readers are more likely to follow the path the author is offering. If the argument requires temporary digression, repetition, or backward motion, help the authors warn the readers so readers can follow and accept where the text is going.
  e. Precision of wording focuses meaning, minimizes digressive or misleading readings, and avoids inappropriate objections. Precise wording can support tight sentences and get rid of extra words. Precise wording and tight sentences allow readers to devote their cognitive energies to understanding and thinking about the ideas presented rather than to figuring out what the author means.
  f. Metaphor and other imagery can be useful to make concepts and stances present and accessible, but they must always be justifiable in advancing the reasoning.
  g. Almost everything improves with cutting.
5. *Keeping the process moving: Create exigence, energy, and timelines*
  a. Keep authors and coeditors informed of how the project is moving forward. Create a sense of deadline, reminding authors and coeditors of work in process, milestones, and next steps. Make deadlines as short as possible, while still being humane and realistic, to keep momentum going.
  b. Don't let one or two people hold up the project. Almost all will come through when you make timely completion a priority. And in the end, triage if necessary.
  c. In choosing collaborators consider their work ethic, timeliness, sense of responsibility, intellectual orientation, and commitment to the project. You are sharing an organizational project as much as an intellectual one. However, if your collaborators cannot fulfill their responsibilities for one reason or another, don't hold the project hostage to issues between editors. Pick up the slack to keep the project going.

CONCLUSIONS

Editorial work and, by extension, other forms of discipline-building work, do not always receive the credit or extrinsic rewards granted authorship. But the intrinsic rewards are great.

Without editorial and discipline-building work, not only would publications be less focused, less intelligible, and less persuasive, there would be no publications or forums. Editing and discipline building imagine the possibility of discussions, give them a place to emerge, and guide their realization. I first was drawn into editorial work because I saw that my own research would gain from being in dialog with others and that together we could have more of an impact. I then saw the value of mentoring others in work related to mine. Eventually I realized the whole disciplinary enterprise rested on communicative infrastructures, and these needed to be in place for all scholars and practitioners in the field to thrive and grow. This volume offers the testimony of many others who have helped build and maintain that communicative infrastructure, though they have come to that commitment through different paths.

Editorial work makes the profession possible and gives us the justified feeling of being part of something bigger than oneself. It also gives us the joys of coming to appreciate the work of others, contributing to its development, and learning from colleagues. It helps extend our vision and deepen our understanding of the subject and practices we have devoted our lives to. It helps us, along with our colleagues, to see just a bit further down the road, which is a pleasure in itself.

NOTES

1. See Winsor 1996; Van Nostrand 1997; Prior 1998; Petraglia-Bahri 1998; Swales 1998; Atkinson 1998; Dias et al. 1999; Flower, Long, and Higgins 2000; Blakeslee 2000; Salazar 2002; and Sauer 2002.
2. See Lauer 2004; Bazerman et al. 2005; Horning and Becker 2006; McLeod 2007; Long 2008; Ramage et al. 2009; Bawarshi and Reiff 2010; Horning and Kraemer 2012; Ray 2015.
3. See Bazerman et al. 2010; Bazerman et al. 2012; Plane et al. 2016; and Bazerman et al. 2019.
4. See Bazerman, Bonini, and Figueiredo 2009; Figueiredo, Bonini, and Bazerman 2007; Bonini, Figueiredo, and Bazerman 2009; Bazerman and Baltar 2010; Parodi and Baltar 2010.
5. See Bork et al. 2014; Tapia-Ladino et al. 2016; and Navarro et al. 2016.

REFERENCES

Atkinson, Dwight. 1998. *Scientific Discourse in Sociohistorical Context: The Philosophical Transactions of the Royal Society of London, 1675–1975*. Mahwah NJ: Lawrence Erlbaum.

Bawarshi, Anis, and Mary-Jo Reiff. 2010. *Genre: An Introduction to History, Theory, Research, and Pedagogy*. Fort Collins CO: WAC Clearinghouse.

Bazerman, Charles. 1983. "Scientific Writing as a Social Act: A Review of the Literature of the Sociology of Science." In *New Essays in Technical Writing and Communication*, edited by Paul Anderson, John Brockmann, and Carolyn Miller, 156–184. Farmingdale, NY: Baywood.

Bazerman, Charles. 1985. "Studies of Scientific Writing: E Pluribus Unum." *4S Review* 3 (2): 13–20.
Bazerman, Charles. 1988. *Shaping Written Knowledge: The Genre and Activity of the Experimental Article in Science.* Madison: University of Wisconsin Press.
Bazerman, Charles. 1989. "Rhetoricians on the Rhetoric of Science (Symposium)." *Science, Technology, & Human Values* 14 (1): 3–6.
Bazerman, Charles. 1991. "How Natural Philosophers Can Cooperate: The Rhetorical Technology of Coordinated Research in Joseph Priestley's History and Present State of Electricity." In *Textual Dynamics of the Professions*, edited by Charles Bazerman and James Paradis, 13–44. Madison: University of Wisconsin Press.
Bazerman, Charles. 2008. *Handbook of Research on Writing: History, Society, School, Individual, Text.* Mahwah, NJ: Lawrence Erlbaum.
Bazerman, Charles, ed. 2018. "Writing Development Across the Lifespan." Special issue, *Writing and Pedagogy* 10 (3).
Bazerman, Charles, Arthur Applebee, Virginia Berninger, Deborah Brandt, Steven Graham, Jill V. Jeffery, Paul Kei Matsuda, Sandra Murphy, Deborah Rowe, Mary Schleppegrell, and Kristen Wilcox. 2018. *Lifespan Development of Writing Abilities.* Urbana, IL: NCTE.
Bazerman, Charles, Arthur Applebee, Deborah Brandt, Virginia Berninger, Steven Graham, Paul Kei Matsuda, Sandra Murphy, Deborah Rowe, and Mary Schleppegrell. 2017. "Taking the Long View on Writing Development." *Research in the Teaching of English* 51 (3): 51–60.
Bazerman, Charles, and Marcos Baltar, eds. 2010. "Genre." Special issue, *Revista Brasileira de linguística aplicada* 10 (2).
Bazerman, Charles, David Blakesley, Michael Palmquist, and David Russell. 2008. "Open-Access Book Publishing in Writing Studies: A Case Study." *First Monday* 13 (1). http://www.uic.edu/htbin/cgiwrap/bin/ojs/index.php/fm/article/view/2088/1920.
Bazerman, Charles, Adair Bonini, and Debra Figueiredo, eds. 2009. *Genre in a Changing World.* Fort Collins, CO: WAC Clearinghouse.
Bazerman, Charles, Christopher Dean, Jessica Early, Karen Lunsford, Suzanne Null, Paul Rogers, and Amanda Stansell, eds. 2012. *International Advances in Writing Research: Cultures, Places, Measures.* Fort Collins, CO: WAC Clearinghouse.
Bazerman, Charles, Blanca Yaneth González Pinzón, David Russell, Paul Rogers, Luis Bernardo Peña, Elizabeth Narváez, Paula Carlino, Montserrat Castelló, and Mónica Tapia-Ladino, eds. 2019. *Conocer la escritura: Investigación más allá de las fronteras; Knowing Writing: Writing Research across Borders.* Bogota: Universidad Javeriana.
Bazerman, Charles, Robert Krut, Karen Lunsford, Susan McLeod, Suzanne Null, Paul Rogers, and Amanda Stansell, eds. 2010. *Traditions of Writing Research.* London: Routledge.
Bazerman, Charles, Joseph Little, Teri Chavkin, Danielle Fouquette, Lisa Bethel, and Janet Garufis. 2005. *Writing Across the Curriculum.* Fort Collins, CO: WAC Clearinghouse.
Bazerman, Charles, and Maria Moritz, eds. 2016. "Writing in Latin American Higher Education." Special issue, *Ilha do Desterro* 69 (3).
Bazerman, Charles, and James Paradis, eds. 1991. *Textual Dynamics of the Professions.* Madison: University of Wisconsin Press.
Bazerman, Charles, and Paul Prior, eds. 2004. *What Writing Does and How It Does It.* Mahwah, NJ: Lawrence Erlbaum.
Bazerman, Charles, and David Russell, eds. 1994. *Landmark Essays in Writing Across the Curriculum.* Davis, CA: Hermagoras.
Bazerman, Charles, and David Russell, eds. 1997. "The Activity of Writing; The Writing of Activity." Special issue, *Mind, Culture and Activity* 4 (4).
Bazerman, Charles, and David Russell, eds. 2003. *Writing Selves, Writing Societies.* Fort Collins, CO: WAC Clearinghouse.

Berthoff, Ann. 1971. "The Problem of Problem Solving." *College Composition and Communication* 22 (3): 237–242.
Blakeslee, Ann. 2000. *Interacting with Audiences: Social and Rhetorical Practice in Ordinary Science*. Mahwah, NJ: Lawrence Erlbaum.
Bonini, Adair, Debra Figueiredo, and Charles C. Bazerman, eds. 2009. "Writing Education in Brazil, L1." Special issue, *Educational Studies in Language and Literature* 9 (2).
Bork, Anna Valeria, Charles Bazerman, Francini Correa, and Vera Cristovão. 2014. "Mapeamento das iniciativas de escrita em língua materna na educação superior: Resultados preliminares." *Revista Prolíngua* 9 (1): 2–14.
Britton, James, Tony Burgess, Nancy Martin, Alex McLeod, and Harold Rosen. 1975. *The Development of Writing Abilities, 11–18*. London: Macmillan Education for the Schools Council.
Figueiredo, Debra, Charles Bazerman, and Adair Bonini, eds. 2007. "Genre and Social Identities." Special issue, *Linguistics and the Human Sciences* 3 (1).
Parodi, Giovanni, and Marcos Baltar, eds. 2010. "Genre." Special issue, *Linguagem em (dis)curso* 10 (3).
Petraglia-Bahri, Joseph. 1998. *Reality by Design: The Rhetoric and Technology of Authenticity and Education*. Mahwah, NJ: Lawrence Erlbaum.
Plane, Sylvie, Charles Bazerman, Fabienne Rondelli, Christiane Donahue, Arthur Applebee, Catherine Boré, Paula Carlino, Martine Marquillo Larruy, Paul Rogers, and David Russell, eds. 2016. *Recherches en écriture: Regards pluriels/Writing Research from Multiple Perspectives*. Metz: University of Metz; Fort Collins, CO: WAC Clearinghouse.
Prior, Paul. 1998. *Writing/Disciplinarity: A Sociohistoric Account of Literate Activity in the Academy*. Mahwah, NJ: Lawrence Erlbaum.
Ramage, John, Michael Callaway, Jennifer Clary-Lemon, and Zachary Waggoner. 2009. *Reference Guide to Argument*. Fort Collins, CO: WAC Clearinghouse.
Ray, Brian. 2015. *Style: An Introduction to History, Theory, Research, and Pedagogy*. Fort Collins, CO: WAC Clearinghouse.
Russell, David. 1991. *Writing in the Academic Disciplines, 1870–1990*. Carbondale: Southern Illinois University Press.
Salazar, Phillippe-Joseph. 2002. *An African Athens: Rhetoric and the Shaping of Democracy in South Africa*. Mahwah, NJ: Lawrence Erlbaum.
Sauer, Beverly. 2002. *Rhetoric Under Uncertainty*. Mahwah, NJ: Lawrence Erlbaum.
Shaughnessy, Mina P. 1977. *Errors and Expectations: A Guide for the Teacher of Basic Writing*. New York: Oxford University Press.
Swales, John. 1998. *Other Floors, Other Voices: Toward Textography and Beyond*. Mahwah, NJ: Lawrence Erlbaum.
Tapia-Ladino, Monica, Natalia Avila Reyes, Federico Navarro, and Charles Bazerman. 2016. "Milestones, Disciplines and the Future of Initiatives of Reading and Writing in Higher Education: An Analysis from Key Scholars in the Field in Latin America." *Ilha do Desterro* 69 (3): 209–222.
Van Nostrand, A. D. 1997. *Fundable Knowledge: The Marketing of Defense Science and Technology*. Mahwah, NJ: Lawrence Erlbaum.
Winsor, Dorothy. 1996. *Writing Like an Engineer: A Rhetorical Education*. Mahwah, NJ: Lawrence Erlbaum.

AFTERWORD

On "Becoming" an Editor

Greg Giberson
Oakland University

My original plan for this afterword was to try to offer some distillation of the chapter contents—some sort of succinct version of the advice offered across the chapters in particular, given that one of the main goals for the collection from the beginning was to bring some transparency to the editorial process for the benefit of those emerging and seasoned scholars who feel forced to navigate it without so much as a compass. When I sat down to begin writing, however, I found that attempts to distill the thoughtful, insightful, and contextually rich advice from the chapter authors quickly turned it into what sounded like cheap platitudes. So, I rejected that idea (which stung just a bit) and decided to go in a different direction.

The majority of the authors in this collection include some sort of narrative history of their work as editors. While they are all different, they also share some similarities. In particular, across the chapters, the narratives tell similar stories of individuals becoming editors—a process, not just an assumed title. There seem to be significant shifts in the ways many of the authors write about their editorial work as they recount the passing of time and their growth through experience. In a sense, the narratives become less synthetic and more descriptive and declarative as time passes, as if the authors' versions of themselves as neophyte editors necessitated detailed explanations and anecdotes that helped explain the early histories of how they traveled to certain editorial "places," why they made certain choices, and the like. However, as the narratives progress and authors discuss their more recent or more mature editorial selves, their language and explanations of what they do and how they approach their work become more direct, lacking the sort of justifying language so many of us have utilized at times in our careers. It's as if their work as editors became tacit implementations of the earlier, neophytic becoming narratives—an editor is something they now are, not just something they do.

I think it might be interesting to explore that idea just a bit more using a personal anecdote that will likely inspire some cringeworthy memories for many readers. As a job candidate and later as a first-year academic, I often found myself citing sources and referencing scholars and specific theories when responding to questions or engaging in discussions with my colleagues in faculty meetings ("I'm a social constructionist who believes in process theory!"). I've seen the same sort of uncomfortable behavior from job candidates and new colleagues over the years, and I'm quite sure we've all had (or will have) similar experiences at some point in our careers. When it was my turn, I recognized what I was doing, and I remember feeling embarrassed and illegitimate, but I also had no idea how *not* to do it ("Back at my graduate institution, we taught . . ."). I had yet to gain enough experience in these positions to recognize myself as having become that which I was supposed to be (at least by title). Now, as a full professor in a department of writing and rhetoric, I only reference other scholars or specific theories and the like when absolutely necessary or in the classroom. That knowledge, those characters, and their impact on my own work and thinking have become a part of me as a scholar, and my thoughts, my stories, my work have become Me—referencing the bibliography of that becoming is only necessary when circumstances necessitate it.

I have to admit that paragraph was fun to write. Those early career moments are the ones that creep into my head when I really need to sleep but my brain wants to torture me for whatever reason by forcing me to relive those silly, embarrassing moments. The point is, from my perspective, that while there is no one way to become or be a successful editor, this collection makes clear that to become an Editor, one must begin by editing. Over time, each of the authors in this collection transitioned from editing their different venues and became the Editor of them—eventually taking tacit ownership of the work they were doing, the decisions they were making, and the like. I want to say a little more about this, but first I want to share the story of the collection.

***

After my third collection was published in 2015, *Writing Majors: 18 Program Profiles*, I promised myself (and my spouse and our two kids) I would not take on another book project, at least not a collection. For those who have never attempted to publish an edited collection, it can *seem* pretty straightforward. Indeed, during my review for promotion to professor in 2020, one of the review committees asked to meet with a member of my department's review committee and myself specifically to discuss the nature of edited collections and the work of editors of such volumes. One of the committee members, I believe a biologist, asked, "How is *this* intellectual work? You just get a bunch of essays together and publish them as a book!" This sentiment is commonly held and a clear example of the lack of understanding and lack of recognition of the important intellectual and scholarly contributions of editors, which several authors in this collection address (in particular Matsuda).

However, developing, organizing, structuring, editing, and ultimately publishing a successful edited collection is no simple endeavor. It takes a great deal of time, patience, dedication, and organization. It takes good communication and organizational skills. Sometimes working with eighteen to thirty different authors can be challenging . . . who would have thought, right? Most important, publishing a successful edited collection takes focus and intellectual clarity regarding the purpose and value of the collection to the scholarly conversations it is meant to contribute to. It takes the vision to identify and secure commitments from the authors most well suited to facilitate accomplishing the goals for the volume. Finally, it takes an editorial ethos to keep contributors focused on the broader goals as they pursue their own individual visions as chapter authors—most of the time this is enjoyable work; at others, not so much. To put it directly, editing a collection is very hard work. But, a little grudgingly, I digress.

Having written off edited collections in 2015, I woke up at 3 a.m. (naturally) in November of 2018 with an almost fully formed idea for a new one—a really good one, I thought. I rolled out of bed, stumbled in the dark to my den, turned on my Mac, and wrote what eventually would become most of the introduction for the proposal for this collection. At the time, I was about three months into my term as managing editor of *Composition Forum*, and I was struggling. I had previously served as an assistant editor for *WPA*, and a section editor at *Composition Forum* and had edited three collections. However, the managing-editor position was different. There were peer reviews to organize and manage. There were missing, late, and conflicting reviews to deal with, decisions to be made about what to publish, and the like. While I had a pretty general understanding of the nature of the work when I started, I didn't know quite how to do it or why, or even if, it should be done a certain way. During those first few months, I was "doing" it, of course. But it still wasn't clear to me why I was doing it the way I was doing it. What drove my decisions on sending out or rejecting submissions? Why was I choosing certain reviewers, and how was I determining the order in which I would contact them? Why did I choose to take a more informal tone in my communications with authors and reviewers than I had been used to as a scholar? There were also more general, but consequential, questions like, "What the hell am I actually doing?" and "What is my connection to the scholarship I am publishing?" Indeed, "How did I get here?" was the question I asked myself the most often. These questions were symptoms of the issue at the heart of this collection—the issue that inspired the subtitle for the collection. While I knew in a general sense the things editors did, I had little idea of *what* they were doing behind that editorial curtain. I woke up at 3 a.m. that November morning because I had finally reached a tipping point with the anxiety the lack of answers to these questions was causing me and decided it was time to ask them intentionally and attempt to answer them as directly as I could.

While the concept for the collection came before I began researching whether or not there were acceptable answers already available, subsequent research demonstrated there were not many answers out there. I found a lot of materials about publishing and editing as an activity. But I didn't find much at all about what it means to be an editor and the role editors play in the intellectual and scholarly work of academic fields. In 2019, *College English* published a special issue on the topic, which reaffirmed for me that there was interest in the subject and that the collection I was working on was timely. But a question I posed on WPA-L well before the *CE* special issue really showed me I was onto something. In a short post to the list, I simply asked people to share the names of editors over the last thirty years who had an important impact on them personally, professionally, or both, and to share some specifics if they wanted to. Over the next few days, the post received more than one hundred responses, most on the list itself, but a few dozen people contacted me directly. As a list member for many years, I was pretty shocked by the number of responses and the enthusiasm of the responders. People wanted to tell their stories—they wanted someone else to know a particular editor (or editors) had dramatically impacted their lives.

So, I made a list of the editors people wrote about and kept track of those who were mentioned most often. I had heard of most of them, but there were a few names new to me. I went about researching each of them while building a sort of editorial biography for each, noting the venues where they served as editors and the time frames. I noted whether or not they were founding editors of any venues. I made lists of noteworthy publications that came out under their editorial direction,

Afterword: On "Becoming" an Editor   233

and so forth. I made sure to cross-reference the WPA-L comments with my biographies to see if there were particular editors who seemed to have the most impact on people or the field. In the end, I had a list of forty different names, each with a unique editorial biography.

I wanted *Behind the Curtain of Scholarly Publishing* to cover the subject in both breadth and depth, so I organized my list of potential authors based on different types of publication venues. I wanted to have somewhat of a balance between those working primarily with journals and those working in book publishing. Of course, many of those on my list had worked as editors of both in some fashion, but I tried to be sure my list of potential authors would allow readers to explore the role of the scholarly editor from as many different perspectives as possible. From my original list of forty potential authors, I narrowed it down to twenty who would receive the first invitations, with the goal of securing between fifteen and eighteen chapter authors. I assumed it would be necessary to go beyond that original list, but, to my surprise, all the authors appearing in this collection were on that original list. Three of the invitees declined because they were retired and not writing anymore, and one, unfortunately, had to drop out during the drafting process. This long anecdote is a roundabout way of saying people seemed, at least to me, very interested in the topic. Since the collection now has potential readers, I sure hope I was right.

***

To bring this afterword and this collection to a close, I want to return to the final point I was making in the first section of this afterword and explore it a bit more as it relates to my different "editor-at-work" stories shared above. The list of questions I offer about my early experiences as managing editor of *Composition Forum* is an example of what someone who is editing a journal for the first time (or their first book, etc.) thinks about. When we're doing something new, and we have little to no understanding of what that thing really is, we tend to fumble around, trying to do what we think it is we are supposed to be doing, while not knowing whether we are doing it correctly or for the correct reasons—in other words, we try to act as if we know what we're doing when we don't. Those in the know likely see right through us ("I'm a social constructionist and believe in process pedagogy"). That was me when I conceived *Behind the Curtain of Scholarly Publishing*—the person at *Composition Forum* who was doing the work of managing editor, but I was not the managing editor, at least not yet; I was barely managing.

I also share the concurrent story of the development of this collection to show I had the idea, worked through the process of researching and developing it into a proposal, selected coeditors and authors, and so forth. Unlike my editing early on at *Composition Forum*, I had no questions about how to do it. I had done it before . . . three times. I already knew how *I* created edited collections. In other words, I had already become an editor of collections. The first one, *The Knowledge Economy Academic and the Commodification of Higher Education* (2009), was a real challenge. My brother/coeditor and I had no idea what we were doing. We fumbled around in the dark, doing the work we thought editors of collections are supposed to do, but we did not feel as if we were really editors (indeed we learned a lot of lessons about how not to be!). That type of editorial work has become tacit, and I don't have to deal with questions about how to do it and why I do what I do. I don't have that anxiety and internal doubt that inspired me to create this collection. I just did it—just like the other editors included in this book—because that's how *I* do it (and, now, after a few years of editing a journal, I feel the same way). That's not to say there's no more to learn but that learning is now contextual. I hope to continue to improve and am always open to change, but I have a framework within which new ideas and new circumstances can be understood and adapted to.

I find these narratives of becoming interesting for several reasons. Most important among them is that they suggest a certain egalitarianism to editing. Most of the authors suggest in one way or another that they didn't set out to be editors. It kind of happened as a result of some decisions they made, or by happenstance, or through some other exigency (Mickey Harris's chapter is a great example of how one thing can lead to another and to another and then you all of the sudden find yourself editing a journal). In other words, the stories suggest to me there are probably a lot of people who would excel at this work but who have not pursued it because so much about it has been mysterious and seemingly inaccessible.

I hope that this collection fulfills the goal I had of pulling back the curtain a bit and that these glimpses behind the scenes and the advice offered in each chapter are beneficial to emerging and accomplished scholars alike. I hope readers will feel better prepared for and more comfortable with the vetting and publishing processes that is, too often, opaque and elusive. I also hope readers will appreciate the hidden histories of journals and other publications offered across chapters. I believe those histories can help us understand a little better where we as a field came from and why we are where we are. I also hope the chapter authors have helped make the case for understanding scholarly editing for the intellectual work it truly is. Scholarly editors play an influential and crucial role in the short-term and long-term intellectual development of their respective fields, as these chapters demonstrate. Finally, I hope this collection inspires others to explore *becoming* editors themselves. As members of a field that values and encourages (and often demands, rightfully so) diversity and inclusion, we will all benefit from continuing to broaden and diversify our field's editorial perspectives and contributions.

REFERENCES

Giberson, Tomas, and Greg Giberson. 2009. *The Knowledge Economy Academic and the Commodification of Higher Education.* Cresskill, NJ: Hampton.

INDEX

accessibility, 21, 172, 177–178; guidelines, 168, 173, 176; web, 84–85, 132, 169–170
accommodation, 42, 53, 146–147
acquisitions, xi
administrator, 75, 125; writing program, 42–43, 48
Alexander, Lynn, 61
American Association for Applied Linguistics (AAAL), 195
Anderson, Rick, 50
Association for Writing Across the Curriculum (AWAC), 122
Atwill, Janet M., 61

Bailie, Brian, 90
Baker, Lewis, 65
Ball, Cheryl, 9, 87, 95, 100, 124, 126, 127, 169, 172, 173, 175, 178
Ballard, Kim, 50
Ballenger, Bruce, 61
Bartholomae, David, 9, 59, 110, 157
Bathgate, Linda, 193
Bawarshi, Anis, 90, 217
Bazerman, Charles, 10, 59, 75, 97, 121, 124, 214, 215, 216, 217, 218, 220, 221
Beale, Walter H., 108
Berlin, James A., 4, 57, 58, 60, 64, 65
Berthoff, Ann, 213
Birkenstein, Cathy, 155
Bizzell, Patricia, 58, 105, 106, 111, 112, 184
Blakesley, David, 71, 74, 123
Blalock, Glenn, 69, 125, 127
Blitz, Michael, 64
Bostdorff, Denise M., 65
Boyle, Casey, 181
Brandt, Deborah, 69, 71
Bratta, Phil, 207, 208
Brereton, John, 106, 107
Britton, James, 214
Brock, Kevin, 84, 86, 89, 90, 132
Brooke, Collin, 186
Brown, Jim, 181
Bruchac, Joe, 204
budget, 21, 34–35, 43, 45, 48, 82, 106, 182
Butler, Judith, 155

call for proposals (CFPs), 4, 25, 96
Campbell, Joann, 106
Carabelli, Jason, 72
Caraher, Brian G., 66
challenges of editing, ix, 4, 42–43, 71, 140, 142, 147, 199–200, 208–209, 217, 219, 234; logistical, 74, 75; technological, 172
challenges of publishing, 82–83, 84, 117
Charm, Stuart L., 67
Chinn, Sarah, 60
Chomsky, Noam, 68
circulation, 19, 107, 129, 133, 179, 183
citation practices, 55, 85, 89, 123, 126, 134–136, 168, 172, 178, 182, 186, 214
co-editing, 94, 194–196
Coles, Nick, 110
collection, 4, 89, 93–94, 193, 195–200
College Composition and Communication (*CCC*), 9, 10, 39, 73, 74, 92–101, 123, 128, 147, 151, 158, 202, 210–211
College English (*CE*), 6, 7, 15, 17–19, 21, 31, 39, 59, 71, 100, 128, 134, 232
community: college, 155, 157; editorial, 41, 74, 101, 174, 209–210, 223; scholarly, 7, 28, 29, 36, 42, 50, 97–99, 123, 146, 147, 172, 206, 208–209, 211
Community Writing, 109
Composition Forum, 70, 78, 80–90, 132, 231–232, 233–234
CompPile, 35, 122, 125, 132
Computers and Composition, 84, 100, 170
Conference on College Composition and Communication (CCCC), 40, 74, 76, 92, 95–96, 101, 111, 120, 121, 122, 124, 126, 132, 158, 160, 166, 178, 188, 189, 195, 196, 206, 207, 210, 214, 218
Connors, Robert, 7, 29, 39, 42, 50, 61, 106
Cooper, Charles, 140
Cooper, Marilyn, 95
Cope, Bill, 106
Cope, Karin M., 60
copyediting, 30–32, 34, 36, 93, 95, 115, 131, 158, 161, 165, 166, 167, 172, 175–176, 178, 203

INDEX

copyright, 31, 35, 80, 123, 129, 130–131, 132, 222
costs, 27, 32, 34, 79, 81–82, 128, 131, 133, 134, 187–188; distribution, 45–46, 87; management, 85; membership dues, 21; subscription, 48, 123
Covino, William, 59
Covino, Deborah A., 60
Cowley, Malcom, 65
Cox, Michelle, 196
Crowley, Sharon, 59, 68, 106, 107, 108
Cullen, Darcy, 142
Cummings, Kate, 60

Davis, Diane, 108
Davis, Matt, 96
Dean, Chris, 218
Dean, Tim, 64
digital edited collections (DECs), 49
Dilger, Bradley, 84, 85, 89, 90, 132
Dingo, Rebecca, 108
Dippre, Ryan, 222
distribution, 79–80, 83, 89, 119, 130, 131, 214, 222, 223
diversity, xi, 34, 38, 83, 89, 92, 96, 126, 140, 141, 145, 178, 182, 189, 194, 198, 206, 210, 235
Donnelly, Michael, 61
Downing, David B., 61
Drew, Julie, 82

Eberly, Rosa A., 61
Ede, Lisa, 57
editorial board (EB), 35, 70, 72, 73, 74, 75, 110, 122, 123, 125, 126, 129, 142, 143, 169, 171, 178, 204
editor: acquisitions, 110, 176; assistant, 4, 28, 51; book review, 83; co, 200, 225; copy, 29, 37, 157, 194, 208; graduate, 3–4, 19, 27, 34, 181, 186; guest, 89; managing, 33, 70, 171, 176, 185, 231–232, 233; special issue, 93, 96
enculturation, 7, 83, 123, 130, 134, 181–190
Enos, Theresa, 62, 66
Epps-Robertson, Candace, 109
Eyman, Douglas, 9, 95, 123, 124, 126, 127, 172, 175, 177

Faigley, Lester, 64, 105, 106, 107, 111
Falkin, Gregory, 63
feedback, 23, 31, 33, 35, 36–37, 44, 51–53, 55, 73, 119, 149, 165, 170–171, 174, 175, 179, 184, 186, 196, 197, 199, 220, 223. *See also* peer-review
Feehan, Michael, 64
fees. *See* costs

Flores, Ralph, 66
Flower, Linda, 151, 213
Fractenberg, David, 57

Gallop, Jane, 68
Gaston, Tom, 94
gatekeeping, 20, 29, 77, 99, 140–141, 144–145, 148, 151, 175, 183, 184
Gebhardt, Rick, 95, 151
Geisler, Cheryl, 218
Gerhart, Mary, 67
Giberson, Greg, viii, 38, 70, 90
Glau, Greg, 71
Gonzales, Laura, 36
grammar, 155–157, 176
Gries, Laurie, 181
Griff, Russell, 63
Guattari, Felix, 60
Gunner, Jeanne, 18

Haas, Lynda, 62
Halloran, Michael, 58
Hansen, Kristine, 70
Hardin, Joe, 81, 82, 90
Harkin, Patricia, 66
Harris, Joe, 95
Harris, Muriel, 8, 124, 139, 234
Hauser, Gerald A., 64
Hawisher, Gail, 100
Hawk, Byron, 10, 95, 108, 123, 124, 189
Hay, Carla, 46
Hay, Richard, 43, 46
Haynes-Burton, Cynthia, 66
Heath, Bob, 65
Hesse, Douglas, 7, 189
Hetzel, Fred, 110
Hewett, Beth, 166
Hidalgo, Alexandra, 208
Hindeman, Jane E., 62
Hollis, Karyn, 64
Holmes, Ashley, 90
Horning, Alice S., 4, 9, 72, 99, 100, 147
Horrigan, Patrick, 60
Huot, Brian, 94
Hurlbert, Mark, 64
hypertext, 87–88, 120, 165, 170–171

inclusion, 141, 198, 205–206, 235
independent journals, 7, 29–30, 34, 82, 185, 189
index, 30, 35–36, 79, 89, 94, 129, 130, 132, 134, 168, 199, 204
Inkster, Robert P., 57
institutional support, 34, 189, 199
intellectual property rights, 123

Interchanges, 97
IRB approval, 149

Jay, Gregory S., 64
Jay, Paul, 65
Johnson, Lamar, 178
Johnstone, Henry, 66
Journal of Rhetoric Theory, 68
Journal of Scholarly Publishing, 140
Journal of Second Language Writing (*JSLW*), 192, 194, 197
Jordan, Jay, 196
Jurecic, Ann, 106, 108

Kalantzis, Mary, 106
Kameen, Paul, 58
Kelly, Kathleen, 63
Kiefer, Kate, 119
Kleinfeld, Elizabeth, 50
Kneupper, Charles, 59
Koerber, Amy, 100
Krause, Steven D., 61
Kuhn, Thomas, 159
Kurtyka, Faith, 90
Kynard, Carmen, 178

Lacan, Jacques, 63, 155
Lamos, Steve, 108
Landmark Essays, 193, 194, 196, 201, 215, 227
Larson, Richard, 94
Latinx, 160, 207
Latour, Bruno, 112
Lauer, Janice, 218
Law, John, 182
Lawlor, Leonard, 67
Lazer, Hank, 64
Leki, Ilona, 197
Lewin, Kurt, 144
Library Publishing Curriculum, 172, 174
licenses, 84, 121, 130–131, 173
Literacy in Composition Studies (*LiCS*), 30–31, 34, 35, 38
Lunsford, Andrea, 106
Lunsford, Karen, 218

Mack, Nancy, 64
Maclean, Norman, 61
Mahala, Daniel, 62
Maier, Carol, 106
Mailloux, Steven, 59
Malinowitz, Harriet, 59
manuscript preparation, 31, 132
Mann, Charles W., 65
marketing, 35, 107, 110
McGinty, Stephen, 145, 146
McKee, Sarah, 174

McLeod, Susan, 121
McLuhan, Marshall, 131
McNabb, Richard, 187
method(ology), 73, 93, 94, 98, 101, 143, 148, 150, 164, 173, 183, 187, 189, 207, 208, 215, 218, 219, 221, 224
Metzger, David, 63
Micciche, Laura R., 8, 29, 31, 124, 190
Miller, Carolyn, 214, 215
Miller, Richard E., 106, 108
Miller, Susan, 107, 155
Miller, Thomas, 107
mission statement, 81, 141–142
Modern Language Association (MLA), ix
Moffett, James, 213
Mol, Annemarie, 182, 188
Monroe, Jonathan, 106
Morey, Sean, 90
Morrison, Margaret, 59
Morrison, Toni, 210, 211
Moshenberg, Daniel, 63
Moss, Roger, 60
Mullin, Joan, 125, 127
Munroe, Randall, 177
Murphy, Jerry, 193
Murray, Mary, 61

National Writing Centers Association (NWCA), 43
National Council of Teachers of English (NCTE), 15, 17, 18, 21, 43, 96, 122, 132, 133, 158, 207, 218
Nelson, Bob, 203
Nelson, William, 58
Nugent, Jim, 70

O'Connor, Patricia, 63
Odoroff, Elizabeth, 66
Ohmann, Richard, 64
Olson, Gary A., 5, 29, 80, 81, 108, 186
Ong, Walter, 157
open access, 21, 34, 35, 79, 129–136, 185, 208, 216–217, 222; benefits, 48–49, 80, 85–89, 123–124; formats, 84–85; in Writing Studies, 81, 83, 120, 122, 182, 207
open journal systems (OJS), 33
Oresick, Peter, 110
Ortmeier-Hooper, Christina, 196
Ottaviani, Jim, 134
Owens, Derek, 90

page limitations, 21, 48, 87
Palmquist, Mike, 9, 119, 124, 125, 127, 133, 217
Paradis, James, 215
Parlor Press, 47, 71, 74, 122, 188

peer-review, 21–22, 24, 31, 50, 54, 84, 96–97, 120–121, 124, 129, 131, 147–148, 168–169, 170–172, 175, 184, 204, 208, 231; anonymous, 72, 97; open, 171
Pell, Derek, 62
Pemberton, Michael A., 9, 32, 34, 38, 50, 75, 77, 99, 124, 126, 127
PMLA, 97
Porter, James E., 60
Prebel, Julie, 50
Priestley, Joseph, 214, 217
Prior, Paul, 218
production cycle, 33, 82
professionalism, 74
promotion, 110, 115
proofread, 32, 74, 166
proposals, 223; book, 100, 111, 115–116, 120, 135, 200, 216, 231, 234; journal article, 25, 93, 96, 97, 187, 193, 195–196, 197–198
Purdy, John, 203, 210

Quiroz, Sharon, 139

race, 83, 109, 112, 178
racism, 161, 178
Ramirez, John, 61
readership, 42, 47–48, 85, 113, 145, 170, 214
Regan, Charles, 67
revision, 24, 33–34, 41, 44, 51–55, 73, 83, 86, 94, 97, 99, 115, 148, 149–151, 170–171, 175, 176, 185, 194, 198–200, 205, 209
Rhodes, Jacqueline, 90, 190
Rice, Jeff, 121, 182
Rickert, Thomas, 88, 106, 108
Rieder, David, 181
Rifenburg, Michael, 121
Ritchie, Joy, 106
Ritter, Kelly, 8, 71, 144
Rodrigues, Dawn, 119
Roehmer, Kenneth, 205
Roen, Duane, 71
Rogers, Paul, 218
Roggenbuck, Ted, 55
Ronald, Kate, 106
Rose, Jeanne, 90
Rose, Richard, 143
Rose, Shirley, 69, 75
Ross, Susan, 63
Rouster, William J., 64
Royster, Jacqueline Jones, 106, 107
Russell, David, 121, 124, 215, 216

Sackey, Donnie, 181
Salem, Lori, 90
Salvo, Michael, 165
Samuels, Robert, 62
schedule, 31, 34, 71, 74, 86, 95–96, 115–116, 204
Scenters-Zapico, John, 62
Schaafsma, David, 107
Scheidt, Donna, 74
Schilb, John, 4, 59, 65, 100
Schoen, Megan, viii, 33, 34, 38
second language writing, 7, 192–197
Shanholtzer, Joshua, 110
Shipka, Jody, 90, 107
Silva, Tony, 192, 193, 194, 195, 197
Sirc, Geoffrey, 62
Smith, Ruth L., 61
Soliday, Mary, 108
Solomon, David, 84
Sommers, Jeff, 100
Sosnoski, James J., 61
Soven, Margot, 121
Stagliano, Anthony, 181
Stanley, Jane, 108
Staples, David, 63
Stedman, Kyle, 88
Stivale, Charles J., 60
Stone, Jonathan, 89
Stromberg, Ernest, 158
Studies in American Indian Literatures (SAIL), 202–207
style guide, 37, 165, 168, 176
submissions, viii, xi, 4, 5, 21–23, 26–27, 30, 31–34, 35, 36, 37–38, 44–46, 48–55, 71–72, 76, 81, 84, 86–87, 97, 99, 125–126, 134, 144–150, 159, 160, 169–172, 179, 184, 187–189, 197, 203–204, 206–207, 209–210, 215, 232
subscriptions, 21, 29, 34–35, 45–46, 48, 79, 83–86, 123, 129, 133, 135
Sutton, Jane, 66
Swales, John, 86
Swearingen, Jan, 59, 67
Sweeney, Robert D., 67
Swilky, Jody, 62
Symposium on Second Language Writing (SSLW), 193, 197

Taczak, Kara, 96
Taylor, Todd, 5, 123
Teachers of English to Speakers of Other Languages (TESOL), 193, 195
tenure and promotion, ix, 21–22, 34, 53, 72, 84, 116, 118, 120, 123–124, 128, 131, 135, 145–146, 199, 204, 206, 208
Tompkins, Phillip K., 65
Trimbur, John, 61
Tuman, Myron, 105, 107, 111

university press, 107, 110, 204
usability, 170, 172–173, 177, 181

Villanueva, Victor, 9, 64, 99, 156, 159, 160, 161

WAC Clearinghouse, 34, 119–122, 124–126, 128, 130–136, 217, 222
Waldrep, Shelton, 60
Wardle, Elizabeth, 90
Warnock, Tilly, 65
Watson, Sam, 58
Weber, Jessica, 50
webtexts, 165, 167, 169–173, 177, 179
WID, 140–145, 147–150. *See also* writing across the curriculum (WAC)
Williams, Joseph, 187
Williams-Farrier, Bonnie J., 178

Winkler, Vickie, 58
Wood, Shane, 90
Worsham, Lynn, 100
WPA: Writing Program Administration, 69–70, 100
Writing Across Borders (WRAB) conference, 219–222
writing across the curriculum (WAC), 9, 119–122, 127–128, 140–145, 147–150, 214–215
writing center, 39–44, 46–52, 54, 119, 165, 166
Writing Lab Newsletter, The (*WLN*), 39, 41–53

Zappen, James P., 66
Zawilski, Bret, 96

www.ingramcontent.com/pod-product-compliance
Lightning Source LLC
Chambersburg PA
CBHW030231100526
44583CB00013BA/707